Thinking Musically

Thinking Musically

∞

EXPERIENCING MUSIC, EXPRESSING CULTURE

∞

THIRD EDITION

BONNIE C. WADE

New York   Oxford
OXFORD UNIVERSITY PRESS

Oxford University Press is a department of the University of Oxford. It furthers the University's objective of excellence in research, scholarship, and education by publishing worldwide.

Oxford   New York
Auckland   Cape Town   Dar es Salaam   Hong Kong   Karachi
Kuala Lumpur   Madrid   Melbourne   Mexico City   Nairobi
New Delhi   Shanghai   Taipei   Toronto

With offices in
Argentina   Austria   Brazil   Chile   Czech Republic   France   Greece
Guatemala   Hungary   Italy   Japan   Poland   Portugal   Singapore
South Korea   Switzerland   Thailand   Turkey   Ukraine   Vietnam

For titles covered by Section 112 of the US Higher Education Opportunity Act, please visit www.oup.com/us/he for the latest information about pricing and alternate formats.

Published by Oxford University Press.
198 Madison Avenue, New York, NY 10016
www.oup.com

Oxford is a registered trademark of Oxford University Press

Library of Congress Cataloging-in-Publication Data

Wade, Bonnie C.
   Thinking musically : experiencing music, expressing culture /
Bonnie C. Wade. — 3rd ed.
      p. cm. — (Global music series)
   Includes bibliographical references and index.
   ISBN 978-0-19-984486-9
      1. Ethnomusicology. I. Title.
ML3798.W33 2013
780.9—dc23   2012036574

Printing number: 9 8 7 6 5 4 3 2 1

Printed in the United States of America
on acid-free paper

Contents

Foreword

In the past four decades interest in music around the world has surged, as evidenced in the proliferation of courses at the college level, the burgeoning "world music" market in the recording business, and the extent to which musical performance is evoked as a lure in the international tourist industry. This has encouraged an explosion in ethnomusicological research and publication, including production of reference works and textbooks. The original model for the "world music" course—if this is Tuesday, this must be Japan—has grown old, as has the format of textbooks for it, either a series of articles in single multi-authored volumes that subscribe to the idea of "a survey" and have created a canon of cultures for study, or single-authored studies purporting to cover world musics or ethnomusicology. The time came for a change and the Global Music Series is that change.

This Global Music Series offers instructors choices. Instructors can now design their own courses; choosing from a set of case study volumes, they can decide which and how much music they will teach. In addition, case studies offer two formats—some focused on a specific culture, some on a discrete geographical area. In either case, each volume offers greater depth than the usual survey. Themes significant in each instance guide the choice of music that is discussed and some of the themes occur in multiple case studies, contributing to depth and permitting comparative study. The contemporary musical situation is the point of departure in all the volumes, with historical information and traditions addressed as they elucidate the present. The framing volume, *Thinking Musically* (Wade), sets the stage for the case studies by introducing topics such as gender and globalization that recur in multiple volumes and other ways to think about how people make music meaningful and useful in their lives. *Thinking Musically* also presents the basic elements of music as they are practiced in musical systems around the world so that authors of each case study do not have to spend time explaining them and can delve immediately into the particular music. A second framing volume, *Teaching Music Globally* (Campbell), guides teachers in the use of *Thinking Musically* and the case studies.

The series subtitle, "Experiencing Music, Expressing Culture," also puts in the forefront the people who make music or in some other way experience it and also through it express shared culture. This resonance with global studies in such disciplines as history and anthropology, with their focus on processes and themes that permit cross-study, occasions the title of this Global Music Series.

Bonnie C. Wade
Patricia Shehan Campbell
General Editors

Preface

This book was written to frame and complement a series of case study volumes in the Global Music Series. Whereas each case study focuses on a specific culture or one designated part of the world, this text offers a basis for the contrast and comparison of diverse musics. Whereas each case study is conceived around themes that are significant in its one area, this book speaks to a set of unifying topics that recur in multiple case studies. Whereas authors of the case studies naturally present their material from ethnomusicological perspectives, this volume addresses the field of ethnomusicology more explicitly.

Comparing is not an intellectual exercise I have cared much for, but as a teacher I know that it is inevitable when diverse materials are presented in a course. My task, then, was to find a way to lay the foundation for careful comparison without actually doing it much myself. In deciding how to lay that foundation in this book, there was another major consideration. As co-general editor of the series, I established a guideline for authors that they were not to spend precious pages introducing basic elements of music; their aim was to provide depth in their particular subject. Yet basic elements need to be explained; therefore, while laying a foundation for comparison, I also took on that task.

How was I to do it? Organization by genre (as in Japanese music study), by historical periods (as in study of the European tradition), or by issues (the purview of the case studies in the series), would not make much sense. Turning to my experience of studying North Indian music, I remembered that my teachers initially focused on *rāga* (melody), and one of the first things I had to do was learn how to play the drone ("harmony") and simultaneously sing melody. Then came a focus on *tāla* ("rhythm"), and I was taught to sing in a *rāga* according to a certain formal structure. That experience resonated with the established order of presentation of Western-style music scholarship, and I first drafted the book on that model. Reflecting on my teaching experience in the course of shaping and reshaping the book, I kept returning to the realization that through the years most nonspecialist students actually relate much more easily to rhythm than to discussions of melody and harmony. A reader of the manuscript for Oxford University Press affirmed this and thus liberated me; I decided to break the mold. Each of the basic ingredients of music is indeed discussed in turn, but rhythm comes first. In chapters 3 and 4, I examine the organization of time and then of pitch (both melodically and harmonically), exploring ways they have been conceived and used in the creative musical imaginations of music makers around the globe. This is not a study of repertoire; it is a study of ideas and practices. Likewise, in chapter 5, I examine the structuring of musical selections. Most examples, but not all, are coordinated with the case studies. While the variety of music in the examples may seem bewildering at first, many of them are considered several times in this volume so that they become very familiar.

Themes that unify the case studies are interwoven throughout the book. Consideration of ways in which people learn the music they know comes in chapter 1. In chapter 2, I present numerous ways of thinking about musical instruments and in chapter 6 speak to issues that are lively in the field of ethnomusicology and that recur in multiple case studies.

A focus of primary significance in ethnomusicology is people. People make music what it is, and *people make music meaningful and useful in their lives*. That last statement encapsulates much of what ethnomusicologists are interested in, and I offer it as a framing perspective throughout the book for ways of thinking about music. The most distinctive method of ethnomusicological research—learning about music from people—is the subject of chapter 7, a practical guide for students doing field research on their own.

I must offer a few caveats. In this volume I have scarcely used three terms with which scholars are grappling: "culture," and its extensions, "a culture," and "a music culture" (see chapter 6). The concept of "culture" resulted when modern European nation-states were emerging, bounded and distinctive. The struggle for recognition by a nation-state causes a rhetoric to develop that defines cultural and historical substance or attributes upon which national existence can be said to rest. Thus the idea of "a culture" emerges—something "authentic" that exists only with "a nation." Recently, however, studies of modernization, with its attendant Westernization, and of globalization, with its flow of people, ideas, and goods around the earth, have problematized that bounded concept of "a culture." More generically, social scientists have used the word "culture" to refer to ideas (values, worldview, concepts) and beliefs of individuals and groups of people as well as practices that emerge from those ideas and beliefs. That sense of "culture" is complemented by the term "society," that is, the systems (kinship, political, economic, etc.) that people construct to manage relationships among themselves. Conflating those different senses, common vernacular usage of "a culture" is likely to refer to the society—that is, the social group or social system—with which the cultural set of ideas, beliefs, and practices are associated. In the few instances where I cautiously use the contested term "music culture," I mean the ways in which people make music meaningful and useful in their lives—the ideas, beliefs, practices, and also the systems in evidence in the sphere of music.

Another extension of the idea of "culture" is the "culture area." Beyond the nation-state, large geographical areas of the world, such as Southeast Asia, have been clustered for political reasons, mostly, and scholars, including ethnomusicologists, have also thought in terms of region. In this book I refer to musical areas carefully and seldom. As we learn more about musics on the planet we are less inclined to feel comfortable with the level of generalization they imply.

A final caveat concerns the rubric of "Western music." It is problematic on several counts. The term "Western music" is all too often invoked when reference is intended to refer specifically to music of or derived from European classical musical practices. The term "Western music" is also problematic when viewed from the perspectives of modernization, colonization, and globalization. Resulting from serious enculturation for more than a century, many peoples around the world consume and create music that is still referred to as "Western music" although it is now arguably just as much theirs as "the West's." "The West" is, on the one hand, a concept and, on the other, a geographical location. In this book I use the term "Western music" carefully, preferring a greater degree of specificity.

In the following pages I speak to a number of musical ideas and practices from around the world. In addition to helping you enjoy many kinds of music, I hope that this book will help you to think musically.

NEW TO THIS EDITION

- Simplified and incorporates recent additions to the Global Music Series
- New charts and diagrams delve into important musical concepts
- Updated companion website includes a new guide to online and print resources, a sample syllabus, and teaching tips

ACKNOWLEDGMENTS

This Global Music Series began as a partnership with myself, Patricia Campbell, and then–Oxford University Press music editor Maribeth Payne. I want to acknowledge here the years of stewardship and support by Payne to help the project come to fruition. I thank Campbell as well, for being such a good colleague in this large and complex endeavor, for creating *Teaching Music Globally*, the complementary book to this, and for stewarding the production of instructional materials that are posted on the website for each case study in the series.

This book, *Thinking Musically*, is the most difficult project I have ever undertaken. I could not have written it without the help of many people, too numerous to mention here. Several of them are noted in the figure and CD credits. I want particularly to acknowledge the teamwork and help of my companion authors in the Global Music Series who are enumerated in the front pages of this book. Dave Brubeck's personal attention to my remarks about his music and Fred Lerdahl's response to the chapter on time remain greatly appreciated. Special thanks also to colleagues Jocelyne Guilbault, for her helpful suggestions on chapter 6, to Karen Rozenak for her encouragement of such a volume and her thoughtful reading of an early draft, to Richard Crocker, Richard Taruskin, Kendra Salois, and Donna Kwon for consultation within their expertises, and Jay Cloidt, Robbie Beahrs, John-Carlos Perea, Eliot Bates for their help with the CD. And I appreciate the help of Department of Music staff member James Coates with the numerous details involved in acquiring licenses. I also thank the anonymous readers of this manuscript in its various incarnations for their insightful comments and helpful suggestions. Special thanks also go to Jan Beatty, Richard Carlin, Marianne Paul and Sheena Kowalski at Oxford University Press.

Last, but not least, I thank the students in my freshman seminar *Thinking Musically* (spring 2001) at the University of California, Berkeley, for their critical reading of a very early draft, their considered suggestions, assistance with compiling the CD, and other creative efforts, some of which are credited individually in the text. Responses from students in classes after that had much to do with the preparation of the second edition. Students Tessa Gregory, Kin Hang Lam, Alex Poska, and Sierra Senzaki in the Undergraduate Research Apprentice Program at the University of California, Berkeley have advised and otherwise assisted in the preparation of this third edition.

CD Track List

Disc 1

1-1   Second *sura* of the *Qur'ān, al-Baqara* (Islamic recitation). Ceremony of the Qadiriya Sufi brotherhood, Mevlevi Sufi, Turkey. *Archives internationales de musique populaire* (*Musée d'ethnographie*, Geneva, 1988).

1-2.   "Zhonghua liuban" ("Moderate Tempo Six Beats"). *Jiangnan sizhu*, excerpt. Field recording collected by Frederick Lau in Shanghai. Reproduced with permission.

1-3.   "Tar Road to Sligo" and "Paddy Clancy's Jig" (Irish jigs). Becky Tracy, fiddle; Stan Scott, mandolin; Dora Hast, whistle. From *Jig Medley* cassette. Courtesy of Becky Tracy, Stan Scott, and Dora Hast.

1-4   Episodes from Gahu dance drumming of the Anlo-Ewe people of Ghana, West Africa. Students in the African Music Ensemble, University of California, Berkeley (2011), directed by C. K. Ladzekpo. Recorded by Alex Poska.

1-5   "The Ballad of César Chávez" (*corrido*). Pablo and Juanita Saludado. From *Las Voces de los Campesinos*, n.d. Courtesy of the Center for the Study of Comparative Folklore and Mythology, UCLA.

1-6.   P. D. "El son del perro." Mariachi "El Capiro de Jalisco," Audio Archive of the National Council for the Traditional Arts (NCTA), *Raices Musicales* tour, Stanford University, Palo Alto, California, November 9, 1990. Bruce Loughry, recording engineer.

1-7   "Ketawang Subakastawa Pathet Sléndro Sanga," Hardo Budoyo, directed by Midiyanto, 2000. Used by permission of Ben Brinner and Midiyanto.

1-8   "Blue Horse Special," Native American (Lakota) intertribal pow-wow song, sung by John-Carlos Perea, December 14, 2011.

1-9 "Hyōjō Netori" (Japanese *gagaku* ensemble). Gagaku Music Society of Tenri University, n.d. Courtesy of Koji Sato, Director, Gagaku Music Society of Tenri University.

1-10 "Liushui" ("Flowing Water"). *Guqin* solo, excerpt. From *Favorite Qin Pieces of Guan Ping-hu*. Guan Ping-hu (*guqin*). ROI: RB-951005-2C. 1995. Courtesy of Frederick Lau.

1-11 *Ālāp-jor-jhālā* excerpts from "Raga Jog," Ravi Shankar, *sitār*. First issued on World Pacific Records WPS 21438, © 1956. Reproduced from *Ravi Shankar: Flowers of India*, reissue by él in association with Cherry Red Records. ACMEM117CD. Used by permission from St. Rose Music Publishing Co.

1-12 *Gat* excerpt from *ibid*.

1-13 "First Wine Offering: A-ak" (Chinese Confucian music in Korea). Confucian ritual ensemble. Orchestra of the National Music Institute, Seoul, Korea, Kim Ki-su, director. Recorded by John Levy. Lyrichord Discs, 1969.

1-14 "Rak Badjalarr" (Lambudju's *wangga*), sung by Bobby Lambudju Lane and Tommy Barrtjap with Nicky Jorrock (*didjeridu*). Recorded in 1986. For *didjeridu*, clapsticks and voice. By permission of the Aboriginal Research Institute.

1-15. Demonstration of different parts in arrangement of "Back Line," recorded by Phase II on Phase II Pan Groove, © 1986. Performed by students and faculty at the University of Washington. Used by permission.

1-16 "*Riachao*" (Brazilian *capoeira*). São Bento Pequeno de Angola e São Bento Grande de Compasso. From *Capoeira: A Saga do Urucungo* (Luzes: Silvio Acaraje, n.d.)

1-17 "Conch call" (Tibetan Buddhist ritual). Conch. From *Musique rituelle tibetaine* (Ocora Records OCR 49, [1970]).

1-18 "Hifumi no Shirabe Hachigaeshi" (Zen Buddhist music). Goro Yamaguchi, *shakuhachi*. Japan Victor, n.d.

1-19 "Unnai Nambinen" (South Indian *Ādi tāla*). *Rāga Kirawāni* (21st *mela*). T. Vishwanathan, singer; David Nelson, *mṛdaṅgam*; Anantha Krishnan, *tāmbūra*. Music by T. M. Swami Pillay. Text by Muttuttandavar. Courtesy of Matthew Allen, T. Vishwanathan, David Nelson, Anantha Krishnan.

1-20 "Festival Music" (offstage [*geza*] ensemble). From *Music from the Kabuki*. Nonesuch H-72012, [1970].

1-21   Korean *"Komungo Sanjo: Chinyangjo, Chungmori, Chungjungmori."* *Sanjo* on the *komungo* zither. Han Kap-deuk *(komungo)*; Anonymous (changgo), Seoul, 1972. Courtesy of the National Kugak Center.

1-22   *Kotekan "norot"* (Balinese *gangsas*). Recorded by Lisa Gold. Used by permission.

1-23   Mary MacNamara (concertina), "The Ash Plant/The Dog Among the Bushes" (reels), recorded by Stan Scott and Dorothea Hast at the MacNamara home. Permission given by Mary MacNamara.

1-24   "Travelling in Soochow" (Chinese folk instrumental music). Chinese *di-tze* (flute). China Records, n.d.

1-25   Analysis of sound of *shakuhachi/syakuhati*. Provided by David Wessel.

1-26   "Kiembara xylophone orchestra," Famankaha, Sous-Prefecture of Korhogo, Ivory Coast, West Africa. From *The Music of the Senufo*. Bärenreiter, UNESCO Collection. *Anthology of African Music*, vol. 8, n.d.

1-27   Cantonese opera (Chinese vocal, Cantonese style). Fung Hang Record Ltd. (Hong Kong, n.d.).

1-28   Georges Bizet, "L'amour est un oiseau rebelle" (Habanera) from *Carmen*. Robert Shaw Chorale and Children's Chorus from l'Elysée Francaise. Robert Shaw, Conductor. Fritz Reiner conducting the RCA Victor Orchestra. Carmen: Rise Stevens; Don José: Jan Peerce; Micaëla: Licia Albanese; Zuniga: Osie Hawkins; Moralès: Hugh Thompson. English translation of the libretto by Alice Berezowsky. RCA Victor Records, © 1951. Under license from SONY BMG Music Entertainment.

1-29   Andean panpipes: three *cortes* (sizes). An example of the Peruvian "Toril" genre, in *conima* style. Performed by Patricia Hinostroza, Jesus Jaramillo *(chili* melody); Vanessa Luyo, Jose Carlos Pomari *(sanja* melody); Illich Ivan Montes, Hubert Yauri *(malta* melody). Followed by a traditional *sikuris* ensemble, including panpipes recorded in the Andean highlands, city of Puno, during the festival La Candelaria, in 1991. Courtesy of Raul R. Cavallo, Instituto de Etnomusicologia, Pontificia Universidad Católica del Perú, Lima.

1-30   Jeff Davis, "Fiat Lux" for carillon duet (2010). Both parts performed by Jeff Davis on the University of California, Berkeley, carillon, December 2011. Courtesy of the composer.

1-31   "Ma Ram" "Dancing Horse" (Thai *pî phât* ensemble). From *Traditional Music of Thailand*, 1968. Institute of Ethnomusicology, UCLA Stereo ier-7502 c. 1968. Used with permission of the Regents of the University of California.

1-32 Paul Desmond "Take Five" (jazz). The Dave Brubeck Quartet (Dave Brubeck, Paul Desmond, Joe Morello, Gene Wright). Copyright © 1960, renewed 1988, Desmond Music Company (USA) Derry Music Company (world except USA); used with permission; all rights reserved.

Disc 2

2-1 "*Aruh li Min*" in *maqām rāst*. Egyptian instrumental ensemble with vocal, © 1958. Umm Kulthum, singer. "*Aruh li min*," composer: Riyad al-Sinbati; poet: `Abd al-Mun 'im al Saba'i. Used by permission of Sono Cairo.

2-2 Witold Lutosławski, "Mini Overture" (1982). Meridian Arts Ensemble: Jon Nelson, Richard Kelley (trumpet), Daniel Grabois (horn), Benjamin Herrington (trombone), Raymond Stewart (tuba). Courtesy of Music Sales Corporation and Channel Classics CCS2191, © 1991.

2-3 Sargam (North Indian vocal solfège). From Bonnie C. Wade, *Khyāl: Creativity within North India's Classical Musical Tradition* (Cambridge: Cambridge University Press, 1984). Cassette tape master in the collection of the author.

2-4 Gamelan Gong Kebyar. "Jaya Semara" (Sanggar Çudamani). Recorded by Lisa Gold. Courtesy of Lisa Gold.

2-5 "Mi bajo y yo" (*salsa*). Oscar d'Leon, bandleader. From *Exitos y Algo mas* Company, n.d.

2-6 "West End Blues" (New Orleans jazz). Louis Armstrong, trumpet, et al. Under license from SONY BMG Music Entertainment.

2-7 Numerical patterns (1-9, articulated with mnemonics) used for rhythmic variety in India's music. Recited by George Ruckert.

2-8 "Marieke." Words and Music by Eric Blau, Jacques Brel, Gerard Jouannest. Recording and text translation courtesy of Suzanne Lake. Recorded by Suzanne Lake, *The Soul of Chanson*, CD. Copyright © 1968 Universal-MCA Music Publishing, a division of Universal Studios, Inc. (ASCAP) International Copyright Secured. All rights reserved.

2-9 Dave Brubeck, "Three to Get Ready and Four to Go" (jazz). The Dave Brubeck Quartet (Dave Brubeck, Paul Desmond, Joe Morello, Gene Wright). Copyright © 1960, renewed 1988, Derry Music Company; used with permission; all rights reserved.

2-10 "Forró em Monteiro" by Arlindo dos Oito Baixos. Arlindo dos Oito Baixos (*sanfona de oito baixos*), Raminho (*zabumba*), Adilson (bass). Field recording by John Murphy, 2001. Used by permission.

2-11   Frédéric Chopin, *Waltz in C-sharp Minor*. Performance by Jean Gray Hargrove. Recording courtesy of Jean Gray Hargrove.

2-12   *Ketawang* colotomic pattern (without gender). Provided by Midiyanto, Berkeley, California, 2008.

2-13   *Ketawang* colotomic pattern (with gender). Provided by Midiyanto, Berkeley, California, 2008.

2-14   North Indian *tāla* patterns (*thekas*): *chautāl, ektāl, tīntāl, tilwādā.* Recited by George Ruckert.

2-15   Three traditional Egyptian eight-beat rhythms, each recited and played four times: *maqsūm, maṣmūdī; ṣaghīr,* and *ṣa'īdī.* Recited and played by Hany El Sawaf. Courtesy of Scott Marcus.

2-16   Richard Strauss, *Also Sprach Zarathustra*, excerpt. Columbia MK 35888, 1980.

2-17   Harmonic and inharmonic sounds, demonstrated by David Wessel.

2-18   "Seki no To" (Japanese *shamisen* and vocal). Example of *Tokiwazu,* a section from the *Kabuki* play *Tsumoru koi yuki no Seki no to,* music by Tobaya Richoo I, text by Takarada Jurai. 1784. From *1,000 Years of Japanese Classical Music*, vol. 7, *Tokiwazu, Tomimoto, Kiyomoto, Shinnai.* Nihon koten ongaku taikei. (Tokyo: Kodansha, 1980–82).

2-19   Balinese *jublag*. Recorded by Lisa Gold.

2-20   Western orchestra tuning process. University Symphony Orchestra, University of California, Berkeley.

2-21   "Frère Jacques" ("Are you sleeping?"). Recorded by Alex Poska.

2-22   Western major (diatonic) scale. Recorded by Alex Poska.

2-23   "Oriental" scale. Excerpt, *Cante Flamenco Agujetas en Paris* (Ocora, 1991).

2-24   *Maqām rāst*, with a lower tetrachord of *rāst* on C (C-D-E^b-F) and an upper tetrachord of *rāst* on G (G –A-B^b-c). Played by James R. Grippo. Courtesy of Scott Marcus.

2-25   *Maqām rāst's* three upper tetrachords: *rāst* on G (G-A-B^b-c)[this flat is half-flat], *nahāwand* on G (G-A –B^b-c), and *hijāz* on G (G-A^b-B-c). Played by James R. Grippo. Courtesy of Scott Marcus.

2-26   Western vertical intervals. Recorded by Alex Poska.

2-27   Western-style overtone singing, overtones 1-12. Sung and recorded by Robbie Beahrs, December 2011.

2-28   Three-part Shop singing from the village of Vrazhdebna, Bulgaria. Timothy Rice, 1972. Courtesy of Timothy Rice.

2-29   Progression of pitches (roots of chords).

2-30   Excerpt from "il-Kalām Da Kabīr." Sung by Hakim. Lyrics composed by 'Abd al-Mun'im Taha; music composed by Aḥmad Shahīn; music arranged by Ḥamīd ish-Sha'rī.

2-31   "Sumer is icumen in" (medieval European *rota*). Courtesy of the Chamber Chorus of the University of California, Berkeley, Paul Flight, director, 2001.

2-32   Episode from *woi-meni-pele* (Kpelle epic performance). Liberian *Womi* epic pourer. Courtesy of Ruth Stone.

2-33   *"Yaegoromo"* (Japanese *sankyoku* ensemble). CD Japon-Ensemble Jiuta Yonin no Kai, C 580069, first published in 1979, re-issued in 1998. Permission from Ocora Radio France.

2-34   Scottish bagpipe drone. Recording by John Pedersen. Courtesy of Lucia Comnes.

2-35   *"Artii-Sayir"* Song in Tuvan (Inner Asian steppe) throat-singing, *kargyraa* style. Sung and recorded by Robbie Beahrs, December 2011.

2-36   Rāga "Miyāṅ ki Toḍi" (North Indian vocal). Dagar Brothers, CD 4137.

2-37   "Iaora I Te Farerei." *Hīmene tārava* (multi-part song) sung by a mixed choir from Papara, French Polynesia. From the album *"Coco's Temaeva"* Royal Folkloric Troupe of Tahiti, MANUITI 65808, c. 1992. Courtesy of Yves Roches.

2-38   Ludwig van Beethoven, *Symphony No. 5*, excerpt. London Symphony Orchestra, Wyn Morris, conductor. MCA Classics, n.d.

2-39   North Indian cadential *tihāī* pattern 1. Recited by George Ruckert. Courtesy of George Ruckert.

2-40   North Indian cadential *tihāī* pattern 2. Recited by George Ruckert. Courtesy of George Ruckert.

2-41   "The Great Ambush." Tsun-yuen Lui, Chinese *pipa*. Courtesy of Tsun-yuen Lui and the UCLA Ethnomusicology Archive.

2-42   "Kumbaya." Kenyan. Courtesy of Greg Barz.

2-43   Kpelle Children's counting song. Totota, 1976. Recorded by Ruth M. and Verlon L. Stone. Courtesy of Ruth Stone.

2-44   Inuit juggling game song. Unidentified singers. Field recording by Beverley Diamond. Courtesy of Beverley Diamond.

2-45 "O brother, stay awake." *Salvesan ami* hymn. Sung by Presbyterian congregants, Pelongk village, Maskelyne Islands, Vanuatu (Melanesia). Field recording by Michael Webb, 2010. Courtesy of Michael Webb.

2-46 Angsel in "Topeng Keras." Balinese music and dance to accompany a strong character in the *topeng* dance form. Courtesy of Lisa Gold.

2-47 *"Aach kapwongen etiwa áámi"* ("Our welcome greetings to you all"). *A kéénún etiwetiw* (welcome song). Sung by a group from Mooch Island, Mortlock Islands, Chuuk (Federated States of Micronesia). Field recording by Brian Diettrich, 2006. Courtesy of Brian Diettrich.

A Note to Readers

Dear Readers,

Please permit me to introduce myself, as I would on the first day of a new course. I am a professor in the field of ethnomusicology, with which you will gradually become acquainted through this book. My special interests in teaching and research lie in the musics of Japan and India. My students always ask how I got there, so here's the story in a nutshell. I grew up as many people in my generation did—studying piano, singing in a church choir, loving to dance, and generally enjoying music. First, I dreamed of becoming a concert pianist. Then I wanted to be a professor of music history; although I didn't realize it at the time, that meant being a professor of the history of European art music only. Then, one day, I experienced an epiphany—a life-changing experience. Friends treated me to a trip to Latin America when I was between my junior and senior years in college. I was too poor to go otherwise, and besides, Latin America was nowhere in my imagination. On that "one day," I was standing at the edge of an Andean mountain precipice near Cuzco, Peru, when up from the chasm below floated music like none I had ever heard before—a flute melody that didn't fit my musical expectations. But it was beautiful! What struck me most that day was that no one in my years of music study had ever mentioned *other* music to me; granted, recordings were relatively few in those days, but really! Not acceptable, I decided. That turned me to ethnomusicology.

As a person, I guess I was just always willing to be open to difference—although I am definitely attracted to some differences more than to others. As an ethnomusicologist, I am quite accustomed to listening to music of any and every sort. As a teacher, I recognize that students' ways of thinking musically range from a clam closed tightly to a giant squid ready to consume anything and everything that comes along. You fit somewhere along that continuum. I hope that, through this book that is about difference—about the infinitely creative imagination of humankind—you will experience something that intrigues you, or moves you, but in any case causes you to think more deeply about music.

I wrote this book with the aim of engaging with you and therefore, I ask certain things of you. If I pose a question that you think is too simple to take seriously, hang in there because you might discover that simple questions don't always have simple answers. When I suggest that you do something (see the Activities through the book), do it, because, in the doing, you will be taking more from the book than if you just read words passively. That is to say, you will experience and internalize the ideas under discussion rather than just receiving them in an abstract way. I suggest that you keep a journal in a notebook or computer file that records what you do in response to the Activities, for purposes of a record and for review. Be prepared to *listen* constantly to the musical examples; the CD icon in the margin signals you to listen, even when I don't direct you to do so in words. The musical examples vary in length, depending on what it takes to demonstrate a point or—in some cases—depending on the availability of rights to the material. Whether long or short, the musical examples are deeply integrated with the prose, and I return to many of them multiple times. Please use the glossary and index as serious tools in the book. Finally, I ask you to enjoy yourself, as you learn more about ways to think musically.

Most sincerely,

Bonnie Wade

Locations mentioned in this text are highlighted.

ID
UKRAINE
DOVA
MANIA
GARIA
TURKEY   AZERBAIJAN
              ÜZBEKISTAN   Beijing   NORTH KOREA
              AFGHANISTAN   SOUTH KOREA   JAPAN
                                  CHINA   (Seoul)
              PAKISTAN   TIBET   Soochow
EGYPT
                   INDIA   Guangzhou

                        THAILAND
                        Bangkok

                        MALAYSIA
GANDA   MICRONESIA
  KENYA   INDONESIA
                                                              POLYNESIA
TANZANIA   JAVA
                        BALI   MELANESIA
MBIA   NORTHWEST
ZIMBABWE   ARNHEMLAND
                                  AUSTRALIA

Thinking about Music

If you can speak you can sing; if you can walk you can dance.
(Zimbabwean Shona proverb)

People make music meaningful and useful in their lives. That statement encapsulates much of what ethnomusicologists are interested in and offers a framing perspective for many ways of thinking both about people and about music all over the world. In this chapter I shall explore each word in the statement with two purposes in mind: to suggest new ways you might think about music that you regularly hear, and to begin to expand your musical horizon. I shall also begin by speaking briefly about the dissemination of music and the ways it is taught and learned, because what you think about music has been influenced by how you have learned it.

PEOPLE

Music Makers.   Who makes music in our familiar world? Music makers are individuals and groups, adults and children, female and male, amateurs and professionals. They are people who make music only for themselves, such as shower singers or secretly-sing-along-with-the-radio types, and they are performers, people who make music purposefully for others. They are people who make music because they are required to and people who do so simply from desire. Some music makers study seriously, while others are content to make music however they can, without special effort.

To think about music makers globally, you might ask whether music makers are regarded in any particular way in a particular place. At one end of a spectrum, some societies expect people who make music to be specialists, born into the role or endowed with a special capacity. At the other end of that spectrum, in some societies it is assumed that the practice of music is a human capacity and that all people will express themselves musically as a normal part of life. Particularly in situations where orality is a viable mode for transmission of knowledge (teaching by sounding), being a musician—or reciter, as in figure 1.1—is an option for visually impaired individuals. In figure 1.1 a sighted sheikh, in company with two blind reciters, participates in a performance of Qur'ānic recitation in Egypt. There, where the aurality of the tradition (learning by hearing) has been culturally affirmed, becoming a reciter has been a potential profession for blind men. Through a long period of premodern Japanese history, blind players of *shamisen* and *koto* (Fig. 1.2) held a governmentally sanctioned monopology on performing and teaching of orally transmitted repertories for their instruments.

FIGURE 1.1   *Egyptian reciter. Multiple reciters of the Qur'ân, accompanied by friends and relatives, participate in a performance at a gathering in Egypt—possibly the opening of a conference. That the illustrious Sheikh Mustafa Ismail is taking his turn (probably last in the program due to his eminence) is ascertained by the positioning of one (sometimes it is both) hand to his face while reciting—a custom for which Kristina Nelson could find no consistent explanation but which undoubtedly helps the reciter focus and better hear his own voice. (Photo by Kristina Nelson)*

FIGURE 1.2 *Japanese* sankyoku *ensemble. From left to right: Keiko Nosaka* (koto), *Satomi Fukami* (syamisen/shamisen), *Kozan Sato* (syakuhati/shakuhachi). *(Courtesy of Keiko Nosaka)*

Local terminology is a clue to the ideas held about music makers.

Shortly after arriving in Sofia in 1969, I took a bus to a nearby village on Mount Vitosha in the Shop (rhymes with "hope") region, home to a subgroup of Bulgarians with a distinct linguistic dialect and musical culture. My goal was to meet some village musicians. Using my dictionary and limited Bulgarian, I asked people in the village square if they could introduce me to some *muzikanti* ("musicians"). One woman helpfully pointed me in the direction of the home of a man who played trumpet and then asked if I would be interested in hearing a women's vocal group that she belonged to. Her response surprised me for two reasons. First, she seemed to understand the word "musician" as referring to someone who played a Western musical instrument, not a traditional one, like the *gaida*. Second, she didn't seem to understand that if I was interested in "musicians," then I would also be interested in "singers."

My first attempt at fieldwork was teaching me what ethnomusicologists know generally, namely, that different cultures have different
ways of thinking about and categorizing music and musical behaviors.
(Timothy Rice, in his book in this series on Bulgaria (2004: 29).

When you hear or use the word "musician," to what sort of music maker
are you referring? Most students in my courses respond to that question with an impression that is clearly derived from the sphere of
Western classical music. In this volume, however, I use the word **musician** more generically, to cover all people who experience music as a
practice (figure 1.3a, 1.3b, 1.3c).

Many questions that can be asked about musicians reveal insights
about their musical and social worlds. Who makes music with whom?
Who learns music from whom? Who is permitted to be a teacher? Who
can perform where? Who can perform for whom? Is anyone prohibited
from making some particular type of music, and if so, why? Who plays
which instrument, and why? Do musicians have high cultural status (i.e.,
is their music-making highly valued by a group)? Do musicians have
high social status (i.e., a prominent ranking in the society)?

ACTIVITY 1.1 *Make an inventory of music makers in your
individual context, including friends and family members. Don't
forget to include yourself, if you make music. Then, for each person, consider whether or not you would categorize him or her as
"a musician" and why or why not. Also, use your list to consider the questions posed in the previous paragraph that particularly interest you.*

Listeners.   When I speak about people making music meaningful and
useful in their lives, I include people who "just" listen. They are, after
all, most of the world's musically involved population. Listeners, like
musicians, are consumers of music. They are the audience to whom performers cater—patrons who are willing to pay to hear performances
and buy recordings.

Answers to questions about listeners reveal a great deal about the musical context in which they live. Do they prefer to listen alone, or is listening
a social activity? Is it more expensive to listen to one kind of music than

FIGURE 1.3   *1.3a: Benedict Tchinburur playing* kenbi [didjeridu] *at Wadeye (Australia). (Photograph by Allan Marett. 7 November 1998)*

1.3b: Sakar Khan Manganiyar playing kamaicha. *Hamira village, Rajasthan, India.   (Photo by Shalini Ayyagari)*

1.3c: Marika Kuzma, Director of Choruses, University of California, Berkeley.   (Photo by Peg Skorpinski) another, and if so, what does that mean for the listener? Are certain types of listeners associated with certain types of music? Is a listening audience restricted by gender or religious belief or membership? Does a listening context foster immediate interaction between performer and listener?

ACTIVITY 1.2 *Agree or disagree with this statement: Listening to music is different from hearing music. Be prepared to give reasons for your opinion.*

MUSIC

In Terms of Sound. I am standing at the edge of a body of water, the ripples sounding alternately like gentle lapping and heavy crashing waves. Nearby, hammers and electric saws are punctuating the air. Above me, soaring and dipping and singing a variety of songs are goldfinches and mockingbirds and cooing doves. The wind whistles across the land. Car horns toot in the distance. In this wonderful sound-scape there is melody and rhythm. Can any of that be called *music?*

ACTIVITY 1.3 *To begin thinking musically, think about sound. Conduct some field research: taking pen and paper with you, listen for ten minutes to the **soundscape** around you and keep a record. Any sound—a motorcycle roaring by, a cluster of people laughing, sounds of nature, the whirring of an elevator's approach, the selection on the radio of a passing motorist, the music you choose to play. Some of the sounds you hear must be what you would automatically call "music." Articulate how you distinguish between what is and what is not music.*

In fact, what is music? The ethnomusicologist John Blacking defined it as "humanly organized sound" (1977), but I suggest that we take that statement one step farther. "Music" is not only a thing—a category of organized sound, or compositions—but also a process. Every known group of people in the world exercises their creative imaginations to organize sound in *some way* that is different from the way they organize sound for speech. No one definition of music exists for all human cultures. Rather, definitions of music are culturally specific.

Calling Something "Music." The ancient Greek word for "music" was adopted into the Arabic language as *musiqa*, but in the Islamic world view, it has been used in a more specific way. The mellifluous recitation of the sacred **Qur'ān** (CD track 1-1, Fig.1.1), which many non-Muslim listeners have called "music," is not considered *musiqa*; *musiqa* is a category encompassing **genres** (that is, types of music) that may elicit negative associations of secular musical practice. Furthermore, the imperative of avoiding inappropriate juxtapositions of the human and the divine has led to a conceptual categorization in Muslim societies that distinguishes between music, on the one hand, and forms of melodic religious expression, on the other hand. Thus, the melodic recitation of the Qur'ān is not considered to be music (Marcus 2007: 94). Clearly, just because something sounds like music to me, I have no right to insist that it is "music" to someone else. It is the local or even personal idea that counts.

In fact, having a word for a particular aesthetic category of organized sound that I as an individual think of as "music" is by no means universal. In Bali, as in many places, the concept of "music" is context specific. Rather than a single category called "music," types of instrumental ensembles, **repertoires** (groups of pieces that are linked in some way), and vocal practices are each named and associated with the specific functions that it fulfills (Gold 2005: 2). Neither does a single one of the hundreds of First Nation Native American groups have a word for "music." In these groups' opinion, the word "music" as a noun creates a category apart from other things; it fails to convey the processes of social action, for example, or of the integration of traditional knowledge and modern knowledge and the relationships that singing and drumming embody in many Native American contexts (Diamond 2008).

Likewise, sociologist Christopher Small has taken the position that music is not a thing at all but an activity, something that people do. Ethnomusicologists generally concur. He calls doing music "musicking": "to music is to take part, in any capacity, in a musical performance, whether by performing, by listening, by rehearsing or practicing, by providing material for performance (what is called composing), or by dancing" (1998: 9). He sometimes—and I always would—extends musicking to all the activities about which I wrote above under "People."

Aesthetic Values in Music. If I, in my American culture, use the expression "that's music to my ears," you will know that I have heard something I want to hear, or in terms of sound, something beautiful. Consensus about desirable quality of vocal sound is behind exclamations such as, "Oh, I don't have a good voice," or "Doesn't she have a wonderful voice!" Ideas about beauty are one aspect of a set of artistic values referred to as **aesthetics**—in this case, music aesthetics. However, aesthetic values are not necessarily shared, even within one society.

ACTIVITY 1.4   *Select one recording in your collection/playlist that you really like, and then find a different version of the same song that you really don't like. Articulate the reason(s) for your aesthetic judgement. Vocal quality? Something else?*

While individual ethnomusicologists have personal ideas about musical beauty in terms of the quality of the sound (**timbre**) that is cultivated, it is a tenet of our field that we will keep our ears and minds open and respect the fact that many timbres are considered beautiful.

Aesthetic ideals are also manifested in the ideas about the relationship between the musical selection and the way a performer is expected to treat it. For many types of music, the ideal is that a composition will be reproduced intact. That is the case with many genres of European art music, for instance, wherein a composition is expected to be performed with a high level of technical proficiency, coupled with artistic expressivity that does not change the musical material. In contrast, the aesthetic process involved in most popular music not only permits, but expects, artists to render pieces in distinctive ways.

The aesthetic ideal of some kind of change in performance is found in untold numbers of musics. In an ensemble rendition of a familiar tune in many amateur music traditions in China, each performer may "add flowers" by embellishing and varying the melody, thus shaping a collecting "sound" that is inclusive of personal styles and voices (CD track 1-2). In a similar manner, Irish musicians practice and discuss the aesthetic of never playing a tune the same way twice, keeping its melodic identity intact, but playing subtle variations each time around. They embellish their playing with ornaments and small melodic or rhythmic variations that make each repetition of a tune slightly different (CD track 1-3).

If, as in Christopher Small's terms, musicking articulates ideals of human relationships, then the aesthetic preference for the content of both music and dance of the West African Kpelle peoples provides a wonderful example (Stone 2005). Short segments (facets) that interlock are highly valued; Kpelle dance movements consist of short, quick, tightly orchestrated steps, for instance. In much African drumming, short rhythmic patterns are repeated in close coordination with other short rhythmic patterns, as an example from CD track 1-4 demonstrates. It is the process of interlocking the short segments that creates "the music"; the musical experience is a social experience.

ACTIVITY 1.5   *By this time you have been directed by the CD icon in the margins to listen to multiple musical examples. In my introductory note, I told you that you would find the musical examples deeply integrated with the prose and that I would return to many of them several times. Information about them and your understanding of them will accumulate gradually. It's time now for you to start a written record of each occurrence of each track; half a page in a notebook allotted to each track or a list of tracks in a computer file should suffice. Make a heading of track number and identifying title and culture for each selection and add information under it each time I refer you to the track. For instance, I have just made a point about an aesthetic preference that is expressed by the content of Ghanaian dance drumming (CD track 1-4). To record it, under the track number and title, enter the page number and the point made. I refer to this track again on p. 92 to make different points.*

For many people, the highest value of music is placed on **affect**, that is, its expressive capacity. Although many years have passed, I still remember vividly the feelings that welled up in me as I heard "Taps" and the American national anthem as I stood with other countrymen in the military cemetery in Manila, the Philippines, where I was just after President Kennedy was assassinated in 1963. As one of my students put it, "It is music that makes me want to dance, or feel. It not only reminds me of times I have felt emotions, but it prompts me to feel emotions" (Lyndsey Brown, 2001). Yes, music has the power to move our hearts, minds, and bodies.

*Student Lucia Comnes: "I feel that the youth in my com-
munity are drawn to this music [reggae] and culture because
it is liberating. We are about to inherit this monster that is
our society—including the government, the educational system, the work force, the media, the capitalist philosophy, the
technology, the developed civilization, the destruction of the
earth, the inequality, the separating illusions of racism, sex-
ism, ageism, homophobia, etc. and the list goes on—I often
find this overwhelming, confusing, and terrifying. When the
communities at home and at school are not strong or secure,
we yearn for another place that speaks to us deeply, a place
that brings us to a higher consciousness. Reggae culture provides this for many—a place where people are brought together
through music, music coming from the heart, speaking to the
power of the people, music that is alive and encouraging, ful-
filling and in the spirit of celebration" (2001).*

MEANING

Having briefly spoken of ways of thinking about people and music in
the main premise of this chapter that *"People make music meaningful and
useful in their lives,"* I now turn to meaning and use. That music is meaningful, no one doubts. However, great debates have ensued over
whether the meaning resides in musical materials themselves or is
ascribed to musical materials by someone for some particular reason.
Is there something really martial about the music played by a brass band
as an army marches by, or is that an association we have learned? Does
a lullaby really put a child to sleep, or is it something else such as loving attention that lulls the child into secure rest? With most ethnomusicologists, I think the latter: people make music meaningful, whether
that meaning is individual or communally agreed upon.

Music and Textual Meaning. Melody set to words constitutes much
of the world's musical repertoire. Perhaps it is because just about everyone can sing, with or without an instrument. Perhaps it is because of the
capacity of music to heighten the expressivity of a text. In the Baroque
period (c. 1600–1750 C.E.) of European music, composers used what was

called "word painting" to heighten expressivity in quite literal ways—a falling melody on the word *morire* (to die), for instance. Blues singers in America improvise expressively to elicit even more meaning from already meaningful texts.

In the Polynesian region of the Pacific Ocean, so highy valued is oral poetry that music is **logogenic** (i.e., word-oriented rather than melody-oriented). Such delight is taken in complex metaphors and indirect references that the song text serves as a kind of process by which listeners become linked in interpretive communities that appreciate the meaning and purpose of the text. Thus, in music-making, the words must be clear (Moulin in Diettrich, Moulin and Webb: 2011: 10-11).

Another reason for singing texts is the license it gives musicians to say something not permitted in ordinary speech. A great deal of covert and overt political protest has been delivered in song. In "Calypso Freedom," Sweet Honey in the Rock reminds listeners of the necessity of the civil rights movement of the 1960s while renewing the protest in 1989 with new text set to an old song.

ACTIVITY 1.6 *Find songs of political protest. You can easily find "Calypso Freedom" on the Internet, and that's a good place to start. Look for others, as well. For one, transcribe the lyrics and then listen to the musical setting. Try to figure out if the musicians use the music in any purposeful way to deliver the message of the text.*

Through the ages narrators have told their tales musically. The Texas-Mexican *corrido* is a genre that has proved to be an effective avenue for protest, as well as a narrative. "The Ballad of César Chávez" (figure 1.4, CD track 1-5) relates an important event in American history: the march of that famed Mexican American leader in the struggle for rights for migrant farmworkers. In spring 1965 the first major strike against grape growers took the form of a march from Delano, California, to the state's capital, Sacramento, to meet with then-Governor Edmund "Pat" Brown. Because of the religious orientation of Mexican culture, the march became a nexus of the religious tradition of pilgrimage and the contemporary form of demonstration. You can follow the route of the demonstrators on a map of California and on CD track 1-6 hear

El Corrido de César Chávez	*The Ballad of César Chávez*
En un día siete de marzo	On the seventh day of March
Jueves santo en la mañana,	Good Thursday in the morning
salió César de Delano	César left Delano
componiendo una campaña.	Organizing a campaign.
Compañeros campesinos	Companion farmers
este va a ser un ejemplo	This is going to be an example
esta marcha la llevamos	This (protest) march we'll take
hasta mero Sacramento.	To Sacramento itself.
Cuando llegamos a Fresno	When we arrived in Fresno
Toda la gente gritaba	All the people chanted
y que viva César Chávez	Long live César Chávez
y la gente que llevaba.	And the people that accompany him.
Nos despedimos de Fresno	We bid good-bye to Fresno
nos despedimos con fe	We bid good-bye with faith
para llegar muy contentos	So we would arrive contented
hasta el pueblo de Merced.	To the town of Merced.
Ya vamos llegando a Stockton	We are almost in Stockton
ya mero la luz se fue	Sunlight is almost gone
pero mi gente gritaba	But the people shouted
sigan con bastante fe.	Keep on with lots of faith.
Cuando llegamos a Stockton	When we arrived at Stockton
los mariachis nos cantaban	The mariachis were singing
que viva César Chávez	Long live César Chávez
y la Virgen que llevaba.	And the Virgin of Guadalupe.

FIGURE 1.4　*Song text: "The Ballad of César Chávez." Texas-Mexican* corrido. *(From Las Voces de los Campesinos: Francisco García and Pablo and Juanita Saludado Sing Corridos about the Farm Workers and Their Union. Reproduced with permission from the Center for the Study of Comparative Folklore and Mythology, UCLA, FMSC-1.)*

mariachis, the sort of musicians who greeted them in Stockton. References to the lady of Guadalupe allude to the Virgin Mary, as she is enshrined at a major shrine in Mexico, the Basilica of the Lady of Guadalupe. In song text, then, we can feel the personal experience of oppressed people.

Among the narrative genres that link music to text for the expression and heightening of meaning, musical drama is perhaps the single best example. In Balinese theater the nexus between music and the narrative, both in terms of mood and action, is so close and so familiar to audiences that the dramatic meaning is automatically remembered when the same musical material occurs without words in a nontheatrical context (Gold 2005).

We might assume that a sung text is meant to be understood. Not necessarily so! Even when a Central Javanese **gamelan** (ensemble) includes vocalists, the text they sing may not be immediately intelligible. Not only do their voices blend into the greater ensemble sound, but the poems are usually in old Javanese language that few listeners know (CD track 1-7; figure 1.5). For the few who can understand, the meaning lies both in the text itself and in the singing of it; for the less knowledgeable, the meaning lies in the recognition that an old text is being sung, in the assurance that tradition continues.

Sometimes melody is sung to text that is not linguistically meaningful—syllables such as "fa la la" in English carols that ethnomusicologists refer to as **vocables**. You might hear people use the phrase "meaningless syllables" for such text, but ethnomusicologists no longer

FIGURE 1.5   *Central Javanese* gamelan *playing for* wayang kulit *(leather puppet play).*   *(Photo by Kathleen Karn)*

do so. Syllables assumed to be meaningless have been found upon further investigation to be archaic language, or mystically meaningful. It also sometimes happens that singers will use linguistically meaningful words as vocables, choosing words for their sound or rhythmic quality rather than for their meaning (Diamond 2008: 108, citing Sam Kronk). Thus, the text of CD track 1-8 consists entirely of vocables. The "Blue Horse Special" was taught to the singer John-Carlos Perea (Mescalero Apache, Irish, German, Chicano) by Barney Hoehner (Hunkpapa and Sihásapa) who used the song for powwow social dancing but also in other contexts, including wakes and honorings. Perea considers one of the beautiful aspects of a vocable song to be that very multifunctionality, wherein the song can accumulate meaning with every new singing (Perea, personal communication, 2011). For this recording, he paced the song slowly, as a way of honoring ethnomusicologist David McAllester, whose work with Navajo music has been inspiring. The closest approximation of the vocables in this song that Perea could give is:

Hey ya hey ya hey ya hey ya hey ha hey yo
Hey ya hey ya hey ya ha hey yo.

For a comparison of this version of the song with a version using hand drum, you can find one sung by John-Carlos Perea for Paul Winter on a 2007 Grammy-award winning Crestone album (http://itunes.apple.com/us/album/crestone/id270770361).

Vocables are practical in the texts of powwow songs, in which participants may speak dozens of different Native American languages. Sometimes there are lexically meaningful words known by the singers who nevertheless may choose to sing the song with vocables (Diamond 2008).

The opposite of texted song without linguistic meaning is **program music**—instrumental music without a text that is treated as if it had one. With its many narrative genres and operatic styles, Chinese music, even instrumental music, is very text-oriented. A title such as "Plum Blossoms" is subject to interpretation, but each instrumentalist may express it differently. The "text" is not in the musical sound but in the musicians' and listeners' meaningful interpretations of the title.

Music as Text. In a subtle pairing of melody and text, the singer of the Alha epic in North India might deliver the bravado words of a warrior to the familiar melody of a woman's song genre. The bravado words are a text certainly, but so is the musical commentary on his womanly personality. Such subtlety requires a knowledgeable audience to be understood.

As that example illustrates, music can acquire meaning from the situation in which it is made or heard and then become a kind of text in itself. Its meaning is then "situated." My favorite theory about the reason that we continue to hate or love (if not get stuck in) the popular music of our teenage years is that it is situated: we absorbed that music when we were experiencing love and other emotions intensely as adolescents. It is not only the style of the music that stays with us, but also the embedded memory of the meaning it had at that crucial time in our lives.

I can think of another important instance of situated music as text. "We Shall Overcome" has a text, but even the melody alone came to be so closely associated with demonstrations that we do not have to hear any text to understand its meaning. That song also provides an illustration of how one song can assume new meanings, assume new functions, and mark different identities. In her book, *Music in America,* in this series, Adelaida Reyes tracks this. "We Shall Overcome" was originally a Christian church hymn; C. A. Tindley, who became America's first important African American gospel songwriter, had written it for his congregation. In the 1960s, it was adopted by the civil rights movement and became an anthem associated in the minds of the nation with the African American struggle for equality and freedom from discrimination.

Reyes recounts her experience of an American Thanksgiving Day celebration in Oxford (United Kingdom) in 1996 to illustrate further how the symbolism of even such a clearly situated song as "We Shall Overcome" may undergo transformation—with shifting senses of "community" and meaning to individuals as well as to a community.

> In the presence of other Americans and guests from the local and international community (mostly Europeans and Africans), one Anglo-American after another stood up to describe their connection to the Pilgrims. Then an African American began to sing "We Shall Overcome." Immediately, the other guests who knew the song joined in. In no time, the one voice had become a rousing chorus.
>
> I hazard to guess that when he began, the singer had intended the song to call attention to his difference from the earlier speakers and to the fact that, though American, he, as an African American, had no connection to the Pilgrims. As the other Americans joined in, the song assumed new meaning. The emphasis shifted from

the difference that the African American singer was signaling to the shared meanings that "We Shall Overcome" has for all Americans. Finally, as the non-American guests added their voices, the scope of the song's meaning expanded beyond the boundaries of one national ideology. The non-Americans may just have been joining in on a party activity. But they may also have been expressing solidarity with the African American individual who initiated the singing in the narrow context of that Thanksgiving celebration. Alternatively, they may have been expressing solidarity with what he stood for in the wider context of racism and universal human rights (Reyes 2005: 56).

While the meaning of "We Shall Overcome" was initially expressed through the text of the song, music entirely without text can be equally meaningful to those who know how to "read" it. In his book on music in Bulgaria, Tim Rice writes on the politics of wedding music, which, in the communist era, had become significant musically and economically (2004). Besides the brilliance of the instrumentalists, he recounts, people's increasing dissatisfaction with the communist government also contributed to the enormous popularity of wedding music. The government had created problems for itself in the 1980s by instituting draconian measures against the Turks and **Roma** (also known as gypsies, figure 1.6), Bulgaria's Muslim minorities. Apparently fearing that these minorities had grown so large in number that they might begin to demand cultural autonomy, the government decided to solve the problem by symbolically erasing them and their culture from the national consciousness. This included banning all forms of "oriental" public cultural display, including the playing of Roma forms of music and dance that Bulgarian cultural officials began to claim that all these practices, including much of what was popular about wedding music, were aggressively antistate. At one level, wedding music was antistate simply because it operated in an economic sphere largely beyond state control. But in the highly charged political environment in Bulgaria in the late 1980s, wedding music, with its emphasis on improvisation, and especially forms of improvisation that broke the bounds of traditional practice (Rice 2001), could be interpreted as an iconic representation of the individual freedom Bulgarians increasingly sought in the political arena. It also provided a new "structure of feeling" (Williams 1977) that allowed people to experience some release and relief within an otherwise repressive and restrictive society (Williams 1977).

FIGURE 1.6 *Bulgarian Roma musicians Mladen Malakov, a brilliant Bulgarian Rom clarinet player, and unknown accordionist play virtuosic, amplified wedding music. (Photo from video by Timothy Rice, 1988.)*

Conde Nast Traveler (CNT), interviewing artist Yo Yo Ma:

CNT: You said that your trip to the Kalahari [Desert in South Africa] in 1993 changed your life. What does a Bushman have to say to a virtuoso Chinese cellist, and vice versa?

Ma: I participated in their transcendent practices, dancing for hours in a circle around the fire. I listened to the old-style music, with people playing for the hunt, for prayer, and for art. That experience was more powerful than almost anything I've done. I asked a woman, "Why do you do this?" She said, "It gives us meaning." How cool is that? That's as good a reason as any to do something.

CNT: How did it affect you?

Ma: It changed my perception of art. It was no longer about high art, low art, medium art. I realized that doesn't matter.

(*Conde Nast Traveler*, May 2007: 42)

USE

Although the meaning and the use of music are inseparable, thinking specifically about use permits us to focus on people's intentions. People make music useful in so many ways that one can think of—socially, as a mode of interaction or to create a romantic mood; politically, to control or unite; spiritually, for sacred expression and worship; economically, to make a living; medically, for soothing or healing; and so many more ways.

I have asked many people about the place of music in their lives. Many have replied: "Oh, I'm not interested in music at all." Then they admit regularly listening to music in their cars, occasionally going to a performance, dancing on a date, exercising with an iPod, or otherwise putting music into their lives. This they may categorize as enjoyment, as entertainment rather than musical activity. However they regard it, they are making music useful.

Untold numbers of people make a living from music—from paid performers to students employed in music libraries and record shops. Students in one of my courses had these comments to make: "Involvement in music looks good on a college application; that's a status function, a statement of self-worth." "Music helps me understand other people and their actions, to place myself in another person's shoes." "It's a stress reliever." "It quiets my anger and otherwise improves my mood." "Music helps me focus while doing repetitive tasks." "I remember things through song." "I use music to escape from chaos!"

One of the most significant uses to which people put music is to express an identity. Performers do this to establish an individual identity as a musician, of course, but music can also be emblematic of a group—a college, as in a school song; a heritage group, as in the Polish polka or the blues; a nationality, as in a national anthem. The meaning of such music is highly situated and useful for purposes ranging from contestation to solidarity. My favorite example is "We Are Family," which was adopted by the 1979 Pittsburgh Pirates baseball team for the purpose of uniting fans in song. In a contrasting use, it is entertainingly employed for irony in the feature film *The Birdcage*, when the conservative senator character and his family, unrecognizable in drag, are generously escorted out incognito through a gay nightclub, past the hovering press, as patrons dance obliviously and joyfully. One day as I waited on campus for a ride home, I heard "We Are Family" blasting forth from the open patio of the UC Berkeley Haas School of Business, where it was being used to send a meaningful message at an alumni fund-raising event. Identity was shifted to "man and fellow man" when the song was adopted in 2001 as the theme for the founding of the post-9/11 We Are Family Foundation, "a non profit dedicated to the vision of a global family by creating and supporting programs that inspire and educate the next generation about respect, understanding, and cultural diversity—while striving to solve some of our biggest global problems at the same time" (www.wearefamilyfoundation.org). Addressed to the young, a music video posted on the foundation's website features over 100 "beloved TV characters" singing for harmony to children in schools throughout the United States and beyond.

In the United States, the assertion of black ethnicity and African roots through music has been extremely effective sociopolitically. So effective, in fact, that some Americans of Asian descent have modeled their political musical activity on that of African Americans. Without a shared musical heritage, Japanese American and Chinese American musicians joined the world of jazz performance in the 1970s, thereby lifting that powerful African American musical voice in the assertion of their Asian American identity and rights. Influenced in the 1970s by the black power movement in the United States and Rastafarianism in Jamaica, black ethnicity became a major sociopolitical issue in Brazil. Music groups endorsed the ideology of the 1940s and 1950s that is still called "negritude;" their songs evoked their African ancestry and the "black is beautiful" theme, but also raised quite vehemently the questions of racism and its resulting socioeconomic injustices (Gerard Behague, personal communication, 2001).

However, music can easily be experienced as utterly decontextualized—divorced from its time and place, cut off from its original makers, meanings, and uses as musicians collect sounds from all over the world to create, as the singer Marc Anthony put it, "world music in a Long Island basement" (Buia 2001: 10). We can no longer assume that ethnic musical materials will serve as markers of particular ethnic identities, for example. Such globally shared music is constantly recontextualized by those who listen to it, given new meanings, and made to perform new as well as the same old functions—a process that some ethnomusicologists call glocalization (global localization). Other musical boundaries are being superseded as well. Senses of musical ownership are routinely challenged by sampling and online filesharing. Boundaries between musical genres such as jazz, rock, and classical are routinely breached. The creative process continues as music and music making become what people want them to be.

ACTIVITY 1.7 *Return to the piece of music you chose for Activity 1.4 and consider whether you can discern the aesthetic values that underlie it. Reflect on emotional stimulations, associations, and memories it invokes for you, to think about its meanings and the ways it has been useful for you as an individual, or for a group to which you belong. Prepare a statement on which you might base a contribution to class discussion.*

TRANSMISSION OF MUSICAL KNOWLEDGE

Three words prevail in writing about music to name the processes by which musical knowledge is passed among people: "dissemination," "circulation," and "transmission." The first two have been used increasingly since the burgeoning of popular music studies in the 1980s; I shall return to them later in the book. "Transmission" is a well-worn word that has mostly been used for one of the most crucial factors for music anywhere—the process by which musical knowledge is taught and learned. Here I focus on transmission and multiple means—tactile, oral, and visual—by which music might be transmitted.

If you have ever taken partner-dance lessons, you know that **tactile** communication of the movements is important. In her book on music in Bali in this series, Lisa Gold describes how, in coaching the remarkably young dancer of the *legong* style (always female), the teacher stands behind and manipulates the student's arms and body while singing the sequence of movements, indicating the melody and drum pattern, and counting out the steps (figure 1.7). In this way, the student learns the entire sequence by feel while integrating it with the music. Tactile transmission can also help in learning to play an instrument; I remember my piano teacher putting his hand over mine on the keys to demonstrate how I should shift my hand to play in another register.

With regard to **oral** means by which music is transmitted, in ethnomusicology we have become increasingly careful to distinguish between oral and aural transmission: oral transmission takes the perspective of the teacher and implies interaction between the teacher and the learner, while aural transmission takes the perspective of the learner, who hears the music through some aural source.

"Written" is the remaining mode of transmission that is usually acknowledged, implying the use of music notation. That is but one mode

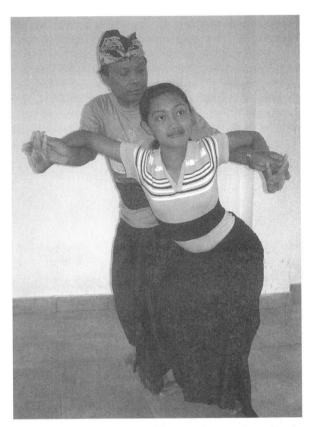

FIGURE 1.7 *Tactile transmission of* legong *dance and coordination with music. Master teacher I Nyoman Cerita with student Ni Made Ayu Septhan. A strong energy is often conveyed as the teacher firmly holds the arms and hands of the student, puts a knee into the arch of the back, holds the head, smacks an elbow up to convey the dynamic power and element of surprise that is so essential to Balinese dance. When the teacher holds or touches the student, it is about technique but also a transmission of energy; for the student it is about learning how your teacher feels something. (Photo and comment by Emiko Saraswati Susilo)*

of **visual transmission**, however. Another is observation; how many have learned to play an instrument by watching musicians! Also, a great deal can be taught and learned from paintings, photographs, film, and the various types of resources obtainable online. One day in a term when I was teaching Music of Japan and had just finished the segment on the Imperial *gagaku* music (CD track 1-9, Fig. 1.8), a student came to me bearing a **hichiriki**—a plastic imitation, but nevertheless a replica of the double-reed aerophone in the *gagaku* ensemble. He had bought it online, he said, and had come to ask if I might show him how to play it. Once I had recovered from surprise at that initiative, I replied regretfully that no, I could not help. Another student who had come along, who happened to be an oboe (double-reed aerophone) player, offered to try to help. Later, I learned that she had found the Japanese instrument totally different and couldn't help. Not to worry, said the determined *hichiriki* player, "I found a manual with video online and I am playing it." I will return to this point about sources for learning at the end of the chapter.

Important to be understood from the outset of this section, however, is that there are different views about whether or not musical knowledge should be shared and, if so, under what conditions. My teachers of North India's music, for instance, related to me instances of other teachers who would transmit certain knowledge only to students from their families. In her book on First Nations peoples, Beverley Diamond informs us that there are currently different views about whether Indigenous beliefs, songs, and customs (including those that constitute "musical knowledge") should be shared with outsiders—both members of other tribes or nations and non-Native Americans. Feeling the pain of being misrepresented by outsiders over and over again, and, some

FIGURE 1.8 *Japanese* Gagaku *ensemble. From left to right: Front row,* shōko, taiko, kakko; *middle,* kotos, ryūteki, hichiriki, biwas; *rear,* ryūtekis, hichirikis, shōs. *Members of the Tenri University Gagaku Ensemble.* (Courtesy of Koji Sato)

believe that nothing should be shared, that Native American knowledge should be accessible only to the Native American community from which it came. In Diamond's experience, that was not the majority view, although she considers it to be an understandable one. It's not that knowledge is secret, but rather that those who are entrusted with knowledge must know how it should be used.

Oral and Aural Transmission. Most music is learned aurally—both by intentional listening and by osmosis, that is, by absorbing what we hear around us. This was already the case before the early twentieth century, when radio and recordings expanded the potential material that was available for learning. The oral mass media of all sorts are without doubt the single greatest teaching force, playing an enormously significant role in the transmission of musical knowledge.

Where music is taught primarily by oral transmission, the teacher plays a significant role, as a repository of knowledge and technique, the individual responsible for musical quality, and often a guide in life (as the Indian *guru* is). The availability of recordings can change the degree of dependence of a pupil on a teacher, as well as the degree of control a teacher has over musical knowledge, but personal instruction provides a qualitatively different learning experience. Student-teacher relationships vary greatly. Particularly where music is being transmitted orally, but within a written tradition as well, a teacher might or might not be willing to make verbal explanations, preferring instead that the student listen, watch, and do.

A student, Nontapat Nimityongskul, remarked to me, "There are two main ways we can keep music. One is to write it down. The other is to know it in your heart." Nontapat raises an issue concerning oral and aural versus written transmission. Will music learned aurally be remembered and preserved? Quite possibly it will fade from memory, unless one or all of three conditions exist. The first and most necessary condition is that one intends to remember the music precisely as learned. This is a matter of personal or group motivation. The motivation would exist, for example, when there is a fear that incorrect rendering will cause some disaster.

The second condition is a system for learning the music so thoroughly that it is not likely to be forgotten. The most evidently successful such system was devised for the chanting of religious texts that have survived in Hindu Indian culture since the Vedic period (roughly 1500–500 B.C.E.). Without any reference to written materials, the chants have been transmitted from Brahmin priests to young Brahmin boys through untold numbers of generations. The teaching priest has his pupils learn the sacred text, using a well-worked-out memorization technique: a set of named patterns that recombine in various ways the words of each sentence of the text. In these patterns, the text is repeated and repeated until truly absorbed.

ACTIVITY 1.8 *Test this method by which Vedic recitation is learned. It involves treating each word in a sentence as a separate entity—to which I am giving a letter. By repeating two of the patterns, try memorizing this unfamiliar sentence: "The gods gave birth to the goddess of speech spoken by animals in all forms."*

- *To get started, write out the sentence. Below each word assign a letter in alphabetical order, as in, The gods gave birth to...*

a   b   c   d   e...

- *Speak (don't write!) the words of the sentence in each of the patterns.*
  Keep repeating each pattern until it comes easily, then move to the next pattern.

  krama pattern: ab / bc /cd / de / etc., to the end of the sentence.
  mālā pattern: ab / ba / ab / bc / cb / bc / cd / dc / cd / de /ed / de / etc.

- *Create your own pattern, and do the sentence with it as well. When you are comfortable with that one, you might well have memorized the sentence.*
- *Try to speak the sentence from memory—just as a sentence. Did the method work for you?*

The third condition is a system of reinforcement: a system that assures that memory of the music will be periodically renewed. "Oldies" radio broadcasts perform this function; recurring music in a religious calendrical cycle does as well, such as carols sung at Christmas or prayers chanted at Passover. In some situations, the responsibility for reinforcing memories is taken by institutions. In Java (Indonesia), musicians at the royal courts hold rehearsals expressly to maintain musical compositions and choreographies that are transmitted mainly through oral tradition (CD track 1-7). Referring to something written is another way to renew the memory periodically.

The best way to maintain musical memory is to have a sound recording available, for so much is excluded from even the most comprehensive system of notation—sensual vocal production that is characteristic of a style, for instance. Preservation was an unintended achievement of the recording industry when it began to record all kinds of musics in the 1890's as a way to sell the new machines. Using that technology, ethnomusicologists, folklorists, and some anthropologists have been motivated to preserve the world's musical treasures, and there are now numerous sound archives around the globe. Touching stories circulate about groups whose traditional music no longer exists for some reason—radical change from international influence, memory loss where no system of reinforcement was in place, or loss of interest on the part of successive generations—but recovery and revival is possible through recordings that someone deposited in an archive.

Visual Transmission in the Form of Notation.   The nature of a notation system depends on the purpose people intend it to serve, and numerous types are in use around the world. If any musician wants to write a brief reminder of music already held in memory, a minimalist notation will suffice, recording only the musician's choice of crucial information. If the minimalist information that is recorded gives a performer instructions on *how* to play the music—what to do on an instrument to sound out the music—it is called **prescriptive notation**. For a xylophone player, for instance, if the notation tells him or her which key to hit, that is prescriptive notation. If a composer or other musician wants to document how the music should "sound," it is called **descriptive notation**. That is the intention of Western staff notation.

Prescriptive notation for stringed and some historic keyboard instruments (often called **tablature**) gives technical instruction to players—where to place their fingers on a stringed instrument and perhaps more. Whereas there are any number of such systems that could illustrate this notation, I chose the historic notation for the **qin** (pronounced "chin" with a rising tone, figure 1.9), a Chinese zither-type instrument (CD track 1-10). Like other **tablature**-type notations, it is intended to transmit performing instructions. Reproduced in figure 1.10 is the beginning of a piece, "Flowing

Water." To read Chinese-language texts, start at the right side of the page and follow the characters in each column, from top to bottom. In figure 1.10, the title of the piece, "Flowing Water," is written at the top of the far right column, and the label for section one is given in the next column toward the left. The musical notation begins at the top of the third column, toward the middle of the page. Basically, the notation specifies left- and right-hand playing techniques and the strings on which they are to be executed. Figure 1.11 shows the Chinese numbers used to indicate the six strings of the instrument. Figure 1.12 shows the right-hand techniques specified in the first column of notation of the piece. Figure 1.13 shows you how indications of playing techniques and string numbers are combined in the first three characters of the piece.

ACTIVITY 1.9   *Your first task is to locate the string numbers in the characters. Fig. 1.11 gives you those numbers. Try copying those numbers to give you a visual feel for them.*

In Fig. 1.10, count to column 5 (from right to left). To get you started, I'll give you the string numbers in the first five characters of column 5, from the top down: 3 & 4, 2, 3, 4, 3. Now try to identify the string numbers in the large characters for the whole of column 3 from the right, that is, from the beginning of the piece. (Small characters written to the right in a column refer to an action to be taken after the main notes have been articulated.)

As you can see, the numbers are embedded within the characters, surrounded by indications of playing techniques. Using Figure 1.12 and 1.13 as a guide for those in column 3, you can see how the player is instructed to play each pitch.

Once you understand what the notation is giving you, try copying the first column of melody to experience the flow of it.

*Most important, think about what this notation does and does not tell you. Each time this notation would be used, the player would render it according to his own **dapu**, a process of realizing the notation in sound. This notation is prescriptive, rather than descriptive.*

FIGURE 1.9   *Chinese qin.*   *(Courtesy of UCLA Ethnomusicology Archives)*

FIGURE 1.10   *Qin notation of "Liushui" ("Flowing Water") (Courtesy of Frederick Lau)*

Numbers indicate the string(s) on which the technique is executed.	
一	1
二	2
三	3
四	4
五	5
六	6

FIGURE 1.11 *Chinese numbers.* *(Chart by Jane Chiu, Viet Nguyen, and Pamela Han)*

At the beginning of the piece (column 3 from the right in Figure 1.10), these right-hand techniques are required.	
勺	Middle finger pulls the string.
尸	Thumb pulls string with nail.
乇	Thumb pushes the string and comes to rest against the next string without sounding it.
早	"Chord" from two simultaneous techniques
厂	Index finger pushes string with tip of fingernail, twice in succession.

FIGURE 1.12   *Right-hand* qin *techniques (Chart by John Groschwitz)*

勺	Middle finger pulls string 1.
居	Thumb pulls string 6 with nails.
毡	Thumb pushes string 6.

FIGURE 1.13   *Techniques and string numbers combined in* qin *notation (Chart by John Groschwitz)*

Notation is a kind of access to information. Whereas in an orally transmitted musical tradition the teacher controls whether or not a pupil may learn something, writing the music down makes it more accessible to greater numbers of people. Unlike in Western music, where all voices and instruments use staff notation (though a few instruments, notably guitar and hip-hop turntable, use specialized tablatures) in Japan each traditional instrument has its own system of notation. Standardized notation assumes that the music is to be shared among the general music-reading public, whereas the Japanese system is tailored to in-group exclusivity.

The five-line **staff notation** system is so detailed that it requires a literacy that is specifically musical. With colonialism, however, its use was disseminated so widely in the world that it now constitutes a kind of international musical language. Because learning some of its basic principles can be of great help as a tool for musical communication, I give a brief guide here. An explanatory list of a few basic elements is given in figure 1.14, and others are added in figure 1.15, a sample of Western notation featuring a portion of the song "Aloha Oe," composed by Queen Liliuokalani of Hawaii (1838–1917).

An adage often voiced by one of my former teachers, Mantle Hood, is one I endorse: "A written tradition is only as strong as the oral tradition that supports it." If you have tried to read any notation system without some further verbal explanation and hearing what is notated, you can recognize that to be true. In the end, an interplay between the oral/aural and written processes for learning music is the reality for most musicians.

In this chapter I have introduced briefly the interests of ethnomusicologists in exploring how people all over the globe learn music and make it meaningful and useful in their lives. Instruments through which people make music are the subject of chapter 2.

Before going there, however, I want you to think about one more basic question. At the beginning of this chapter, concepts of "music" in general were explored. But what about "the music" or, as is frequently said, "the music itself"—TMI? What constitutes "the music itself—the ubiquitous TMI?" asked music historian Nicholas Mathew in a class I observed. He was speaking to the assumption of many of his students that the notated piece or the single recording (think MP3 file) is TMI. "But is it?" he queried and wrote across the board: Composer, performer, audience. Demonstrating the importance of the question, he showed us a clip from the 1947 feature film *Song of Love*. In the scene, the flambuoyant and fabulously

1. The basic unit is a staff of five lines (▤); staves meant to be read simultaneously are joined by a vertical line at the left margin.
2. Individual musical sounds are represented by notes. ♩ ♩
3. Pitch is indicated by placing notes both on staff lines and in spaces between staff lines.
4. Melodic contour is visible: Even if pitches cannot be identified, the rising and falling of the pitches can be followed.
5. When multiple musical parts are intended to be sounded together, they are aligned vertically.
6. Rhythm is shown by altering the appearance of notes. "Black" notes (with filled-in noteheads) are of shorter duration than "white" notes. A flag on the stem (♪) attached to a note shortens the duration. Additional time on the pitch is indicated by a dot after the note. For example:

   ♩ = 1 count
   ♪ = ½ count (half-counts are often linked by a beam ♫)
   ♩. = 1.5 counts
   ♩ = 2 counts
   ♩. = 3 counts

7. Meter (grouping of counts) is shown by vertical lines called bar lines. The space between two bar lines is called a measure. (In "Aloha Oe" each measure consists of four counts.) See chapter 3.

FIGURE 1.14 *Basic Guideline to Western Staff Notation*

famous nineteenth-century performer-composer, Franz Liszt, was playing his transcription for piano of composer Robert Schumann's romantic "Widmung" ("Dedication") that he had written for his beloved wife Clara, who sat listening in the intimate salon gathering. The select, elite audience applauded Liszt's bombastically virtuosic version of the piece with the sort of admiring adulation that Liszt hoped to receive from the transcriptions he made of other composers' compositions; the audience valued virtuosity, and he gave them just that. As other guests wandered off, Clara sat at the piano and played the piece as her husband had intended it to be—a quiet, lyrically tender love song. Before we could see Liszt's reaction in the film, Mathew brought the showing to an end. It was up to the students to think about what "the music" was in that instance. Their

FIGURE 1.15   *Five-line staff notation of "Aloha Oe."* (with the assistance of Joseph Dales)

conclusion: the composers, the performers, and the audience all con-tributed to what "the music" was. It certainly wasn't any one thing.

In the ensuing chapters of this book, I turn to thinking about music in additional ways. Chapter 2 is devoted to instruments (including the voice as an instrument), both in terms of ideas about them and in terms of ways in which they are used in musical practices. Chapters 3, 4, and 5 focus on three basic parameters of musical content—time, pitch and structure—as musicians have used them creatively. As in this introductory chapter, I have drawn examples from a variety of musics from around the world. In Chapter 6 I return to thinking about music through issues that ethnomusicologists have found to be important as they have studied many different musics and that authors of the case study volumes of this Global Music Series address at greater length. In some senses, Chapter 6 comes full circle back to this introductory chapter, to pull some things together. Chapter 7 guides you to musical investigations of your own. As I said in my "Note to Readers" (pp. xxiv), by the time you finish this book that is about the infinitely creative imagination of humankind, you will have experienced something that intrigues you or moves you, but in any case, causes you to think more deeply about music.

CHAPTER 2

Thinking about Instruments

The countless and varied musical instruments that have existed through time are evidence of how people make music meaningful and useful in their lives. Because people have taken them wherever they have gone— for signals in war, for entertainment on expeditions, as items for trade, as gifts for foreign potentates—instruments also provide evidence of cultural diffusion. A notice posted by Craig McCrae on the Society for Ethnomusicology internet list offers an excellent example of this, with the accordion as example:

> One vital but little-known accordion tradition is found in the Khorezm region of Uzbekistan, in recent centuries seat of the Khiva khanate and an important center of high civilization since ancient times. The most typical Khorezmian ensembles combine the diatonic accordion with vocals, *doyra* (frame drum) and the Azerbaijani *tar* (a plucked, fretted lute with sympathetic strings, a bit smaller than the Iranian *tar*). . . . Russian colonists brought the accordion to the region in the late nineteenth century and the locals quickly adopted it for their own use. A high point in Khorezmian accordion history was in the 1930s when Soviets organized women's ensembles with forty or fifty accordions. (27 July 2000; cited with permission)

When people design and craft instruments, they both express cultural values and create musical practices through them. One basic question is whether instruments should be standardized. "Definitely!" say music makers and instrument makers wherever mass production and ensemble practice foster standardization. "Definitely not!" says the player of *sitār* in North India. "Add a string for me" (CD tracks 1-11, 1-12). Most Indian music ensembles are small, and mass production of instruments is still low, so the idea of idiosyncratic instruments flourishes.

34

"Standardize the pitch of all instruments in this ensemble for me," says a Javanese purchaser to a smithy, "but make its tuning slightly different from the tuning of all other *gamelan*s" (CD track 1-7, fig. 1.5). Where ensemble-specific pitch is an ideal, individuals in Java do not bring their own personal instrument to play in a *gamelan*; instead, they gather to play a set owned by a person, company, or club.

Indeed, instruments are items of expressive culture as well as material culture, works of art, symbols, technological inventions, tools for earning a livelihood. In this chapter I examine various ways in which people have thought about instruments, considering them first as physical objects apart from the music made with them, then as instruments in music, that is, as people use them musically. I include both voices and bodies among musical instruments.

INSTRUMENTS AS OBJECTS

Ideas about Instrument Types. In two of the world's oldest civilizations—China and India—musical instruments have for millenia been considered particularly significant items of culture. While individual instruments had their specific meanings and uses, in China and India people also thought systematically about them to develop **classification** systems for instrument types.

The ancient Chinese classification system resonated with the value that culture placed on nature. Chinese classified their instruments according to the natural material that produced each instrument's sound. The "eight sounds" (*ba yin*) were those of metal, stone, skin, vegetable gourd, bamboo, wood, silk, and earth (i.e., pottery). As shown in figure 2.1, the sounds were associated with cardinal directions and seasons. When musicians performed on specified instruments, the "eight sounds" were incorporated into significant rituals—not to provide musical variety, but to manifest a link with nature (CD track 1-13).

ACTIVITY 2.1 *Identify the natural sounds in CD track 1-13, Confucian ritual music. It originated in China but has been preserved in Korea, as a–ak. Figure 2.2 may help you hear the different instruments.*

Ba yin system of instrument classification from the Zhou Dynasty
(c. 1000–200 B.C.E.)

Type	Direction	Season	Instruments
Metal	West	Autumn	Bell-chimes
Stone	Northwest	Autumn to Winter	Stone-chimes
Skin	Northwest	Winter	Drums
Gourd	Northwest	Winter to Spring	Mouth Organ
Bamboo	East	Spring	Flutes, pipes
Wood	Southeast	Spring to Summer	Wooden tiger (scraper)
Silk	Southeast	Summer	Zithers
Earth	Southwest	Summer to Autumn	Ocarinas, vessel flutes

FIGURE 2.1   *Ba yin chart.*   (Chart by Kin Hang Lam.)

FIGURE 2.2   *Instruments of the Korean* a-ak *ensemble. Transverse bamboo flute (ji) played by seated musicians on left; in rear just to their right—wooden barrel-shaped drum (jin'go) and hanging stone lithophone slabs (p'yeon'gyeong); hanging large bronze bell in center (teukjong); set of hanging bronze elliptical bells played by musician on right (p'yeonjong).* (Photo courtesy of Donna Kwon)

The *ba yin* classification system has fallen out of use, but the phrase "silk and bamboo" (*sizhu*) is still widely used in Chinese music to designate a string and wind ensemble. The phrase still names natural materials, but the intention now is to suggest a pleasing combination of different timbres (CD track 1-2).

Scholars in ancient India also cultivated an intellectual tradition of systematic thinking. They loved to classify and devised a variety of exhaustive categorizations—from character types in drama (in the *Nātya Sāstra* treatise) to physical positions in lovemaking (in the *Kāma Sūtra*). The classification system for musical instruments, dating from the early centuries of the Common Era and still viable today, identifies four basic types, according to the primary sound-producing medium: the vibrating body of the instrument itself, a vibrating membrane, a vibrating string, and a vibrating column of air.

In the European system of classification, there are four groups of instruments, based on the selection in the largest ensemble, an orchestra: strings, winds, percussion, and keyboard. Wind instruments are also referred to in more specific categories, brass and woodwind (figure 2.3).

FIGURE 2.3 *European instrument classification system: Winds (Brass). From left to right: Michael Fraser (tuba), Christy Dana (trumpet), Karen Baccaro (trumpet), Beth Milne (horn), Suzanne Mudge (trombone).* (Photo by Kathleen Karn)

This system mixes the criteria for classification: strings and winds name the sound-producing medium; percussion and keyboard refer to the means of playing; and brass and woodwind pertain to the material of construction.

Nineteenth-century Europeans, in the interest of science (but to a large extent as a result of imperialistic colonialism), began to gather instruments from around the world and to deposit them in museum collections, where they were documented as physical objects rather than meaningful items of culture. The task of cataloguing them presented a challenge. While efficient in their own musical context, the basic European criteria were too inconsistent to be useful for scientific classification. In the late nineteenth century, searching for a consistent system, the Belgian curator Victor Mahillon turned to the ancient Indian system with its one consistent criterion—the primary sound-producing medium of the instrument—and named the four types of instrument as **idiophone** (from the Latin *idem*, the thing itself), **membranophone**, **chordophone**, and **aerophone** (see figure 2.4). Some instruments draw on more than one sound source, but this system designates only the primary one.

Early in the twentieth century, the German scholars Curt Sachs and Erich von Hornbostel espoused and expanded Mahillon's system, which is now used by museums and scholars worldwide. For greater specificity, they devised criteria for distinguishing instruments within each of the four major categories. A complete explanation of the system is found in Baines and Wachsmann (1961); here I incorporate into figure 2.4 only a few helpful definitions from that source. Note particularly the numbering system that allows for subdivisions within each category by a criterion that is sensible for the instrument type. The Sachs-Hornbostel system allows for further subdivisions, as shown in figure 2.4 for the chordophones and aerophones. Even further subdivisions than are shown in figure 2.4 are provided in the system. Membranophones, for instance, are further subdivided by shape (see figure 2.5), then by number of heads and playing method. All chordophones, as another example, are further subdivided by playing technique—struck, plucked, bowed. You might be surprised to think of a piano as a zither-type chordophone played by keyboard (Fig. 2.6)

Updating the Sachs-Hornbostel system calls for some adjustments, because it is designed only for acoustically generated sounds. Figure 2.5 includes mechanical and electrical instruments. A category of **corpophones** is another possibility, to include handclapping, finger snapping, body slapping, and the like into the system. In addition, the idea

1. Idiophones (sound produced by the instrument's vibrating body) are subdivided by playing technique.

   11 Struck

   12 Plucked

   13 Friction

   14 Blown

2. Membranophones (sound produced by a vibrating string) are sub-divided first by playing technique.

   21 Struck

   22 Plucked

   23 Friction

   24 Singing membrane

3. Chordophones (sound produced by a vibrating string) are subdi-vided by construction.

   31 A zither (simple chordophone) consists solely of a string bearer; the strings are parallel to the sounding body and run almost the entire length.

   32 Composite chordophones

       321 A lute has a neck along which strings run, and the plane of the strings runs parallel with the sound table.

       321.1 Lyres, classified as a type of lute, are important in Africa. The strings are attached to a yoke, which lies in the same plane as the sounds table and consists of two arms and a crossbar.

       322 On a harp the plane of the strings lies at right angles to the sound table, and a line joining the lower ends of the strings points toward the neck.

4. Aerophones (sound produced by a vibrating column of air) are sub-divided into

   41 Free aerophones and

   42 Wind instruments proper, on which the column of air is con-fined.

       421 On flutes a stream of air is directed against an edge.

       422 On reed pipes the air stream has through means of a reed placed at the head of the instrument, intermittent

access to the column of air that is to be made to vibrate. Reed pipes are subdivided into:

422.1 Double reeds, on which a double layer of reed vibrates against itself

422.2 Single reeds, which vibrate against a plane

422.2 Free reeds, where a reed secured inside vibrates freely.

423 Horn and trumpet-type instruments, on which the air stream passes through the player's vibrating lips, so gaining intermittent access to the air column that is to be made to vibrate.

FIGURE 2.4 *International instrument classification system (Sachs-Hornbostel) based on the ancient Indian system.* *(Chart by Kin Hang Lam)*

of membrane as animal skin requires stretching to include fiberglass heads of drums in the category of membranophones. While a number of instruments are hybrids and do not fit neatly into the categories of the Sachs-Hornbostel system, it continues to be extremely useful for the study of musical instruments.

ACTIVITY 2.2 *To correlate the numerical listing of the Sachs-Hornbostel system with Figure 2.5, add the numerals to the figure.*

To understand the subdivisions in the classification system, investigate these: Among the struck idiophones, what distinguishes a bell from a gong and then a xylophone, a lithophone, and metallophone from each other? Among the aerophones, what distinguishes a trumpet from a horn, an oboe from a bassoon? Try your hand at classifying the reed aerophones in Figure 2.7; it will take some investigating.

An electronic instrument depends on electricity to produce a sound; if you unplug it—no sound. If you're feeling really adventurous, experiment with devising a classification system for electronophones. Start by listing a few instruments you think belong in this category and work from there.

A number of relatively more contemporary ideas about grouping musical instruments are in use, meant not for worldwide comparative study but for local purposes. The Kpelle of West Africa, for example, categorize instruments by playing technique, as either struck (including plucked strings and drums) or blown. This local classification works because all Kpelle stringed instruments are plucked, rather than bowed, and the finger in their view strikes the string (Stone 2005: 20). In Javanese *gamelan* the two major groupings are "loud-playing" (drums and louder bronze instruments) and "soft-playing" (flute, strings, and quieter bronze instruments). Those Javanese groupings are explained by historians as dating to the use of different ensembles for different performance contexts, but instruments from the two groupings have probably been combined in ensembles for about four hundred years.

The West African Igbo provide two conjunct systems for categorizing their musical instruments: according to the sounding material or the technique of sound production (Nzewi 1991: 57). At the same time they acknowledge musical roles and sociocultural musical importance informed by variety and popularity, as follows.

1. The most popular and varied are the wooden, metal, and membrane instruments. Without producing definite pitches, these are capable of a wide range of phonic manipulation: to "sing," to "talk," and to play percussion roles in ensembles. Nzewi uses the term *melorhythm instruments* for these.

2. The second in importance are blown instruments, which are melody or phonic-effects-producing instruments.

3. Next are the shaken and pot instruments, which play percussive roles in ensembles.

4. Finally there are plucked (soft-toned) melody instruments, which are played primarily as solo instruments.

ACTIVITY 2.3 *Choose an instrument in each of the four basic categories of the Sachs-Hornbostel classification system that you see pictured in this book. Classify each of them in the other systems just above. If classifying in one of the systems doesn't seem to work, articulate the reason or reasons.*

Electro-mechanical instru
Radio-electric instru
Electric organs
Electric guitars
Mechanical instruments
Mechanical organs
Automatic pianos
Mechanical music makers
Carillons and chimes
Music boxes
Pianoforte
Clavichord
Dulcimer
Spinet
Virginal
Harpsichord
Psaltery
Long zithers
Stick zithers
Raft zithers
Tube zithers
Trough zithers
Ground zithers
Fiddles
Fretted lutes
Flat-backed lutes
Round-backed lutes
Frame harps
Angle harps
Bow harps
Bowl lyres
Box lyres
Multiple bows
Mouth bows
Resonated bows
Simple bows

Mecha
and ele

Chordophones

Membranoph

Mirlitons
Friction drums
Frame drums
Vessel drums
Long drums
Footed drums

42

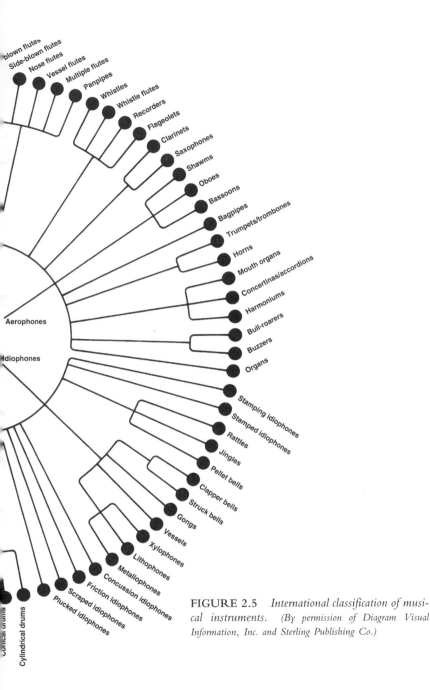

FIGURE 2.5 *International classification of musical instruments. (By permission of Diagram Visual Information, Inc. and Sterling Publishing Co.)*

43

FIGURE 2.6   *In the European instrument classification system, these instruments are keyboard and string. In the Sachs-Hornbostel, they are both chordophones (strings)—of the zither (piano, played by Nalini Ghuman) and harp (played by Henry Spiller) types respectively.   (Photo by Kathleen Karn)*

Some classification systems then, facilitate the comparison of instruments of the same basic type as they are found in various places around the world. One need only think of lute-type instruments, which most historians agree originated in the Middle East and spread gradually by the process of diffusion. Middle Eastern plucked lutes traveled different routes across the continent of Asia—to the east, for instance, where one form became the Chinese *pipa* (Fig. 2.8), and west to Europe and beyond, where another form became the guitar in its many manifestations (Fig. 2.9). A Middle Eastern bowed lute is the origin of the fiddle/violin, which, recycled back to Asia, was adopted into contemporary Middle Eastern and Indian music.

The most natural of all musical instruments—the human voice—is totally neglected in the classification systems to which I have introduced you thus far. However, it was of primary significance in

FIGURE 2.7 *Irish session in Ocean View, Miltown Malbay, County Clare. Michael Falsey (pipes), Mary Ann Sexton (accordion), Gabi Wooff (flute). (Peter Laban, Miltown Malbay, Co. Clare). The pipes are uilleann pipes; a full set consists of a bag (under the player's left arm), bellows (pumped using the left elbow), chanter (being fingered, resting on Mr. Falsey's knee), three drone pipes and three regulator pipes (both sets resting over his right knee, the regulators lying on top and played with the side of his right hand). The accordion is a two-row button accordion made in Italy by Paolo Soprani; the fingers of the right hand play the melody notes and the fingers of the left hand play the bass notes. The flute is made from blackwood, a model in the simple flute system (pre-Theobald Boehm) that ranges from keyless to eight keys. (Dora Hast, personal communication, 2011). (Peter Laban, Miltown Malbay, Co. Clare)*

the ancient Greek system that classified instruments into two categories—voice and non-voice, i.e., the animate (the "human vocal") and the inanimate. Inanimate instruments were subdivided into string and wind.

Classification with regard to voice types has been of interest mostly in European-based practices. There, attention has been given in choral music to dividing parts based on the range (span) of pitches a singer is asked to perform (classified from high to low as soprano, alto, tenor,

FIGURE 2.8 *Tsun-yuen Lui playing Chinese* pipa. *(Courtesy of the UCLA Ethnomusicology Archives)*

bass). For soloists, tessitura—the most comfortable range for a given singer and that in which (s)he presents the best vocal quality—has been the subject of most attention.

The expectation that a singer will probably expand a naturally comfortable range only slightly is a culture-specific idea about the use of the voice (and there have been exceptions in the demands of some European composers). In other musical traditions, the expectation for pitch range is entirely different. In North Indian (Hindustani)

FIGURE 2.9   *Principal instruments of a Mexican* mariachi *ensemble. From left to right:* vihuela, *Armando Quintero;* guitarrón, *Francisco "El Capiro" Castro; violin, Hilario Cervantes; trumpet, Luis "El Loco" Pérez.*   *(Courtesy of Daniel Sheehy)*

classical music, the ideal is to sing in three pitch registers, (high, middle, and low), displaying a range that is considerably wider than most people's "natural voice." The same can be said for Japanese traditional vocal practices, wherein a very wide range is expected, to the extent that it is sometimes impossible to discern if a woman or man is singing.

Beyond classification of voices by range, the matter of vocal production and resulting qualities of vocal sound emerges. I will return to that below.

Ideas about Particular Instruments.   Some instruments carry extramusical associations so clear and strong that the mere sound of them will transmit meaning to anyone in a knowledgeable group. The *didjeridu* (CD track 1-14, figure 1.1a), used as background music in television promotionals, evokes images of the Australian outback, *Crocodile Dundee,* or the lone Aboriginal on walkabout. Because of its historical association with court culture, European classical music imparts high class status in advertisements for expensive automobiles and expensive perfumes. The saxophone connotes "cool": a student, Tamina Spurney, noted, "When I hear it, I think of jazz and sunglasses and nightclubs and sophistication" (2001). Because of international circulation of sound recordings, performances by émigré musicians and the adoption of it for instruction in many American schools, the distinctive sound of the **steel band** (CD track 1-15) immediately invokes the Caribbean—or specifically Trinidad—for many of us.

> **ACTIVITY 2.4** *To focus on extra musical associations with instruments, watch for a few in TV ads and other contexts. Then, to think further about this, look for bands on YouTube that include instruments from two or three different cultures. (One example is banjo player Béla Fleck and the multi-musical collaborations in his "Tales from the Acoustic Planet" project.) Do you ascribe extra musical associations to them, or do you think the musicians are suggesting some?*

Brazilians recognize in the distinctive sound of the **berimbau** the spirit of rebellion, resistance, and liberation that the present practitioners of **capoeira** are able to draw from it (CD track 1-16, Fig. 2.10). A common story has it that *capoeira* was a martial art developed by slaves to aid in rebellions and escapes, but that it had to be disguised as a dance to fool the masters, who had forbidden all martial art training to slaves. *Capoeira* players agree that even after the abolition of slavery, a *capoeirista* would never carry a gun or even use one if captured in a fight. It was a matter of pride that one did not need a firearm to emerge victorious. Today this spirit is directed toward socially engaged projects that are intended to improve the lives of Brazilians of African heritage, and the legacy of slavery is remembered in the names of *capoeira* groups (Murphy 2006: 62).

For Native Americans, the vertical bass drum became the horizontal powwow drum. It was "turned"—a concept that is often used to describe how the energy or power of an object may be changed, in this

FIGURE 2.10   *The* bateria, *or* capoeira *ensemble, at a children's* capoeira *ring in the* Grupo de Capoeira Angola Pelourinho. *On the left can be seen the* agogô, *the double bell-gong, as well as a child playing a tambourine-like* pandeiro, *and three* berimbaus *(the* gunga *with the largest gourd is the leftmost in the hands of the child leading the singing). Another student plays a* pandeiro, *and on the right end of the bench is the tall* atabaque. *(Photo courtesy of Greg Downey)*

case to change its energy and its related meaning from war to peace. Multiple men sitting around one drum to play in a spirit of peace become "the drum" (Diamond 2007).

Associations of Sexuality and Gender.   Referring to the physical body, and specifically biological attributes of male and female, some instruments are accorded sexual associations. Is not B. B. King's guitar named

Lucille, and do not instrument teachers sometimes tell pupils to hold the instrument as they would a loved one? The flute of the Hindu god Krishna is playfully suggestive of phallic sexual innuendo, enjoyed by poets and singers and devotees. In Liberia and other places in Africa, drums might be thought of as female. In surprising contradiction to "our" ideas of female and male physicality, in Bali (Indonesia), some sets of instruments have two large gongs: the larger of the pair (lower in pitch) is considered female, while the smaller (higher) is considered the male (Gold 2005: 41).

Ideas about **gender** sometimes dictate who may and may not play an instrument. In Bulgaria traditionally only men played musical instruments, and the playing of an instrument was an enactment of maleness. Women who played were so exceptional that they were the immediate targets of gossip. There are exceptions, of course. Returning to the powwow for a gendered perspective, it is meaningful that women have historically been excluded from sitting around the powwow drum. The explanation for this exclusion, however, sometimes surprises non-Native students, says Beverley Diamond in her book in this series, since it relates, not to any restrictions on women's expressive potential, but to the power of their bodies. Women have the ability to purify their bodies monthly when they menstruate. Men, on the other hand, do not have this power and must drum to acquire the same spiritual strength. In some communities, the prohibition against women touching the drum has been relaxed, but in other places, it is still respected. A role that women do play is to form a circle around the drum, symbolically holding the circle together and participate in the singing (Diamond 2008).

ACTIVITY 2.5   *If you play a musical instrument, think back to how you came to select your instrument. Was there some instrument you considered but did not pursue? Did gender or sex have anything to do with the choice? Even now, do you perceive the instrument to be played predominantly by musicians of one particular gender or sex?*

As several authors have noted in case study volumes in this series, gender and sex restrictions are decreasing in contemporary life. In Mexican and Mexican American cultures, for example, whereas women were typically excluded from public mariachi *performance, except as singers, many are now taking*

up the instrumental genre (CD track 1-6). Have you witnessed such a process of change in any musical sphere?
  More generally, what does the instrument you play mean to you and your peers? Does it have a particular cultural status—associated, for instance, with certain social classes or ethnicities, or is it even perhaps a "national" instrument somewhere in the world? Is the instrument used in religious music, or mainly for secular music, or for both in your experience? Are there interesting stories surrounding the instrument and its meaning? Are you likely to see it a lot in films, TV shows and advertisements, or does it appear in poems or novels you have read?

Spiritual Associations. We find throughout the world the idea of an instrument's giving voice to a sacred spirit. In the Poro or Sande secret society of the Kpelle people of West Africa, an official plays pottery flutes to produce the voice of the spirits. In Buddhism, the conch shell produces the voice of Buddha symbolically; the call on CD track 1-17 invites monks to assemble at a Tibetan monastery temple at dawn. Not the voice of a sacred spirit, but a spiritual connection with nature and Zen Buddhist meditation, distinguishes the Japanese *shakuhachi* (figure 1.2, CD track 1-18).

  Religious associations suggest many other meanings. To some Christian Protestant groups the fiddle is "the Devil's instrument," and the names of fiddle tunes and legends certify it: "Devil's Dream," "Devil in the Kitchen," "Devil Went Down to Georgia." The harp, on the other hand, is the instrument of angels. While conservative elements within Islam have condemned many instruments for distracting the faithful, followers of Sufism, who pursue a more mystical interpretation of Islam, often embrace specific instruments in their ritual practices. The Mevlevi Sufis, for example, place the *ney* (flute) in the center of their rituals and philosophy. In the Hindu pantheon the *mṛdaṅgam* drum (CD track 1-19) is associated with Ganesh, the deity of auspicious beginnings, and drummers in South India perform a brief ritual in praise of him to initiate instruction on the instrument. From the offstage instrument room beside the traditional Japanese stage of the *kabuki* theater the deep-sounding strokes of a bell invoke the meditative atmosphere of a Buddhist temple or of impending death, while

FIGURE 2.11 *The* komungo *is a very unusual zither-type instrument in that it has both frets and individual bridges. Its six strings are made of twisted silk. Strings 2, 3, and 4 rest on 16 graduated frets, while strings 1, 5, and 6 are supported by moveable bridges shaped like the foot of a crane. Fine tuning of the strings is executed by round wooden pegs at the playing end of the instrument. (The context for this photo by Donna Kwon is an educational pre-concert instrument demonstration in the lobby of a concert hall in Seoul)*

 the chipper combo of flute, drums, and lute invokes the fun of a Shinto shrine festival to complement the dramatization that the audience sees on stage (CD track 1-20).

Cultural Status. Some individual instruments are accorded more prestige than others. Many peoples give primary status to the voice as the best of instruments. In South India vocal music is so dominant that there is no independent instrumental repertoire of compositions; instrumentalists perform songs (CD track 1-19). The reason for this is that the voice is the vehicle for sacred chant, from which Indian music evolved, and music remains primarily a treasured mode for the expression of religious devotion (see Activity 1.8).

In Japan as in Western countries, the piano holds a high status. When European music was adopted there in the process of modernizing the nation in the nineteenth- and early twentieth centuries, the piano was a rare item; only relatively wealthy persons could afford one or had the space to house one. By the time it became widely accessible from Japanese manufacturers such as Yamaha and Kawai, the piano had accrued the prestigious socio-economic associations that it still holds. Americans can understand this easily, thinking of grand pianos that sit unplayed in living rooms as a piece of furniture, transmitting visually the aura of high cultural status.

An instrument's status can be transferred to players and makers of that instrument, so that a sociomusical pecking order develops. In the prestigious Korean court music ensemble the zither-type **komungo** is the instrument of highest status (figure 2.11, CD track 1-21); consequently, until a few years ago, when the present, more democratic system was introduced, the musician who played it held the highest personnel rank. Drums in South India are an interesting case: although the skins of dead animals are considered polluting, drums are considered powerful instruments. Whereas makers of drums, who work with the skins, are of lowest status, players who invoke the power of the instrument are Brahmins, with the highest caste status.

ACTIVITY 2.6 *With a classmate or two, plan a mini-fieldwork project to inquire further among your peers and in the media to discover other examples of the sorts of ideas about instruments that I have pointed out—ideas about particular instruments, associations of sexuality and gender, spiritual associations, and cultural status—and others if you wish. See particularly "Picking a Project" and "Planning the Project" in Chapter 7 for guidance. If this proves interesting to you, you may decide actually to conduct the research.*

Aesthetic Value.   As exhibitions in museums around the world attest, an instrument may be treated as an object of aesthetic value apart from its musical capacity. A drum inlaid with mother-of-pearl, a harpsichord lid embellished with painted flowers and birds, the wooden body of a grand piano gently undulating around a sturdy steel frame—craftsmanship endows these physical objects with artistic beauty.

You can find multiple meanings in the carved case of a bamboo xylophone from *gamelan Jegog* of West Bali (figure 2.12): elaborate embellishment of a valued instrument, yes, but also invocation of Bhoma, son of the forest in the Hindu Balinese pantheon, the fanged protector whose face is often carved over doorways to the inner courtyard in temples and over house doorways to prevent evil from entering.

Item of Technology.   Instruments have always been items of technology. It takes only one experience with trying to make one to appreciate the extent to which that is true. However, it took mass production and

FIGURE 2.12   *Bamboo xylophones from* gamelan Jegog *of West Bali. Carved on the center instrument is Bhoma, fanged protector against evil.*   (Photo by Lisa Gold)

the burgeoning popularity of electronic instruments to make most of us think of them in technological terms. An average popular music band carts around and sets up an astounding amount of equipment; "the technology" is a member of the band.

People change instruments technologically on a regular basis. For example, the piano did not have even a marginally successful steel frame until about the 1820s. Only after the frame was universally in place, after the middle of the nineteenth century, could thicker and higher-tension strings increase the tonal power, brilliance, and therefore expressive capacity of the piano. Bluhmel added valves for brass instruments in 1818, and Boehm developed a system of mechanical keys for woodwinds in 1832–39. Various durable materials are being used to replace animal skins (i.e., membranes) on drums and strings of natural material on chordophones, and tuning mechanisms have been added to many instruments around the world, from drums to zithers.

No matter how technological a process, the manufacturing of an instrument can become imbued with deep meaning and the maker of an instrument be deemed a person of special cultural significance. The making of gongs in Java and Bali is a spiritually charged craft. Forging a large gong (figure 2.13) is a formidable task, requiring special skills and precise coordination among the members of a team of five or more men. From fieldwork observation, Lisa Gold wrote this description of the process.

> Watching a gong being forged is almost like witnessing a musical performance: a number of gongsmiths work together so that every movement is coordinated. First copper and tin are melded together to produce molten bronze, which is poured into a mold in the shape of a pancake. When hardened it is placed in a fire and hammered into the three-dimensional, bossed gong shape. One person operates the handheld bellow to fan the fire while another holds the gong with tongs and turns it to allow two other people to hammer it into shape. The hammers strike consecutively after each turn of the gong, sounding in a rhythm that recalls interlocking parts in *gamelan* music (Gold 2005: 31; CD track 1-22).

The bronze is unpredictable, and even an experienced team will occasionally fail, having to melt down and reforge. But gongsmiths have long believed that it is a spiritually dangerous task as well, requiring

FIGURE 2.13   *Balinese gong.*   *(Photo by Lisa Gold)*

the smith and his men to make particular offerings and take on the names of characters from the medieval Panji legends.

Returning to Activity 2.2—the classification of electronic instruments (electronophones)—you can think of all sorts of relatively more recent instruments that are items of technology. For instance, the varieties of electronic keyboards have revolutionized the possibilities for that ilk of instrument. I count the computer as the ultimate keyboard. And the turntable has morphed into being an instrument in itself, requiring considerable skill to manipulate for musical purposes. In the hands of a vocalist, the microphone can rightfully be considered a musical instrument. In most popular music, it plays an important role in projecting the voice. By manipulating the distance of the microphone from the mouth, a singer can apply subtle control to the dynamics and timbre of the voice.

Electronic instruments are playing an increasingly important role in music making in so many ways. For instance, electronic keyboards and synthesizers, connected to powerful computers and driven by sophisticated software, offer an infinite variety of sonic possibilities, allowing musicians not only to play the notes but actually to design the sounds that their instrument makes. One further example: computers equipped with sensors that capture body gestures are now used as musical instruments. They can offer the same level of intimate control as their acoustic counterparts (Wessel & Wright 2002). In such computer-based musical instruments, software plays an essential role in interpreting the gestures and applying them to the control of processes that generate sound and musical patterns.

Item of Commodity.   Another way to think about instruments is in economic terms—as items to be manufactured, bought and sold. Besides the economic side of instruments as items of commodity, there may be interesting effects of such economic activity on musical practice. The concertina in Ireland is a case in point (CD track 1-23). The **concertina** belongs to the free reed family of instruments (see the Hornbostel classification 422.2), including accordions and melodeons, all of which are popular in Ireland today. The concertina came to Ireland by the late 1800s. Mass produced in Germany and England, the instruments were poorly made but extremely loud and therefore good for accompanying dances. While they were soon supplanted in most places by the even louder accordion, concertinas continued to remain popular in County Clare. Many houses had concertinas that were used for practice and for house dances. A large number of cheap German models flooded the market there from 1900 to 1950. Because of their poor quality, the instruments had to be replaced often; they were your quintessential consumer product in a capitalist economy. Women were able to buy them at local hardware stores, and because of this, the concertina became, and remains, known as a woman's instrument. One by-result of the concertina trade in the nineteenth century, on the other hand, was the decline of the distinctive Irish uilleann bagpipe, shown in Fig 2.7. (See Scott and Hast 2004)

ACTIVITY 2.7 *If you think of the incredibly complex set of instruments, amplifiers, and speakers (and lights, risers, backdrops, and so forth) that adorn the stages of most popular music concerts at present, it is clear that technology reigns in that sphere of musicking. Agree or disagree with this statement and be prepared to say why: in addition to musical values, other aesthetic, economic, and cultural values are being expressed in the degree to which technology is used and displayed on such occasions.*

Timbre and Aesthetics of Sound. Finally, in this discussion of instruments as objects, there is the matter of **timbre**—the quality of the sound of an instrument or voice. "Reedy," "nasal," "growly," "dark," "golden": timbres are difficult to describe precisely in words.

It is remarkable how different instruments whose construction is similar can be made to sound so different. The sound of a basic bamboo flute is modified on the Chinese *di-tze* by placing a paper membrane near the blow hole; the resulting reedy sound can be contrasted with that of the *shakuhachi* without membrane (*syakuhati* hereinafter, as per Japanese preference), for instance (CD track 1-24, compared with CD track 1-18).

In recent years the analysis and synthesis of the sounds of musical instruments has reached a high level of refinement (Risset & Wessel 1999). These acoustical analysis techniques have helped us better understand the ingredients of musical timbre and the corresponding synthesis methods provide composers with an expanded palette of sounds. An example of the analysis and synthesis of the *syakuhati* is provided on CD track 1-25. First, one hears the full sound of the *syakuhati* with its characteristic noiselike transients. The sound is then decomposed into its constituent frequency components. First, only the fundamental frequency is played. Then harmonics are added one by one to build up the tone. The noisy transients are then played alone, and finally the sound of the *syakuhati* is completely reassembled. The synthesized sound is virtually indistinguishable from the original.

Perhaps the most meaningful question about timbre brings us to the matter of aesthetics, in this case, values concerning the qualities of musical sound. In accordance with the sound aesthetics of many African groups, the natural sounds of instruments are likely to be disguised or complemented in some way. In CD track 1-26, a recording of the Kiembara group of the Senofo (Ivory Coast, West Africa), you can hear several examples of this. The ensemble consists of four xylophones and three bowl-shaped drums of different sizes; rattle-type idiophones attached to the xylophone players' wrists add to the sound. On the xylophones, each wooden bar is resonated by a gourd; each gourd has one or two membranes, which cover specially bored holes to alter the timbre of the sound as they vibrate. The membranes are made from the webs with which certain spiders protect their eggs. In addition, jingles made of pieces of tin and metal rings are fitted to both the smaller kettledrums.

For variety of timbre, perhaps no instrument is more flexible than the human voice. While the variety of timbres produced on chordophones, aerophones, idiophones, and membranophones can be significantly different from instrument to instrument, the variety of timbres that are cultivated by singers around the world is perhaps equalled or surpassed only by sounds created technologically on electronophones. Compare, for example, the aesthetic choice for a beautiful sound in Cantonese opera's female vocal style (CD track 1-27) and that of European bel canto opera style (CD track 1-28). Those two examples offer a contrast in the cultivation of nasality as opposed to a clear, open sound.

ACTIVITY 2.8 *Pick one instrument type that you like to listen to—flute, plucked lute, double reed, or drum, for example. Using the Internet or another source, find at least three greatly contrasting timbres produced on instruments of this type. Explore the reasons why the sounds are so different.*

If the aesthetics of vocal timbre particularly interest you, there are plenty of examples on CD tracks 1-1, 1-5, 1-8 and others to be introduced later.

INSTRUMENTS IN MUSICAL PRACTICE

Put a person together with a musical instrument and a world of possibilities opens up. Such different kinds of music can be made on the same instrument! One need only think of the violin in the hands of a Romanian Roma musician, a bluegrass fiddler, a Cajun fiddler, an Irish fiddler, a South Indian classical violinist, and a European classical violinist to realize that it is not so much the instrument as human creativity that determines the music's character.

Instrumental Capacity. On the other hand, an instrument must have certain capabilities to meet the expectations of the players or the performing context. Instruments with small sounds (low volume) are appropriate for relatively intimate music making circumstances, and adjustments have to be made if they are to be heard in a large concert hall. Amplification techniques have made a considerable difference there, but some instruments have actually been changed—the piano among them, as European keyboard performance moved from the chamber to the concert hall.

Instruments have their own peculiar characteristics that present the players options that are idiomatic to them. One important physical characteristic is the length of the decay once a sound has been initiated. On some instruments the decay will be relatively rapid (CD track 1-21), and sustaining a sound means developing a specific technique. It is possible to sustain a pitch on a fiddle with repeated bowing across a string. Singers work on their breath control, as do players of aerophones (particularly those whose instruments have no mechanism for storing air, such as the bladder on a bagpipe). On some instruments a sustained sound is not achievable, so the effect of a sustain is created by other means; on a hammered dulcimer, a xylophone, or a drum, repeated striking will do it.

The Peruvian Andean *siku* panpipe provides a good example of achieving a sustained tone both by breath control and cooperative music making (figure 2.14). In *sikuri* ensemble practice, a melody is played on a pair of instruments, requiring two musicians to interlock their parts (each of the first three segments of CD track 1-29). Within the large circle formation in which *sikuri* ensembles usually play, the paired musicians who interlock parts typically stand next to each other, listening most closely to their partners. Ethnomusicologist Tom Turino has often heard the musical value stated that ensembles should

FIGURE 2.14   *Peruvian* sikuri *ensemble in procession.*   *(Courtesy of Raul Romero, Center for Andean Ethnomusicology, Catholic University of Peru)*

"play as one" or "sound like one instrument" and that there should be no "holes" (rests, silences) in a group's sound. This and other aspects of the panpipe ensemble music appear to him to be strongly guided by the broader ethical system of the community that is characterized by close cooperation and reciprocity that underpin social life more generally (Turino 2008). Each member of the pair usually holds his note, slightly overlapping with his partner's so that there are no gaps of silence in the melody due to decay of sound (Turino 1993: 44).

Conversely, the long decay of the sound of a gong or a bell must be coped with; one possibility is to assign a sparse musical role to those instruments in an ensemble in order to avoid a muddle of sound, while another possibility is to develop damping techniques. Composers for carillon have a special challenge (CD track 1-30).

ACTIVITY 2.9 *The beginning moments of Chinese ensemble music on CD track 1-2 illustrate a sustained pitch played on flute and plucked lute. Once you understand the principle of listening for the different techniques for achieving a sustained pitch, listen to CD track 1-31, played by a Thai* **pî phât** *ensemble (figure 2.15). Try to identify the instrument types. Then listen for the characteristic pattern of decay on each instrument, and how each musician handles the decay in a way that is idiomatic to that instrument.*

FIGURE 2.15 *Thai* pî phât *ensemble from the Fine Arts Department in Bangkok, Thailand, performing a ritual to honor teachers, 1986. On* ranât êk, *Natthaphong Sowat, on* pî nai, *Pip Khonglai Thong. These are some of the best musicians in Central Thailand. From left to right:* taphôn, ranât êk, pî nai, ching, ranât thun. *(Courtesy of Deborah Wong)*

Another aspect of the construction of instruments has been considered by scholars of music cognition: spatial properties, such as the arrangement of slabs or lamellae on an idiophone, relative to the movements that occur in the process of playing that instrument. Several scholars have focused on this spatiality for African musics (von Hornbostel 1928, Blacking 1955, Berliner 1978, Kubik 1979), as have Baily for Afghani (1985) and Brinner for Javanese (1995) musics. Analyzing tunes played on the Nsenga *kalimba* (thumb piano) and considering the layout of the lamellae relative to the motions of playing, for example, Blacking concluded that "the most significant common factors of the kalimba tunes are not their melodic structures, but the recurring patterns of 'fingering' which, combined with different patterns of polyrhythms between the two thumbs, produce a variety of melodies . . . the tunes are variations on a theme, but the theme is physical and not purely musical" (1961: 6–7). Musical style, then, can be partially a result of the idiomatic morphology of an instrument, and "creativity in music may often consist of deliberately finding new ways to move on an instrument" (Baily 1985: 257).

Ideas about Ensemble.   When musicians play together, the possibilities are infinite. Many factors can obtain, depending on the situation—whether they are jamming or performing formally, or the extent to which they expect to improvise music on the spot as opposed to playing what a composer or arranger provides, or whether a sociomusical hierarchy among the music makers gives one player authority. There is a great deal to listen to and think about with ensemble music making.

A good way to begin listening to music made by a group is to identify the instruments (remembering to include the voice as an instrument). In some performances or compositions or even musical styles the **instrumentation** is clear. As performed by the Dave Brubeck Quartet, for instance, the instrumentation in "Take Five" is clear (CD track 1-32). Each instrument can be tracked as it enters the performance. The drummer starts the piece, then the pianist comes in. They are joined by the string bass player and finally the sax, in prominent position. The instrumentation of the jazz quartet is nicely balanced, including all of the major categories of instrument types. The drum set incorporates membranophones and an idiophone (high hat cymbal); two chordophones and an aerophone round out the ensemble.

Heterogeneous and Homogeneous Sound Ideals. This performance of "Take Five" demonstrates both the principles of heterogeneous and homogeneous sound ideals played out in one ensemble. It would be completely heterogeneous (instruments producing clearly different timbres), were it not for the string bass's sounding so similar to the low keys on the piano. Those two sounds are homogeneous, having similar timbre.

The **heterogeneous sound ideal**, the love of timbral variety, is widespread. Prominent examples can be found in African music (CD track 1-26) and in African musics in diaspora—of which jazz is one, of course (Wilson 1992). It is also enjoyed in eastern Arab music; the Egyptian ensemble on CD track 2-1 includes violin, flute, *qanun* (struck board zither) and vocalist (figure 2.16). Figure 2.15 explains why the Thai

FIGURE 2.16 *The Michigan Arab Orchestra Takht Ensemble (MAOTE, part of the non-profit Michigan Arab Orchestra (MAO)) in performance on April 1st, 2011 at Wayne State University's Community Arts Auditorium. From left to right: on double bass, Jonathan Hammonds; on tableh, Roger Kashou; on riqq, Gursharan "Yash" Singh Sandhu; on 'oud, Nashwan Fadhel; on qanun, Victor Ghannam; vocalist, Usama Baalbaki; on violin, Nady Benyamine; on nay, Music Director Michael Ibrahim.* (Photo courtesy of Donna Kwon)

ensemble in CD track 1-29 presents a heterogeneous sound ideal; some of the instruments are very different from each other.

A second reason why the instrumental parts are clear in "Take Five" is that each instrument enters separately, therefore noticeably. The heterogeneous sound ideal and the same principle of bringing in instruments in clear succession occurs in other ensemble music—in the ancient Japanese court music, *gagaku,* for instance (CD track 1-9; figure 1.8). In the brief prelude in CD track 1-9, the instruments enter in almost ritualized order; this has become standardized in the approximately thirteen hundred years of the music's existence.

ACTIVITY 2.10   *Listen to the* gagaku *selection (***netori***, a prelude) on CD track 1-9. Listen for the sound of each instrument as you hear it in this order of entry: organlike free reed (shō), double-reed (hichiriki), flute (ryūteki), and sharp-sounding drum (kakko), zither and lute (koto and biwa). It will help to match sounds with instruments if you find a gagaku performance on YouTube. Two instruments—the small gong (shoko) and the large frame drum (taiko) are not played in a* netori, *so if you see them being played, you are watching a named piece rather than a prelude.*

Conversely, the idea of a timbral blend—a **homogeneous sound ideal**—occurs in countless ensembles around the globe. A quintessential example is a brass quintet (CD track 2-2, figure 2.3). Sometimes, *seeing* the ensemble playing is the only way to *hear* the instruments individually. You might hear Central Javanese *gamelan* music in that way (CD track 1-7, figure 1.5); the homogeneous sound on primarily bronze **metallophones** (pitched metal percussion instrument) and the style of the music create a kind of floating, calm sound. Santosa (2001) writes eloquently about the quality in *gamelan* music desired by villagers with whom he did field research. Listening mostly to radio broadcasts, they sought an atmosphere that evokes the contemplative state: "I want to cite an example in which a middle-aged man claimed that the atmosphere of gamelan performance is similar to that [atmosphere] people want to get when meditating. . . . When conducting meditations he felt *nganyut-nyut,* the state of mind that brought him close to God." It is music meant to hold desire in check. Above all, Santosa found that the *gamelan* tradition is an activity that conserves relations not only among patrons and musicians but also among members of the community; it is a communal practice in which no one individual stands out. Thus the homogeneous sound of the *gamelan* expresses Javanese culture.

The idea of the homogeneous sound ideal is stretched somewhat when an ensemble consists of instruments whose sounds are basically similar but are distinguished by difference in the pitch range—the brass instruments in CD track 2-2, for instance (figure 2.3).

Dividing a large pitch range among several instruments of the same type occurs in much larger ensembles as well. An instance of this is the Peruvian *sikuri* ensemble, which consists of three (sometimes five) sizes (*cortes*) of the *siku* panpipe (figure 2.14) plus drum, usually the wooden double-headed *bombo* drum. Playing the same melody in multiple pitch registers simultaneously greatly enriches the sound of the ensemble. The first thirty seconds of CD track 1-29 features the *cortes* called *chili* or *suli* playing a melody of the "Toril" genre, at the highest pitch register of the three sizes of the panpipe demonstrated here. The next thirty seconds gives the same melody played on the middle-register *corte* called *malta*; musicians identify the *malta* as the principal melody carrier of the sizes of *siku* panpipe. The unmistakably lower-register *sanja* is played in a third segment of thirty seconds. For the final portion of CD track 1-29, all three are featured, entering one by one. For this recorded example an ensemble of twenty to twenty-four performers is pared down to six, two playing interlocking parts on each size of panpipe. A large ensemble might even include two more sizes of the instrument (Turino 1993: 41–47).

The practice of dividing a large pitch range among several instruments of the same type occurs in a number of ensembles in Southeast Asia, as well. In figure 1.5 you can see two of the three sizes of **saron** in the Central Javanese *gamelan*; the lowest-pitched in the third row has bigger, thicker slabs than the middle-pitched in the center. (The highest-pitched is not visible.) Their musical parts are quite different: the higher the register of the instrument, the faster the musical part moves. The performance practice, then, is different from that of the Peruvian *sikuri* ensembles.

One final example brings into play all three ideas I have presented thus far about ensemble: timbral mix, multiple sizes of similar instruments, and highlighting of selected instruments. The sound of the mariachi ensemble combines both homogeneity and heterogeneity (CD track 1-6). Homogeneity is there instrumentally with the two plucked lutes: the *vihuela* and *guitarrón* that are special to the mariachi ensemble. They were created in Mexico, and although they were based on earlier instruments brought from Spain, they are unique in origin and to western Mexico and are easily recognizable by their shape and sound (figure 2.9, CD track 1-6). When combined with the violin, as was often the case before the 1940s, the ensemble sound was still relatively homogeneous. Dynamic heterogeneity is assured by the trumpet that was added to the string ensemble in the latter half of the twentieth century, as well as by the voices in contrast with instruments and the one voice contrasting with the vocal duo.

ACTIVITY 2.11 *Pick three of your favorite musical performing groups and think about the instrumentation. Do the instruments contribute to a homogeneous or heterogeneous sound ideal, or a bit of both?*

Musical Roles. An additional way to think about ensembles is to consider the nature of the musical roles assigned to the instruments. In an ensemble making North Indian classical music, three musical roles will be filled: the playing or singing of a melody, maintenance on an instrument of a basic pitch reference (a drone), and rhythmic accompaniment on a percussion instrument (CD track 1-12, 2-3). In large steelband ensembles, in which there are multiple sizes of pans and complex arrangements, the musical roles are likewise delineated: the high-pitched tenor pans play melody, the lowest-pitched bass pans play a bass line (figure 2.17), and mid-range pans "strum" as if they were the plucked lute (*quatro*) of Trinidadian calypso. CD track 1-15 permits you to hear parts separately for "Back Line," a composition for steelband by arranger Len "Boogsie" Sharpe (Activity 2.12); you can hear the full ensemble, Phase II Pan Groove, playing "Back Line" on the CD of Shannon Dudley's book on Trinidad in this series.

ACTIVITY 2.12 *CD track 1-15, separate steelband parts of "Back Line," is played by a small group of six people instead of twenty-five, students at the University of Washington, Seattle, and friends of Shannon Dudley. A full ensemble would include more instruments—including a whole battery of other percussion referred to as "the engine room." This recording starts with only a pair of conga drums to give the steady underlying beat. Follow this guide as you listen.*

0:15   1. Bass pans playing bass line.
0:34   2. Bass + double second pans strumming chords. (Notice that the seconds' strum is constantly off-beat, contrasting with the on-beat pulse of the bass.)
0:53   3. Bass + double seconds + tenor pan playing melody
1:12   4. Adding double tenor to double the melody at the octave. The double tenor is a pan that is similar to the seconds that adds depth and power to the melody by playing it in a lower register.
1:32   5. Adds triple cellos strumming chords (played twice). Cellos enrich the harmony and play a strum that contrasts somewhat with the seconds; you can hear the low-pitched cellos strum best in the second half of the section.

FIGURE 2.17   *Barry Nanton of Desperadoes steelband (Trinidad) playing a set of nine barrels (bass pans), each with three notes tuned on the surface. Each note is bordered by a hammered groove that helps isolate the pitch so that when the player strikes one, he does not set another one ringing simultaneously. The grooves that delineate notes can be seen most clearly in the bottom center pan. On the pans to the left that are raised and tilted toward Barry Nanton, there are three convex notes with a triangle of dead space in the center.* (Courtesy of Shannon Dudley)

Although melody is often the easiest part to identify, all the parts together greatly influence how one hears and feels music.

The words **solo** and **accompaniment** delineate musical roles. "Soloist" is a somewhat confusing word, since on the one hand it means someone who makes music totally alone and on the other refers to a person in an ensemble whose music is meant to stand out most prominently— like the opera singer on CD track 1-28 and the North Indian singer on CD track 2-3. We are likely to assume that a musical hierarchy is at work, with the "soloist" more important than the "accompanist(s)." Beware of that, however! In musical styles like jazz (CD track 1-32 "Take Five") and North Indian instrumental genres the "soloist" role might pass from music maker to music maker, so the role of "accompanist" shifts too (CD track 1-12).

FIGURE 2.18   *West African Music Ensemble. C.K. Ladzekpo, master drummer, teaching a class at the University of California, Berkeley. Left to right:* gangokui *(bell); C. K. Ladzekpo, standing (playing* atsimevu *[lead drum]); George Glikman, standing (playing* gangokui*); Tsz Hin Ng, sitting (playing* sogo*); Katherine Bones, sitting (playing* kidi *[2]); Kevelyn Hare, sitting (playing* kagan*).*
(Photo by Kathleen Karn)

The words "conductor" and "leader", "master" and "concert master" also name musical roles. In some performance traditions, a leader is visually obvious: the conductor of a Western orchestra, for example. In both the Central Javanese *gamelan* (CD track 1-7) and Balinese gamelan (CD track 2-4) however, a drummer leads the timing of the performance; he sends musical signals by drumming patterns that are embedded in the fabric of the music. There are, then, both highly visible and clearly audible types of "conductor." The master drummer in an African musical ensemble is both visible and audible; he is the one musician who is free to improvise, and he signals through drumming when the other musicians should change their musical parts (figure 2.18, CD track 1-4).

Aesthetics of Ensembles. Perhaps the most important ideal for an ensemble is the way the musicians are intended to interact during performance, in order to achieve a certain aesthetic. Interaction can take any number of forms, such as the shifting of musical roles in a jazz ensemble or the precise coordination of interlocking drum patterns that create the rhythmic feel of salsa (CD track 2-5). With communal spirit, Native American musicians around a drum at a powwow—comprising a group called "the drum"—strive for "harmony"; each singer will adjust the strength of his accompanying drum strokes so that no one person plays louder than the others (Browner 2002: 74).

For an individual Balinese musician, the ultimate goal is to contribute to a sense of oneness with a group of musicians, whether the group is a duo or a forty-five-member ensemble. This oneness results from years of training and practicing together, working toward the ultimate aesthetic of tight precision, called *kompak* ("compact") or *sip* ("tight"). Balinese music is a deeply communal practice.

In this chapter I have considered several ways of thinking about instruments. As objects they have been classified in different ways in different cultures, have accrued extra-musical associations, and expressed aesthetic values both visually and in terms of sound quality. Interrelationships among musicians, their instruments, and the music they make were explored through ideas about ensemble. In the next chapter I turn my attention to the organization of musical time, focusing first on rhythm, then on speed.

Thinking about Time

In this chapter I explore the ways in which musicians organize time in music. Except when there is a constant drone, there is always **rhythm** in musical sound, created by successions of durations. In a context filled with sound, the absence of sound (i.e., silence) becomes significant as well. In English, a consistent set of terms is used in talking about time in music, including "rhythm," "pulse," "beat," "count," "feel," "groove," "rhythmic mode," "meter," and others.

ACTIVITY 3.1 *Conduct this mini-fieldwork project with at least four of your friends. (1) Before you read further, write definitions of these terms: "pulse," "beat," "count," "feel," "groove," "rhythm," "meter." (2) Ask your friends to define the terms. Where is there consenus, where difference, among the definitions? (3) Play for each friend a musical piece of your choice and ask them to talk about it using those words. If they also use other words to describe time in the music, keep track of them. Finally ask if they would use different words for different music. You will emerge with a sense of your and their perceptions about the flow of musical sound.*

In coordinating the definitions of terms as authors are using them in the case studies in this Global Music Series, I found the greatest differences in the way we understand the practices encompassed by terms pertinent to the organization of time. That is because concepts of musical time differ greatly in different traditions. Our teachers have explained the ideas in their own ways, and we ethnomusicologists assume the task of translating them. In so doing, we draw on a vocabulary that is small because

relatively little attention has been paid to time in European art music—
the source of most musical terminology in English-language writing. This
has caused single words to have multiple meanings; the term "meter," for
instance, is applied to qualitatively different concepts about the organization of musical time. The implications of the words "rhythm" as opposed
to "meter" and "pulse" as opposed to "beat" are particularly confusing.

RHYTHM

It is useful to distinguish between **rhythm** in general and "a rhythm."
By "rhythm" I mean the aspect of music having to do with the duration of sonic events in time—any succession of durations. "A rhythm,"
in contrast, is a specific succession of durations such as a repetitive
rhythm pattern.

More often than not, musicians organize rhythm in some purposeful fashion—rhythm in dance music, for example, or in rap, or in music
for a marching band. In some music, however, musicians purposefully
leave the rhythm unorganized, or "free." In the sections that follow,
both those musical possibilities are illustrated as they are carried out in
a variety of ways.

Free Rhythm. Music in "free rhythm" refers to music with little or no
sense of predictability about the organization of time. Scholars speak of
such music in various ways: as being **nonmetrical**, as (*parlando*) **rubato**,
or as freely flowing in time. On CD track 1-31, an entire Thai *pî phât*
ensemble plays nonmetrical rhythm (not organized in regular units) to
initiate a piece (figure 2.15). Louis Armstrong chose to begin "West End
Blues" (CD track 2-6) with a trumpet solo in free rhythm.

Coordinating through "breathing rhythm," the members of the con-
ductorless Japanese *gagaku* ensemble (figure 1.8) introduce the melodic
mode of the selection they are about to play with an introductory
prelude called *netori*. Trying to find regular durations through CD track
1-9 is fruitless; breathing with it is a more appropriate idea. This prelude
would be followed in performance by a piece with organized time. In
much Japanese *syakuhati* music (figure 1.2), however, the rhythm of
an entire selection (beyond an excerpt such as that on CD track 1-18)
is nonmetrical, sustaining a meditative mood. The music is precomposed to be that way.

Rhythm for the Text Alone. In some music the rhythm is the servant
of the text. **Recitative** in Western opera is one example of this. As its name

implies, recitative is singing that imitates and emphasizes in both rhythm and pitch the natural flow of speech. Although the melody has been pre-composed, an opera singer can have fun with the rhythm as Carmen does in her four-line response to the soldiers who are anxious for her attention: "When will I love you? Really, I don't know. Perhaps never, perhaps tomorrow. But not today. That's certain!" (CD track 1-28, from 0:32 to 1:01).

Traditions of religious chant exist for the purpose of rendering sacred texts, so the rhythmic setting of the text is of particular concern. On CD track 1-1, moments of recitation of the second chapter (*sura*) of the Qur'ān express these words: "In the Name of God, the Merciful, the Compassionate." Not only these devotees of the Qadiriya Sufi brother-hood in Turkey but all Muslims everywhere adhere to rules for the rhythm that were established to elucidate the text when reciting the sacred text revealed to the Prophet Muhammad.

Qur'ānic recitation is a unique art form in which, while there are detailed rules for rhythm and also for pronunciation and sectioning, melody is completely free (Nelson, in Frischkopf and Nelson 2011).

From Free Rhythm to Relatively More Organized Time. In Indian classi-cal music, the contrast between free and organized rhythm is played with purposefully, when a soloist works through a sequence of sections in a pro-longed selection. (See p. 141.) CD track 1-11, the first portions of an impro-vised selection by a North Indian (Hindustani) *sitārist* demonstrates this. At the beginning, tradition dictates that the soloist must focus attention on melody; in order to do that with maximum effectiveness, the rhythm is kept free, essentially unorganized. Just beyond three minutes into CD track 1-11, however, the soloist eases into attention to rhythm by adding pulsa-tion. At about 3:40, rhythmic play of a more complicated nature starts, but time is still not organized into regular units. All the while, the accompa-nying drummer in the ensemble has sat on stage in his position (Fig. 3.1); not yet playing, he is like a member of the audience, responding with a shake of the head or a quiet exclamation to particularly creative moments in the improvisation. He will begin to play in the next section of the sequence when time is organized into units (CD track 1-12).

ACTIVITY 3.2 *Pick up whatever object you have at hand to use as a percussion instrument and play with creating rhythm that is first regular, then free, then regular, then free. This will help you embody these two different senses of rhythm in time.*

FIGURE 3.1   *Hindustani ensemble performing at the Julia Morgan Center for the Arts in Berkeley, California. From left to right: Abhiman Kaushal* (tablā), *Shujaat Khan* (sitār), *Sudev Sheth* (tablā). *(Photo by Shivang Rajendra Dave. Courtesy of Sudev Sheth)*

Pulse/Beat.   We can sense a purposeful organization of time in music most intuitively perhaps if we orient to consistent, equal-length durations of time such as we hear in the ticking of an analog clock or see in the passage of time on a digital one. I think of this as **pulse** as in the experience of the human heartbeat; perhaps you think of it as **beat**. If you call consistent, equal-length durations "beats," however, you must remember that the word "beat" also has other meanings. Among American Indian dancers on the Northern Plains, "one beat" is a common designation for speed—not any fixed speed, but an ideal speed: "Every reservation's "one-beat" is its concept of a good tempo for dancing" (Browner 2002:74). And in some musical systems, "beat" is the term for long and short subgroups of a rhythm (see below).

The best way to orient to the pulse/beat is to try to find it in a number of different kinds of music. You can see others find it by watching dance videos. The best way for you to find it, however, is for you to feel it—for you yourself to move with the music—tap a finger, clap, pat your foot, or—best of all—get up and move in time with the music—march, or dance.

ACTIVITY 3.3 *Go to your playlist to practice finding a pulse/beat—consistent, equal-length durations of time—in multiple selections. If it doesn't include "Born in the USA," find a recording of that classic and move with the beat; once you "have the beat," count out how many beats you feel in the whole song. Then try it with other selections—at least four. You might also count how many beats you feel per minute in each selection and then rank them by your musical preference for a **tempo** (speed).*

Once you are truly comfortable with finding the beat in a variety of musical pieces of your own selection, return to the CD tracks for this book that I have referred to thus far for the purpose of taking note of whether you feel a pulse/beat—or not. This is a good time to be sure that your accumulative record of each track is complete.

ORGANIZING TIME INTO UNITS

At the Level of the Single Beat.   Beats can be subdivided. They can also be grouped—or both grouped and subdivided (see below).

The most systematically worked out organization for subdividing beats that I have encountered was developed long ago in India. It is articulated as a repertoire of nine patterns that are learned by speaking syllables: "Ta" constitutes the single beat, "Taka" a subdivision of Ta by two, and "Takita" a subdivision of Ta by three. The result is a quantitative increase in rhythmic density.

In the list below, items 2–4 constitute the basic subdivisions, then 5–9 use those again, in combinations. Capital T's make that clear.

1. Ta
2. Taka
3. Takita
4. Takadimi
5. TakaTakita (2 +3)
6. TakaTakadimi (2 +4)

7. TakitaTakadimi (3 +4)

8. TakitaTakitaTaka (3 +3 +2)

9. TakaTakitaTakadimi (2 +3 +4)

ACTIVITY 3.4 *On CD track 2-7, you will hear George Ruckert recite the nine patterns. When you have listened sufficiently to follow what he is doing, experience this principle of increasing the rhythmic density yourself. Either speak it with Ruckert or set your own slower, steady beat. Clap to sound it out or ask a classmate to do it for you. If you find it too difficult to speak the syllables, substitute numbers. To experience this principle of increasing the rhythmic density, set a very slow, steady beat (•) and clap to sound it out. Then start speaking these patterns to fill in the beats, keeping the pace of the beat steady. If you feel really ambitious, carry it through the nine patterns.*

•	•	•	•
Ta	Ta	Ta	Ta
Ta ka	Ta ka	Ta ka	Ta ka
Ta ki ta	Ta ki ta	Ta ki ta	Ta ki ta
Ta ka di mi	Ta ka di mi	Ta ka di mi	Ta ka di mi
Ta kaTakita	Ta kaTakita	Ta kaTa kita	Ta kaTakita

Through subdivisions of the beat, musicians in an ensemble can play different instruments at different speeds, with all parts linked by a common basic pulse. Music played on the Central Javanese *gamelan*s demonstrates this clearly. The register (see chapter 4) on each instrument correlates with the rhythmic density of its musical part: the higher the pitch, the denser the part. When you hear an extremely slow basic melody in this music, listen for extremely fast playing on some instruments. To hear this, I refer you to CD track 1-7 and Activity 3.10.

Metric Structures with Flexible Means of Articulation. In most of the world's music, musicians organize time into units longer than one pulse/beat/count. Terms for the different sorts of units are "meter," "rhythmic mode," "clave," and others. In the rest of this chapter, I provide examples of different sorts of units—meters of several varieties, rhythmic modes, polyrhythm, and such. I lay them out for you with two perspectives—quantitative and qualitative.

The quantitative perspective is numerical, giving us, for instance, the basic defining feature of units of musical time: some total number of beats. The quantity can be anything—from a three-beat *waltz* meter to a South Indian *tāla* cycle of 128 counts. In every case, the unit functions to mark off musical flow through time. The qualitative perspective takes into consideration, for instance, how the unit may be articulated—performed so that you feel it (or not) in musical practice.

There is one more general point for you to think about. In the case of the first types of meter I present—duple and triple, some other meters, and then South Indian *tāla*—performers and composers can choose whatever qualitative way they wish to make listeners aware of the metric structure—melody, harmony, instrumentation, drum pattern, dance pattern, hand clapping, or something else. In the systems I get to beyond those, the means of articulating the meter is "given" in some way.

Duple and Triple Meters.   Quantitatively, the simplest meters have two or three counts; the former is called "duple," the latter is called "triple." Each unit of two or three counts constitutes a **measure** or **bar**, terminology from Western music notation, which puts vertical bars (measure bars) between units (figure 1.14).

Meters with multiples of two counts are considered to be duple meters—units of four counts, for instance: **1** 2 3 4 | **1** 2 3 4 |. It is common for a four-count unit to feel like it comprises subunits (2 + 2), owing to stress being put on count 3 in addition to the expected strong stress placed on count 1 (the **downbeat**): | ♩ ● ♩ ● | ♩ ● ♩ ● |. The great majority of popular dance music—samba, rhumba, techno, and house, for example—are in duple meter.

ACTIVITY 3.5   *Listen to CD track 2-6 "West End Blues," past the beginning trumpet solo; in the first chorus the pianist clearly articulates the counts 1 2 3 4 | 1 2 3 4 |. Each chorus is twelve measures long; this is a perfect example of what is known as "twelve-bar blues," with each bar being four counts long.*

A three-beat unit, triple meter, is demonstrated by "Marieke" (CD track 2-8), most often associated with the late Belgian poet, songwriter, and cabaret performer Jacques Brel. The triple meter is articulated clearly in the bass with a primary stress on 1 but a secondary stress on 3 that anticipates the next count 1. In addition, waltzes are in triple meter; if you have danced a waltz, you have already embodied the feeling of it.

ACTIVITY 3.6 *To challenge your hearing of triple and duple meters, listen to CD track 2-9, Dave Brubeck's "Three to Get Ready and Four to Go," until you find it easy to count out the measures.*

The piece begins entirely in triple measures, with four phrases of three measures each, for a total of twelve measures. The piano gives the melody, while the bass plays on each count 1. Listen for the hi-hat (idiophone cymbal in the drum set) being struck offbeat, on count 2.

Phrase 1: 1 2 3 | 1 2 3 | 1 2 3 |
Phrase 2: 1 2 3 | 1 2 3 | 1 2 3 |
Phrase 3: 1 2 3 | 1 2 3 | 1 2 3 |
Phrase 4: 1 2 3 | 1 2 3 | 1 2 3 |

For the second chorus (from 0:12) the alto sax takes the melody. The metric pattern changes to phrases of two measures of triple plus two measures of duple (4) from that point to the end.

Phrase 1: 1 2 3 | 1 2 3 | 1 2 3 4 | 1 2 3 4 |
Phrase 2: 1 2 3 | 1 2 3 | 1 2 3 4 | 1 2 3 4 |
Phrase 3: 1 2 3 | 1 2 3 | 1 2 3 4 | 1 2 3 4 |
Phrase 4: 1 2 3 | 1 2 3 | 1 2 3 4 | 1 2 3 4 |

If you can count the pattern easily, you are very secure with duple and triple meter. If so, listen for another detail: It is in the duple measures that the instrumentalists take brief solos and play around.

Most music in duple and triple meter is composed so that each beat is felt to be subdivided into two equal parts so that you can count "1 and 2 and 3 and 4 and" or "1 and 2 and 3 and." The tune in CD track 2-10, a northeast Brazilian *forró*, is in a quick duple meter that you should be able to count in fast four-beat bars from the first downbeat (the fourth pitch you hear).

Another option is to subdivide each beat into three equal divisions, as shown here with dots.

Beat: | •   • | and | •   •   • |
Subdivision: | • • • • • • | | • • • • • • • • • |

That is the case with duple meter Irish **jigs** as on CD track 1-3. The beats are stressed musically in performance, so you should be able to feel them. Saying, "1 and uh 2 and uh" or "jiggity jiggity" with "Tar Road to Sligo" (beginning to 1:31) and "Paddy Clancy's Jig" (from 1:32) may help you feel the subdivision.

Some Other Meters. To reiterate: the total number of beats in a unit of musical time can be anything—duple and triple as just presented, or an uneven number of beats more than three, or a unit as long as a South Indian *tāla* of 128 counts—and so on. Paul Desmond's famous piece "Take Five" serves to demonstrate a meter with five beats to a measure. He composed it so that subunits of 3 + 2 are felt; the structure is there in the initial drum introduction in the performance by the Dave Brubeck Quartet (CD track 1-32). When the pianist and bassist come in, they articulate the subunits with a pitch pattern—pitches 1 and 5.

Counts: 1 2 3 4 5 | 1 2 3 4 5 | 1 2 3 4 5 |
Pitches: 1 • • 5 • | 1 • • 5 • | 1 • • 5 • |

The bass player is given the musical role of keeping the metric pattern through most of the piece, with that recurring 1–5 pitch pattern. It is reinforced by chord changes, at times on the piano. (Pitch—including chords—is explained in chapter 4).

ACTIVITY 3.7 *To help you hear the meter in the jazz piece "Take Five" (CD track 1-32) practice this first without listening: Clap on the stressed counts 1 and 4 while speaking the 5 counts in a measure.*

After a while, keep clapping but stop speaking the counts. Let yourself feel the short and long subgroups with a kind of swing. Then put on the recording and listen again.

South Indian Tāla. In the South Indian *tāla* system, the number of counts in a meter (*tāla*) depends on the total number of counts called for in subunits. There are three types of subunit: a 1-count subunit, a

2-count subunit, and a subunit that can have either 3, 4, 5, 7, or 9 counts. Most Karnatak *tāla*s consist of particular combinations of those types. The *tāla* most frequently drawn on for compositions is **ādi tāla**; its eight-count grouping is 4 + 2 + 2 (CD track 1-19)—subunits of four, two, and two counts, respectively.

ACTIVITY 3.8 *On CD track 1-19, T. Viswanathan sings a portion of a song, clapping out* ādi tāla *so that you can hear the strongest counts. Count it out as you listen. The first line of text is repeated several times, and you can get the* tāla *from it. Count 1 of the* tāla *falls on "Un" of "unnai."*

Count	1		2	3		4	5	6		7		8	
Subunit	4						2			2			
Count placement	•		•	•		•	•	•		•		•	|
Text				Unnai namibinen ayya caranam, nan									

"I worshiped you, lord, I prostrated at your feet."

Permit me to reiterate a point: When making music in all the types of meters discussed thus far, performers and composers can choose whatever qualitative way they wish to make listeners aware of the metric structure (or to obscure it)—melody, harmony, instrumentation, drum pattern, dance pattern, hand clapping, or something else. Put another way: the means by which the meter is articulated is not part of what characterizes the meter. I pointed out to you that in "Marieke" (CD track 2-8) the triple meter is articulated by the bass stressing counts 1 and 3. In "Take Five," it is the bass, but also chord changes, that articulates the meter (CD track 1-32). In the Irish jigs performed on CD track 1-3, the violinist stresses many of the main counts by the technique of down-bowing. In "Unnai namibinen" the *tāla* is articulated musically by the text and its setting and physically by handclaps (CD track 1-19), but South Indian musicians relish the musical play of going against the metric structure.

Meter is usually defined as a pattern of strong and weak counts. That definition is qualitative, rather than quantitative, telling you how you might expect the unit to be articulated. The stress pattern of the meter is not always so clearly performed, however, so that definition does not always work well.

Whether or not to articulate the pattern clearly is a musical option. CD track 2-11, the Waltz in C-sharp Minor by the Polish composer Frédéric Chopin (1810–49), for instance, is a waltz meant for concert presentation. Its speed is too fast for dancing, and there is considerable ebb and flow in the pace of the counts, as appropriate in the rubato performing style. If you were to listen to the entire piece, you would notice moments when the triple meter is hard to feel because it is not being articulated by musical stresses; it is still there however—in theory.

In fact, some musical practices that add rhythmic interest can confuse the sense of the metric unit. One of those is rhythmic **syncopation** that puts subdivision of a beat into play. (With syncopation, the word "beat" is more usual than "count" or "pulse.") Once a regular beat is firmly established, rhythmic interest can be added by putting an accent in an unexpected place. If you count 1 and 2 and 3 AND 4, stressing the AND, you have got the sense of "offbeat" syncopation. Another type of syncopation consists of accenting a beat where stress is not expected: If, in a regular grouping of four counts, you put stress on the "weak" counts 2 and 4 rather than the "strong" counts 1 and 3, that is a kind of syncopation sometimes called a "backbeat." If the backbeat stress continues for very long, you can lose the sense of the "regular" beat. That happens, for example; in Bruce Springsteen's "Born in the USA." What defines the offbeat as offbeat is the framework that locates the strong "on" beat; because of that, syncopated music commonly combines strong downbeats with offbeat and backbeat stresses. Syncopation is a basic ingredient in African and African diaspora musics, but it occurs in many other musical traditions as well.

Metric Structures with Given Means of Articulation. Thinking more qualitatively, I now turn to structures in which a particular performance practice is an essential part of what characterizes the system for organizing musical time. This encompasses such systems as colotomic meter, North Indian *tāla*, and rhythmic mode.

Southeast Asian Colotomic Meter. A clear example of an essential performance practice that articulates the metric structure is found in most Southeast Asian ensemble music: **colotomic meter**, in which one or more instruments in an ensemble is consistently assigned the musical role of articulating the metric structure. In Central Javanese *gamelan* music, the instruments assigned to do this are pitched gongs.

In the *gamelan* music of Central Java, the number of counts in a metric unit will be duple—8 or 16 or 32 or 64, and so forth. Interestingly, the *last* count of a grouping—count 8 or 16, for instance—is the most significant count. That beat is clearly marked by a stroke on the largest gong (*ageng*) in the ensemble; it literally holds together the metric structure.

> **ACTIVITY 3.9** *Feeling the last count as the point of greatest emphasis requires considerable reorientation for those of us who are accustomed to placing the stress on count 1. Without listening to music, count out cycles of eight beats, giving the greatest weight to the eighth beat by saying the word "GONG" in deep tones. If you do this while walking, you will get the sense of it quite easily. Also, putting a slight stress on beats 2, 4, and 6 as points of arrival will help you feel the approach of that important last count in the cycle. Do this until it feels right for the cycle to culminate in count 8.*

The roles of the instruments that articulate the colotomic meter are as follows:

- The **gong ageng** (G), a large hanging gong marks off the whole cycle (called a *gongan*)
  - • The **kenong** (N), a large kettle gong, subdivides the *gongan* into two *kenongan*:
    - ••• The **kempul** (P), a medium-sized hanging gong, subdivides the *kenongan*
    - ••• The **kethuk** (t) and *kampyang* (p), two small kettle gongs, further subdivide the *kenongan*. The *kethuk* is played with a damped stroke, usually two or three times in rapid succession. The *kempyang* is the highest-pitched colotomic gong.

These roles can be heard on CD tracks 2-12 and 2-13, which illustrate a particular colotomic pattern—that of the 16-beat **ketawang** form.

Because this same pattern is played over and over again through a musical composition, it is considered to be cyclical. The last count (here 16), functions as both a beginning and ending count, so the structure is cyclic in two senses of the word.

Collapsed into a single line, you can easily see that the only count on which there is no stroke in this colotomic pattern is count 4; a **rest** occurs there. Indeed, the only count where two strokes coincide is the last count of the cycle, stressing its structural significance. A piece will end with a stroke on the *gong ageng* that is a little delayed, for climactic finality.

16	1	2	3	4	5	6	7	8	9	10	11	12	13	14	15	16
N	p	t	p		p	t	p	N	p	t	p	P	p	t	p	N
G																G

ACTIVITY 3.10 *Speak the Central Javanese* gamelan *colotomic meter of it.* Ketawang, *saying "gong" for G, "nong" for N, "pyang" for p, "tuk" (as in "took") for t, "pul" (as in "pool") for P. You will feel the interlocking nature of it if you do it with friends, dividing the instrumental parts among you.*

When you have the flow of it, including the stress pattern, listen to CD track 1-7, a composition with that metric cycle of sixteen counts. You should recognize the beginning from listening to this selection before: the short nonmetrical passage played on the gendèr *(a metallophone struck with padded mallets).*

At 0:05 the gendèr *is joined by the drummer who begins to slow the pace.*

0:09 The first GONG stroke. From this point the other musicians begin to play. It will take a complete cycle through the colotomic meter for the speed of the counts to settle down and you may not feel the beat yet. But try: the most basic melody (played on a metallophone) is sounded only on the even-numbered counts in this piece. Under the guidance of the drummer, all gradually slow down through the first cycle. A female vocalist begins to sing at 0:27 as the end of the first cycle approaches.

0.31 The second GONG stroke. Try to feel the beats. Listen for Nong at 0:47 and Pul at 0:55. There, you can hear the vocalist and rebab (bowed lute) player shift the melody to a higher pitch register and the end of the cycle approaches.

> *1:04 The third GONG stroke. At 1:08 the male chorus enters. Keep trying to count and feel the beats. Listen for Nong at count 8 (1:20) and Pul at count 12 (1:28).*
> *1:36 The fourth GONG stroke. Nong at count 8 (2:26). At 2:28 the drummer begins to give subtle cues to slow the pace further and bring the piece to a close. The last beat is stretched greatly as the musicians wait for the gong to sound before playing their last note.*
> *2:50 Last GONG stroke.*

Because the gongs that perform the colotomic meter are playing pitches in the melody, the marking of the important counts is greatly submerged in the ensemble sound. If you were sitting in the ensemble, however, you would be consciously listening to or automatically hearing them.

Javanese colotomic meters are articulated qualitatively by other musical content as well: each meter is associated with its own drum pattern. This and Javanese colotomic meter in general are discussed at length by Ben Brinner in his book on Central Java in this series.

North Indian Tāla.   North Indian *tāla* is another example of a metric system in which a given means of articulation is part of what characterizes a particular meter. Two North India *tālas* that are the same quantitatively—the same number of total counts and the same subunit structure—will be distinguished qualitatively—by a way they are articulated on drums. That way is through a one-cycle-long pattern of drumstrokes (a brief composition, really) called **theka.** A Hindustani musician, if asked to demonstrate a particular *tāla* will speak the *theka*, using syllables to indicate the strokes that would be played on the drum. The syllables have some relationship (though sometimes not much) to the sound that the stroke will produce on the drum.

For example, two *tālas* with the same structure played on the *tablā* (drum pair, figure 3.1)—*tīntāl* and *tilwāḍā tāla*, are each sixteen counts (4 + 4 + 4 + 4). The two *tālas* are distinguished partially by the *theka* through which they are articulated. (*Tilwāḍā* is used for slow selections, while *tīntāl* is used for any speed.) Here are those patterns as taught by Pandit Swapan Chaudhuri (slight variants exist). Underlining indicates multiple syllables spoken in one count; a + indicates count one.

Tīntāl *(played on* tablā*) 4 + 4 + 4 + 4*

+   2   0   3

dha dhin dhin dha | *dha dhin dhin dha* | *na tin tin ta* | *ta dhin dhin dha*

Tilwāḍā *(played on* tablā*) 4 + 4 + 4 + 4*

+   2

Dha -kra *dhin dhin* | *dha dha tin* terekita |

0   3

ta -kra dhin dhin | *dha dha dhin* terekita

ACTIVITY 3.11   *Listen to those two* thekas *spoken on CD track 2-14 by George Ruckert, author of the volume on North India in this series. Then concentrate on* tīntāl, *as follows:*

(1) Team up with a classmate or two to speak the theka *syllables without worrying about counting numbers or thinking about subdivisions. Practice this by yourself and then do it with your classmates until you can all speak the* theka *easily. Ideally, memorize it.*

(2) Now you need to get comfortable with the quantitative structure of the tāla—*the feeling of counting out 16, coming to completion on a next count 1, and the subdivisions into groups of counts. To do this as Indians do, you will need to do physical motions to embody the pattern: for this* tāla, *clap three times—on counts 1, 5, and 13. Wave on count 9; as you will feel, that divides the cycle in half. Just do the motions until you are comfortable with the pattern.*

(3) Once comfortable, speak the numbers of the counts as you do the motion.

(4) When you are comfortable speaking the theka, *rather than the numbers, while doing the motion pattern, you will have really accomplished something.*

(5) The final step is to hear the cycle in performed music. CD track 1-12 gives excerpts from a performance in tīntāl *that features* sitārist *Ravi Shankar and* tablā *player Chatur Lal. You have 18 seconds to prepare yourself to hear the*

tāla: *the first clear count 1 occurs at 0:19. To feel the beat from 0:05 to 0:18, you need to listen to the melody— not to hear the tune, but to sense beats that are just about a second apart. It will be impossible to feel the beat from the drummer because he is enjoying a quick moment for a virtuosic solo.*

The first eight beats of the tune are the clearest, as shown here,

x			2					o			
Pa	Pa	Pa	Ma	Ma	Pa	Ni	(Ni)	sa	sa	ga	ma...
5	5	5	4	4	5	7	(7)	1	1	3	4...
G	G	G	F	F	G	B♭	(B♭)	c	c	e	f...

At 0:18-9 start speaking the beats: 1, 2, 3, etc., to 16. Count 1 comes again at 0:33-4, 0:48-9, 1:03. (A fade-out at 1:06 marks omitted improvisation after 1:06 in the full performance.) When you have listened to the first 1:06 several times and feel secure in the beat, speak the theka *rather than speaking beat numbers. Do that several times as you listen.*

Perhaps you have noticed this: while count 1 is (obviously) the first count in the tāla, *it is also the count on which Hindustani musicians will bring a musical unit to an end. Count 1 is thus a beginning and ending point musically; because of this, North India metric practice is thought of as cyclical.*

Notice in the theka *that some of the syllables start with "dh" and some with "t." A heavier sound occurs for "dh" syllables because both hands strike the drums (Figure 3.1). Only the right hand produces the lighter "t" sound on the drum. To embody the feeling of this, produce imaginary drum strokes with your hands as you speak the* theka. *Once you physically get that pattern, listen to the drumming on the recording. The drummer is free to vary the pattern a bit, so do not be surprised if he does not stick to the "textbook* theka." *Just keep listening.*

After 1:10, my excerpting on CD track 1-12 resumes 13 seconds before the next count 1, so you have time to get ready. At 1:23, start counting 1 and try to follow the tāla. *The pace of the beats accelerates a bit. The next count 1 comes at 1:36, but Shankar is improvising through two cycles of the* tāla, *so you won't feel an ending. Shankar does end his improvisational passage at 1:49 (count 1) and turns the soloist role over to Chatur Lal on* tablā *for a one-cycle chance to shine. During that cycle, listen to the* sitār *for the beats because the two players have traded roles temporarily. At 2:01 Shankar retakes the soloist role so you can listen to the drum again. Keep trying to follow the* tāla *as the speed accelerates. Counts 1 come at 2:14-5, 2:27-8, and 2:40-1—the end of the performance.*

Middle Eastern Rhythmic Modes.   The Arabic term *iqá* is usually translated as "rhythmic mode" rather than "meter," suggesting the qualitative nature of the rhythmic aspect of traditional Arab and Turkish music. A **rhythmic mode** is a metric structure that also bears particular expressive qualities. (Mode, as related to mood, I discuss in chapter 4.)

So many rhythmic modes have the same total number of counts that distinguishing them quantitatively makes no sense. Instead, each rhythmic mode is defined by the way it is articulated, that is, performed on a drum. (You can see in this how Hindustani drumming was influenced by the concepts and practices taken to North India by immigrant musicians from West Asia over a period of several hundred years, climaxing in the seventeenth century.)

In the Middle East there is a great variety of drums, each capable of producing a variety of sounds. Only two sounds, however, *dumm* and *takk* (Arabic language) are used to define the individual rhythmic modes. *Dumm* is the deepest or lowest sound the instrument can produce. *Takk* is high pitched, the sound produced when striking where the head meets the rim of the drum.

Each rhythmic mode is defined by a unique skeletal pattern of *dumm*s and *takk*s that create a distinctive rhythmic quality. A comparison of three different eight-count rhythmic modes should make this point clear: *D* indicates *dumm*, *T* indicates *takk*, and a dash (−) indicates a rest.

The names of the modes here are those used in the eastern Arab world; they are called by different names in different places.

Count	1	2	3	4	5	6	7	8
Maqsum	D	T	–	T	D	–	T	–
Masmudi saghir	D	D	–	T	D	–	T	–
Sáidi	D	D	–	D	D	–	T	–

ACTIVITY 3.12 *Listen first to CD track 2-15 to hear the three rhythmic modes drummed and also spoken by Scott Marcus, author of the volume on Egypt in this series. Then it's your turn: speak the patterns, making deep and high (heavy and light) sounds for* dumm *and* takk. *Do this at several speeds and you will feel the relative weighting of the mode caused by the defining strokes. Another way to feel the modes is to create a dance movement pattern for each one.*

Now listen to CD track 2-1. A nonmetrical *rubato* section *begins the ensemble introduction (*muqaddima*) to the song that will follow. The* rubato *section extends to 1:27, encompassing a beginning by full ensemble, followed by interaction between a soloist on* qanun *(frame zither) and the ensemble response. The next section of the introduction, starting at 1:28, is measured— in* **maqsum** *rhythmic mode. Listen particularly for the* **riqq** *(tambourine with jingling cymbals in the frame, Figure 2.16).*

In performing music in a rhythmic mode, drummers can make some substitutions or embellishments to the patterns in the interest of timbral and expressive variety, but the mode's defining weighting needs to be maintained. The extent of the embellishment should tastefully reflect the overall context in which the rhythm occurs—little, perhaps, when accompanying a slowly moving section of a lyrical song, and much, perhaps, when accompanying a rousing dance.

Shifts in rhythmic mode might also occur for the expression of mood. Returning to CD track 2-1, you can hear this. As composed by Riyad al-Sinbati, the selection is in *maqsum* rhythmic mode beginning at 1:28. Contrasting with that, the song (3:02, just as the track ends) starts in *wahdah* rhythmic mode: Dumm – – Takk – – Takk –. The composer's reason is a change of mood, as *wahdah* is weightier and more appropriate for a serious song.

The Arabian Peninsula, like Egypt, has a number of unique rhythms, including *sa'ûdî*, named after the country Saudi Arabia, and *'adanî*, named after the city Aden, in Yemen. In Iraqi music, the ten-beat *jurjûna* is a characteristic rhythm not generally found in music of the rest of the eastern Arab world (for example, Egypt or Lebanon). For Lebanese, Saudi, Yemeni, and Iraqi people, then, these specific rhythms play an important role in the creation, maintenance, and celebration of their unique cultural identities.

Rhythmic Groupings. In a "grouping" as opposed to a meter, the total number of counts in a unit is not emphasized as a particularly important trait in the organization of time (Lerdahl and Jackendoff 1983). The two examples presented here are Korean *changdan* and polyrhythm in music of sub-Saharan Africa and the Caribbean.

Korean Changdan. A *changdan* is a rhythmic grouping (or pattern) of accented and unaccented beats wherein an aesthetic feeling of tension and release is maintained in the course of a rhythmic cycle. Rhythmic groups/patterns vary in length. Unlike any other time-organizing units I have presented here, some of the rhythmic patterns (*changdan*) occur in nonmetrical music and others in metered contexts.

Two other defining characteristics of *changdan* are new in this discussion of time. One is speed; *changdan* are performed at specified (though relative) speeds. (Speed is of some consideration in Middle Eastern and North Indian *tāla*s but takes relatively less of a defining role there than in *changdan*.) Secondly, the amount of repetition of a particular *changdan* that can occur in a musical selection is another defining trait—free repetition or a set number of repetitions, for example. This elaborate system for the organization of time indicates the importance of rhythm in Korean traditional music: most Korean ensembles, like Middle Eastern and Indian ensembles, include a percussionist.

Within a *changdan* drumming pattern an aesthetic sense of tension and release should be discernible. *Kutkŏri changdan*, for instance, is a pattern of twelve counts, with four groups of three counts each. Drummed on the double-headed hourglass-shaped drum *changgo* (figure 3.2), you can feel gathering intensity from the first six beats, climaxing during beats 7–9, and letting down during the last three beats.

FIGURE 3.2   *Ensemble EGO at the University of California, Berkeley, poses in front of Sproul Hall after performing Pangut P'ungmul for their annual fall showcase. EGO, the campus's Korean traditional percussion group, aims to spread awareness of Korean culture through their music. Three instrument types are visible. With students in the front row are six two-sided barrel-shaped drums called* puk. *Jokingly resting on the head of a student in the front row, second from right, is the* ching, *a low-pitched gong. Held over the shoulder of the student at the right end of the front row is the* soe, *the small lead gong (also called the* kkwaenggwari); *two other* soe *of slightly different size can be found if you look closely. Students in the second row on the left have the two-sided hourglass-shaped* changgo *suspended in playing position by a strap over one shoulder, and one other can be seen mid-group. Hardly visible is a double reed-type instrument (but trumpet-shaped) held by the tall student in the second row, fourth from left.   (Photo by Justin Kwon, permission by EGO)*

ACTIVITY 3.13   *To feel the triple rhythm of* kutkŏri *chang-dan, first count* **1** *2 3 slowly several times. Stand up to try this exercise. Korean musicians think of it as a rhythmic pulse based on breath, so you think the counts as you exhale on* **1** *and inhale on 2 and 3. Continue to think* **1** *2 3 slowly.*

Now bend your knees so that you drop down slightly on **1** *and rise slowly on 2 and 3. This is* ogum, *deep up-and-down movement of the body, coordinated with breathing. Do this exercise again several*

*times, counting from 1 to 12 but keeping up the triple pattern. In
this way you will feel the whole length of* kutkŏri *changdan.*

Now speak the syllables for the strokes on the changgo, *proceeding through the* kutkŏri *pattern to feel the sense of the aesthetic cycle.*

1	2 3	4	5	6	7	8 9	10	11 12
Dong	dak Kung	[da da]	dak	Kung	dak	Kung dak		

Dong *indicates hitting both heads at the same time.*
Dak *indicates hitting the right head with a thin, flat stick.*
Da *is a lighter version of* dak, *hitting with just the tip rather
than the flat part of the stick;* [ ] *indicates filler strokes.*
Kung *indicates hitting left or right head with a wooden mallet.*

*Now speed it up to about one-third faster than you've been
doing it. (In* kutkŏri *changdan, each beat should be counted at
approximately 92–108 beats per minute.)*

Chungmori changdan *exercise*

A more stately rhythmic cycle, **chungmori** *should be counted at
68–88 beats per minute and is usually taught with the following
drum syllables. Make sure to emphasize the accent on the ninth
beat; this is an essential identifying characteristic of the* **changdan**. *Also note that the "dak-i" pattern on the fifth beat should
be articulated so that the "dak" lasts for three-quarters of the pulse
while the "i" lasts only for one-quarter of the pulse. In contrast,
the "dak dak" pattern on the sixth beat should be articulated evenly.
"I" is another way to indicate a lighter "dak" stroke.*

1	2	3	4	5	6	7	8	9	10	11 12
Dong	Kung	Dak	Kung	dak—i	dak dak	Kung	Dak		Kung	Kung

*Like "da", "i" is another way to indicate a lighter "dak" stroke.
(Exercise courtesy of Donna Kwon)*

As in Middle Eastern and Hindustani drumming, the drumming patterns that articulate Korean rhythmic units can be varied in performance. The extent and the ways in which a drummer can do that, of
course, are learned within each tradition.

Polyrhythm. **Polyrhythm** is the musical texture of performing multiple rhythmic patterns simultaneously. Here, the sense of "a rhythm" is clearly delineated from "rhythm in general" (see p. 72). Polyrhythm occurs in many musical practices around the world, but this text focuses on Africa and the Caribbean.

In much African ensemble music south of the Sahara desert, different instruments have their own rhythmic patterns that are repeated many times, in effect multiple rhythmic ostinatos. (An **ostinato** is a constantly recurring motive.) Each rhythmic pattern functions to mark off a time span in the musical flow; musicians feel the rhythm in units of some number of beats—not in meter, where there will be stronger and weaker beats, but a grouping of beats without metrical accent.

The example of polyrhythm in African music that is provided here is *gahu*, a popular West African secular dance-drumming practice that originated in Benin, but was transmitted to places like southeastern Ghana by traveling fisherman from Nigeria. It is communal popular entertainment, comprised of different dance episodes based on loosely choreographed communal dances and "performed whenever the community finds the excuse to celebrate life such as weddings, funerals, and other formal celebrations" (C. K. Ladzekpo, *Gahu Song Book*). The music consists of songs and drumming to accompany the dancing. Each instrument has its pattern(s), with the master drummer (likely a man) providing melodic and rhythmic contrast for a texture that Shannon Dudley defines as featuring "a constant rhythmic feel or 'groove' that is created by the interaction of repeating and contrasting parts" (Dudley 2004). On CD track 1-4 *gahu* dance-drumming of the Anlo-Ewe people of Ghana is demonstrated by a community of students of master drummer C. K. Ladzekpo (figure 2.18).

ACTIVITY 3.14 *Listen a number of times to CD track 1-4, following this guide. Singers are very much in the background in this recording, to give precedence to the instrumental parts. Notations given here are transcriptions by C. K. Ladzekpo.*

0:00 *The recording begins with a basic beat-and-unit pattern being set by the shakers (**axatse**) and double bell (**gankogui**). To hear this, first feel units of four strong beats—1 2 3 4—and keep time with that. The pattern* *played on the shakers clearly gives out the four beats. The pattern played on the* gankogui *features syncopation so that beat 1 is clearly articulated on the lower-pitched bell, but the higher-pitched bell is hit on the off-beats of 2 3 4.*

TIN GO GO GO GO TIN GO GO GO GO

PA PATI PA PA APTI PA PA PATI PA PA PATI PA

The composite sound is very dense because the lead drum **(atsimevu)** *and support drums* **(sogo, kidi,** *and* **kaganu)** *also play a composite of the* gankogui *and main beats.*

0:55 *The second episode of the song fades in. The support drums each play different rhythmic patterns; the* kidi 1, kidi 2, *and* sogo *parts are also melodic with multiple sounds possible on the drums. Even if you cannot read the notation here, you can see that the patterns are different.*

KA GA KA GA KA GA KA GA KA GA KA GA KA GA KA GA

KI DI GO TO KI DI GI TO KI DI GI TO KI DI

KU DI KU DI KI DI KU TU KU TU, KI DI KI DI KU TU, KU DI KU DI KI DI KU TU KU TU, KI DI KI DI KU TU,

KU DE KU KU DE KU KU DE KU DE DE GE DE KU

> *Within the dense texture of the sounds, all musicians lis-*
> *ten for the steady beat and also for the lead drum, on*
> *which a variety of predetermined melodies will be played*
> *to indicate what choreography the dancers should follow.*
> *Try to hear changes and note the timings.*
>
> *Do not forget that the drummers are accompanying*
> *dancers; you can hear the tempo of the drum patterns*
> *increase when the full ensemble is playing to facilitate vig-*
> *orous dancing.*
>
> 3:30 *The final statement, called the prayer, is played by the*
> *instrumental ensemble. It is called in by the lead drum-*
> *mer and played in unison to end the song.*
>
> *If you and a few classmates are able to read the notation, team*
> *up with them to try to tap out the patterns. You may want to*
> *designate one person to keep a steady beat as well. Keep repeat-*
> *ing these patterns until you coordinate smoothly.*

Ruth Stone identifies this rhythmic practice as one manifestation of an aesthetic idea, a love of what she calls "faceting." Each participant contributes a facet (a segment) to the whole.

As I talked to Kpelle musicians about what kinds of performance they most valued, they told me that in Liberia the highest form of performance, from their viewpoint, was when musicians combined . . . short sound facets to create the synchronized whole. Such faceting was considered to be quite wonderful and much to be valued over everyone singing or playing in unison—that is, performing the same music together at the same time.

It's fascinating that as a ruler, such as a chief, appeared at an official function, his (there are a few women chiefs) bearing and presence were enhanced by the sounds that were played. A few chiefs had horn ensembles using carved ivory instruments, but more commonplace were the horns carved from a lightweight wood.

The audience that observed this spectacle had come to value the horn players who created a composition that required split-second timing and how the ensemble symbolized the ultimate in cooperation between multiple players. The most valued form of music was attached to the political leader who used these sounds to reinforce his status.

Strikingly, this most performative practice for the organization of musical time reveals ways in which people make music meaningful and useful in their lives.

A number of musical genres of the African diaspora feature polyrhythmic organization of time. In Caribbean and Latin American dance genres such as *salsa*, *rumba*, *tango*, and *cha cha*, the bell pattern is transformed to **clave**—a rhythmic pattern that is repeated constantly and without change as a rhythmic foundation for a musical selection; it organizes the rhythmic feel of the music. In her volume on the United States in this series, Reyes discusses *clave* as a musical marker of ethnic identity: "Heard by itself or as part of an ensemble, it is immediately identifiable as Latino, or more specifically, Afro-Caribbean, by those who identify themselves as such."

Salsa, with its three-drum percussion coordination plus other instruments, displays a thickening of the rhythmic texture beyond *clave*. Each instrument has a distinctive rhythm or rhythms (*ritmo*) to play (figure 3.3). *Ritmo* refers to the quality of each one of them and also to the overall effect when they coordinate. The quality is defined by timing, volume, timbre, and the manner of blending with other rhythms. Perhaps most significantly, rhythmic thinking is crucial for everyone, because both melodic and percussion instruments are approached like drums. Musicians talk about playing *afincao* (i.e., locked together), meaning that if the rhythms are not happening "together," the music is "not happening." The quality of the rhythmic ensemble, which ultimately is all the ensemble, is of utmost importance (Marisol Berrios-Miranda, personal communication, 2001).

Revealing a synthesis of different musical ideas, about the organization of time, the rhythmic groupings of Afro-Caribbean and Afro-North and South American polyrhythm are not held together by the African timeline; rather, the rhythmic groupings work within the context of meter. *Salsa* is in duple meter with measures of four counts, but it is a two-measure long *clave* pattern that really identifies it. On CD track 2-5, moments from a *salsa*, the *clave* can be heard played on the wooden idiophone called *clave*, whose timbre stands out from the drums and other instruments and voice.

With the evidence of just the systems discussed in this chapter, it is clear that the organization of time in music reveals the remarkable

FIGURE 3.3 *Salsa Band. Left front, Héctor Pérez (bongos); right center, Rafael Angel Irizarry (Puerto Rican cuatro); right front, Jorgé Martínez (guitarrón); right rear, Marisol Berrios-Miranda (güiro); rear left, Karim A. Imes (drum set); rear right, Allan Stone (bass). The bongo drums (front left) are tuned the interval of a fourth apart. Note the bridges on the sounding board of each of the plucked lutes, and the frets up the necks, as well as the tuning pegs on the guitar on the left rear.* (Photo by Kathleen Karn)

musical imagination of humankind. I shall now move to another element having to do with musical time—tempo, or speed.

SPEED

Speed (or *tempo*) in music refers to the pace. Most composers of the Western tradition, since the 17th century, have used Italian indications (Fig. 3.4) as instruction to performers, although some composers go so far as to state the precise number of beats per minute (bpm) in which the movement or piece is to be played. Ultimately, however, performers get to decide the speed in which they will render a piece. Tempo markings are also intended to reveal the character and mood of the piece of music. *Allegro* not only means fast, but implies also a cheerful feeling. Similarly, *adagio* usually implies an "at ease" feeling through the slow speed at which it is to be performed.

> **ACTIVITY 3.15** *Compare the pace of the basic beat of your favorite dances or other types of music. What is the slowest? What is the fastest? To answer this you have to go back to that basic point: find the beat! The important question is this: Why did the musicians set the pieces at the tempos they chose?*

Once a speed is established for the basic beat, both **acceleration** (speeding up) and **deceleration** (slowing down) might be used in the structuring of time in a musical selection. You have already learned about *rubato*—ebb and flow in the pace of the basic beat. But tradition dictates that North Indian classical instrumentalists will gradually accelerate the beat of a selection; never falling back, they sometimes attain a breath-taking speed that requires incredible virtuosity (CD track 1-12). Conversely, gradually slowing down, **ritardando**, to end a piece occurs in many styles.

In the performance of "Marieke" on CD track 2-8, the effect of changing the pace of the basic beat is quite dramatic. Rather than slowing at the end, the speed accelerates. "Marieke" invokes images of World War I (1914–18) in the songwriter Jacques Brel's native Belgium. As a way of bypassing French defenses and attacking Paris directly, German forces marched across the fields of Flanders, resulting in some of the bloodiest fighting of the war. Buildings, roads, nature were completely destroyed, leaving only mud and leveled land. In the churned-up soil, wild poppies began to grow. Heralded in the poem "In Flanders Fields" by the Canadian poet John McCrae, published shortly thereafter, the poppies came to symbolize the tragedy and sacrifice of the war: "In Flanders fields the poppies blow/Between the crosses, row on row." In "Marieke" the loss of a loved one (a woman) is mourned (expressed in English), as is the damage to "my flemishland" (in Flemish), with its once-flourishing cities of Bruges and Ghent (in French, at 2:45 on CD track 2-8) (figure 3.5). As if running to escape both memories, "the day is done" comes faster and faster until the song ends in shrill hopelessness.

	Term	Approximate Beats Per Minute
Largo	Very slow	40–60
Adagio	Slow	66–76
Andante	Walking pace	76–108
Moderato	Moderate	90–115
Allegro	Fast	120–168
Vivace	Lively	140
Presto	Very fast	168–200

FIGURE 3.4   *Italian terms for speed (tempo) in music*   (Chart by Kin Hang Lam)

"MARIEKE"
Ay, Marieke, Marieke, the Flanders sun
  shuns the sky, since you are gone.
Ay, Marieke, Marieke, in Flanders Fields
  the poppies die since you are gone.

Zonder liefde, warmede liefde	*Without love, warm love,*
wait de wind de stomme wind.	*wails the wind, the speechless wind.*
Zonder liefde, warmede liefde	*Without love, warm love,*
weent de zee, de grijze zee.	*Moans the sea, the grizzled sea*
Zonder liefde, warmede liefde	*Without love, warm love,*
Lijdt het licht, het donker licht.	*Suffers the light with darkening sky*
En schuurt het zand over mign land.	*And scours the sand o'er my land*
Mijn platte land, mijn Vlaanderen land.	*My leveled land, my Flemish land.*

Ay, Marieke, Marieke, the stars look down
So soon, so soon, the day is done
Ay, Marieke, Marieke,
The Flanders moon won't light your way,
The day is done.

Zonder liefde, warmede liefde	*Without love, warm love*
wait de wind, (c'est fini)	*Wails the wind (it's over)*
Zonder liefde, warmede liefde	*Without love, warm love*
Weent de zee (déjà fini)	*Wails the sea (already ended)*
Zonder liefde, warmede liefde	*Without love, warm love*
Lijdt het licht (toute est fini)	*Suffers the light (all is over)*
En schuurt het zand over mign land	*And scours the sand o'er my land*
Mijn platte land, mijn Vlaanderen land.	*My leveled land, my Flemish land*

Ay, Marieke, Marieke, the bells have rung
the echoes sound. The day is done
Ay, Marieke, Marieke. In Flanders fields
The echoes sound, the day is done.

Zonder liefde, warmede liefde	*Without love, warm love*
Lacht de duivel, de zwarte duivel.	*Laughs the devil, the dark black devil.*
Zonder liefde, warmede liefde	*Without love, warm love,*
Brandt mijn hart, mijn oude hart.	*Burns up my heart, my aging heart.*
Zonder liefde, warmede liefde	*Without love, warm love,*
Sterft de zomer, de droeve zomer.	*Dies the summer, the pitiful summer.*
En schuurt het zand over mign land.	*And scours the sand o'er my land,*
mijn platte land, mijn Vlaanderen land.	*My leveled land, my Flemish land.*

FIGURE 3.5   *"Marieke." words and music by Eric Blau, Jacques Brel, Gerard Jouannest.   © Copyright 1968 Universal-MCA Music Publishing, a Division of Universal Studios, Inc. (ASCAP) International copyright secured. All rights reserved. (Translation courtesy of Suzanne Lake)*

Rather than accelerate the pace of the basic beat, however, musicians might create a sense of great speed by increasing the subdivisions within the beat; this is perception rather than acceleration. What changes is the rhythmic density—a technique demonstrated in Activity 3.4 through an Indian system of spoken patterns.

In this chapter on the organization of time I have presented some ideas and practices by which musicians mark the passage of time through musical selections. Those ideas range from successions of unequal durations in freely floating rhythm, to a single regular unit—a pulse—to various kinds of meters, and to colotomic meter, rhythmic mode, and polyrhythm. Finally, I considered the element of speed, the pace of moving through time. In chapter 4 I take up the musical element of pitch.

CHAPTER 4

Thinking about Pitch

∞

I treat the subject of pitch at some length in this book for the following two connected reasons: pitch is the fundamental element in both melody and harmony, and ideas about pitch need to be explored in order to understand how melody and harmony are cultivated in different traditions. Accordingly, I will start by analyzing pitch in basic terms—as single **tones** and in the formation of intervals and scales. Then I will proceed to the use of pitch in melody and in harmony.

In its most generic sense, **melody** can be defined as any selection of pitches in succession. A particular melody will have one of several forms. It might be short—as in a **motive** (CD track 2-16). It might be relatively longer, as in an Irish tune (CD track 1-3) or a mariachi strophe (CD track 1-6), or even longer, as in a jazz riff of several sections or the solos of a Japanese *syakuhati* (vertical bamboo flute) player (figure 1.2, CD track 1-18). A melody can be easy to sing or play for those familiar with the melodic system, or difficult to remember.

In its most generic sense, **harmony** can be defined as pitches heard simultaneously. How the relationship between those pitches is understood differs from system to system.

PITCH

∞

"Ken McIntyre once commented that a great improviser could play an entire solo based on one pitch alone. Coincidentally, during an interview with a young drummer, a soft background recording featured flugelhornist Wilbur Hardin, who was generating tremendous excitement with a stream of single-pitched rhythmic patterns at his solo's opening. . . . The drummer

suddenly burst out laughing and, with an apology for his distraction, added: 'Did you hear that? That's what our music's about. Listen to all that brother can say with one note!'" (Berliner, 1994: 147).

The term **pitch** as a relative quality of "highness" or "lowness" of sound is not limited to musical terminology: we speak metaphorically of the high-pitched squeal of tires and the low-pitched roar of a powerful motorcycle engine. Musical pitch is a more focused idea, referring to a sound that is produced more purposefully in some area, high to low.

In terms of musical practice around the world, it is useful to think of a continuum of ideas about pitch placement. At one end is a sense of satisfaction when the pitch lies anywhere within an expected general compass. In his case study of East African music in this series, Greg Barz cites the distinguished Ugandan musician Centurio Balikoowa as saying: "The temperature in our country is sometimes a bit hot, and the instruments, apart from the flutes, they respond to the weather. If it's hot they go very high. If it's cool it goes very low. So people just play without thinking that this is [this pitch] or this is [that pitch as on a keyboard]." At the other end of the continuum is the ideal of precise placement, a pitch that results when a string, a column of air, or other sound-producing body vibrates at a particular **frequency** (rate) such as 440 **Hertz** (cycles per second). I will return to this concept later.

Some instruments can produce clearer or more well-defined pitches than others. Wind, brass, and bowed string instruments have patterns of vibration that are periodic. The repetition rate, known as the fundamental frequency, determines the perceived pitch. Other instruments like wood blocks, snare drums, and cymbals do not produce periodic patterns of vibration, and although they may sound higher or lower, they do not have clear pitches. Periodic sounds have frequency components that fall along the harmonic series in that the constituent frequencies are integer multiples of the fundamental or repetition rate of the waveform. We say these sounds are harmonic. On the other hand, nonperiodic sounds like those from many percussion instruments are said to be inharmonic. CD track 2-16 demonstrates the difference between harmonic and inharmonic sounds. The harmonic sound has frequency components at 220, 440, 660, and 880 Hertz (cycles per second), whereas the inharmonic sound has frequency components at 220, 395, 678, and 845 Hertz.

Pitch Names.   For communication about music and as an aid to memory (mnemonic), it is convenient to assign names to pitches. This has been done in various places around the world, using syllables, numbers, or letters. A few examples are given here.

Syllables.   Syllables used to name pitches (and percussion strokes) are generically called by the term **solfège**. In India historically syllables have been assigned to seven pitches in ascending order as *sa, re* (in North India, *ri* in South India), *ga, ma, pa, dha* (in North India, *da* in South India), and *ni*. On CD track 2-3, those syllables are incorporated into vocal music as text for melody; this brief excerpt sung by the late great Pandit Amir Khan begins "*re—ni sa.*" Indian musicians notate music by writing those syllables, and they appear prominently in the case studies on North and South India in this series.

> **ACTIVITY 4.1**   *Make a transcription of the pitch syllables from CD track 2-3. Then invent a notation to show the melody spatially—showing the contour. Once you have completely plotted the melodic contour, redo the notation to show indications of relative durations. Are some pitches prolonged rhythmically or sung relatively quickly? When you finish, try to sing with the recording from your notation.*

Solfège syllables have been used in European music since about 1600, as follows: *do, re, mi, fa, sol, la,* and *ti* (or *si*), in ascending order. The song "Doe, a deer, a female deer," from the Broadway musical *The Sound of Music*, plays with those syllables, as in "Ray, a drop of golden sun;/Me, a name I call myself" as the nanny is giving the children a singing lesson. In fact, that system of solfège is used for teaching music around the world; it has been widely adopted throughout the Middle East, and musicians in Arab countries, Turkey, and Iran are masters at singing and sight-reading in solfège.

Numbers. Numbers are used in music in at least two different ways. One is to indicate pitch (1 = *do* fixed to pitch C in the French system; 2 = *re*, etc.). The other use is technical, instructing musicians how to produce a particular pitch on an instrument. This is the case with the tablature for the Chinese *qin* (figures 1.10 to 1.13), where notation tells the player only which string to pluck. In Javanese music, where basic melodies are played out on metal xylophone-type instruments, theslabs are numbered (figure 1.5). On the *qin* and the metallophone, the resulting melodies depend on which pitches the strings or slabs are tuned to.

Letters. In the European system, letters as well as syllables and numbers are used for identifying pitches. Adopted from the Greeks, via the Romans, c.500 C.E. the letters in ascent are A, B, C, D, E, F, and G.

SETTING THE PITCH

Questions arise. Where is pitch *sa* or pitch 1 or pitch A? Who sets the pitch, and how?

Who Sets the Pitch. On many instruments the pitch is fixed in construction. During manufacture, a flute will have pitch holes drilled at some points. If a flute, as the typical Tanzanian **filulu** flute is, is invariably played alone for one's own enjoyment there is no need to worry about drilling holes to obtain pitches that will match some other flute's (Barz 2004:10). On a metallophone, the metal will be forged and then trimmed to produce a certain pitch when struck. Tuning a bar is accomplished by scraping or filing away different parts of the bar. If the pitch is too low, metal is filed off the end of the bar, thus decreasing its mass and raising its pitch. If the pitch of the bar is too high, metal is filed off underneath the middle of the bar, thus increasing the flexibility of the bar and lowering the pitch. On the metal surface of a steel drum discretely tuned spots will be hammered out (figure 2.17). On a chordophone, **frets** (a raised appendage on the neck of an instrument) are one mechanism for indicating the pitch placement; the player presses the string down to the fret (called "stopping the string") to indicate the place of other desired pitches. Most but not all fretted stringed instruments are lutes (figure 4.1); the zither-type Korean *komungo* has frets (figure 2.11, CD track 1-22). If they are to be fixed in place, the instrument maker will have to know the musical system in order to set the pitches properly.

If the pitches are not fixed on the instrument, the musician has responsibility for setting them. While a North Indian maker of *sitārs* (figure 3.1, CD tracks 1-11, 1-12) will put frets on an instrument, he will strap them onto the neck, rather than fix them in place, so that the player can set them according to the melody (**rāga**) to be performed. On the Japanese *koto* (figure 1.2), the player positions a moveable **bridge** under each string to set its pitch, and a player of a lute-type instrument, such as the *syamisen* in figure 1.2, tightens the strings to a certain basic pitch. Beyond that, fretless bowed and plucked lutes present great challenges for players. To obtain pitches beyond those on their open strings, all the musicians in figure 4.1 and the *syamisen* player in figure 1.2 (CD track 2-18) have to memorize where to press their fingers down on the strings along the neck. They must literally embody the sense of pitch as they train their muscles what to do.

FIGURE 4.1   *Displaying three of the four sizes of the violin family of bowed lutes is the Kin Lam String Quartet.   From left to right: on viola, Haley Mulstein; on cello, Jonathan Chang; on violin, Kin Hang Lam; on violin, Justin Uang—all students at the University of California, Berkeley.   For the string bass, see Fig. 2.16.* (Chart by Kin Hang Lam)

Student Kin Hang Lim: *"Learning the violin can be a frustrating process in the beginning, since we don't have frets on our instruments to instruct us where to place our fingers. We do so entirely by ear and experience. In fact, a violinist's fingers can be compared to lightning. We never strike the exact same place twice."*

ACTIVITY 4.2 *If you know how to tune an instrument, articulate that process to someone who is unfamiliar with it. In addition, get someone to explain the process on an instrument you are less familiar with.*

Pitch Placement. At what sound levels pitches should lie is a matter of choice in a musical style, deeply embedded in tradition.

All musicians have an ideal of pitch precision, but the ideals differ widely. Indonesian traditions provide a good example of this. In Central Java, each ensemble (*gamelan*) of instruments is manufactured to have its own distinctive set of pitches (figure 1.5). No two ensembles are tuned alike, and the aesthetic effect of its tuning gives each *gamelan* a musical identity.

In Bali, precise tuning is done with pairs of instruments. However, the two instruments in a pair are tuned precisely *unalike*: the frequencies (the rate of vibration of the sound waves) of their pitches are very close but intentionally set far enough apart in order to produce **beats**. Beats occur when two sound waves with different frequencies overlap; what we hear are resulting periodic variations in amplitude. This is demonstrated on CD track 2-18, with each instrument played alone, then the two instruments together. The practice of paired tunings creates the desired bright, shimmering metallic timbre that you hear in CD track 2-4. When played together, the higher instrument, known as the "inhaler," and the lower, the "exhaler," create this pulsing effect, metaphorically breathing and thus bringing the sound of the *gamelan* to life. When there is more than one of a single instrument, such as in the metallophone section of the *gamelan*, the inhalers are all tuned alike, and the exhalers are all tuned alike (Gold 2005: 33). The contrasting pitch ideals in the Central Javanese *gamelan* on CD track 1-7 and the Balinese *gamelan* on CD track 2-4 make the ensemble sounds unmistakably different. (I am assuming that you are remembering to take the initiative to listen when I refer to a CD track, even if I do not tell you to do so.)

In classical music in the European system the named pitches (A, B, C, D, etc.) are expected to lie at some precise place, that is, at a precise frequency: by agreement in recent times, the pitch called "A above middle C" vibrates at 440 Hertz (with some preference also for the slightly higher pitch of 442 hz). Instruments with fixed pitch are manufactured to this standard, and instrumentalists without fixed pitch are expected to adjust to it. This adjustment can be witnessed and heard through the tuning practice that initiates an orchestra concert (CD track 2-20). Before the conductor of the orchestra comes onstage and the performance begins in a formal sense, the **concertmaster** (the male or female leader of the violin section, who acts as an assistant to the conductor) stands to face the orchestra and instructs the lead player of the oboe section to produce the pitch A. In turn, in a ritualized order the sections of the orchestra tune. From the cacophony that soon results, it is clear that this is also an opportunity to warm up onstage. Furthermore, the tuning cues the audience to settle into silence for the performance, a practice derived from and idiosyncratic of European classical music performance.

With a sense of "in-tuneness" firmly established in one's musical soundscape, playing against it can be an aesthetic choice. One need only think of the "bent notes" that play around with pitches' "in-tuneness"; modern keyboard synthesizers have pitch bend wheels so the keyboardist can bend the notes. The *salsa* musician Gerardo Rosales insists that *salsa* is not authentic *salsa* unless the trombonist plays a little bit out of tune; not all *salsa* musicians agree, however (Berrios-Miranda 1999).

For a performer to produce pitches at desired frequencies is known as "having good **intonation**." An ideal once held by musicians of European classical music was to "have **perfect pitch**," wherein one could identify or produce a desired letter-named musical pitch at its established frequency even if asked on the spot; now it is considered far more useful to "have excellent relative pitch." That is certainly the case if you want to enjoy music of traditions with different senses of intonation. A sensible, flexible way to think about "good intonation" is to appreciate musicians' exceptional good aural memory, in whatever pitch system they cultivate.

A finely cultivated sense of pitch is crucial also in the classical music of North India. Producing pitches that are out of tune with the expected pitch placement is sufficient in contemporary times to ruin a musician's reputation, but it has always been so; from the *Nāradīya Śikṣā* (c. fourth century C.E.): "Wrong musical intonation is a crime in which one risks one's life, one's progeny, and one's cattle" (te Nijenhuis 1974: 36). Flexibility is embedded within the system, however: there is no standardized pitch frequency (cycles per second) for the pitch called *sa*. *Sa* can be placed anywhere a singer is comfortable placing it—not so high or so low as to prevent reaching all the pitches desired in the improvisatory moments to come.

ACTIVITY 4.3 *Pick a starting pitch 1 and experiment with singing a straight ascending row of eight pitches. If the pitches get too high for comfort as you go up, start over on a lower pitch 1 until you find your comfort zone; you are finding "your sa." When you have it, sing the ascending row with the syllables* sa re ga ma pa dha ni sa—*and also trying singing back down on those syllables. It's fun too to make brief melodic phrases, using the syllables as text. To cement your sense of* "sa" *at your own level, ask a classmate to sing it (or play it on an instrument), keeping it sustained as a drone while you improvise little phrases over it.*

All of the preceding discussion about pitch assumes that a pitch is a discrete entity, a sound. To musicians in some traditions there is much more to it. In Korean musical aesthetics, for instance, the moments of the sounding are just part of the aural experiencing of a pitch. Its dying away, its decay as a string gradually ceases to vibrate audibly, is at the heart of the aesthetic sense, as well: the beauty of "sound into silence." This should be clear to you from listening to CD track 1-21—the fretted zither *komungo*—particularly through the first minute and a half.
The player creates vibrato with fingers of the left hand (figure 2.11) until the sound of the string plucked with a small bamboo rod dies away; the decay is even more obvious when a pitch is allowed to die without vibrato.

PITCHES IN SUCCESSION

Intervals. In the discussion above I focused primarily on single pitches, but here I want to move to thinking about pitches in relationship to each other. That relationship can be in a succession of pitches as in melody or as in some kind of harmonic simultaneity. In either case, it is the distance spanned between pitches that comes into play. The English-language term for that distance is **interval**. The matter of intervals is more important in music in the European system than in any other, because that system cultivates harmonic relationships. Nevertheless, I shall approach intervals first as pitches occurring one after another, as in melody.

Naming Intervals. So important are intervals in European music theory that they are given names. Two factors are involved in the naming. One is the number of pitches that the interval spans. Figure 4.2 depicts a keyboard with the white keys labeled A, B, C, D, E, F, and G.

Ascending from A to B involves two pitch letters; the interval from A to B is thus called a second. Going up from A to C spans across A, B, and C (i.e., three pitch letters), so the interval is called a third, and so forth. The interval from one note to another note with the same letter name spans eight pitch letters and is called an **octave** (*octo-*, "eight"), as in A to the next higher (or lower) A.

The second factor involved in the naming of intervals in the European system is quantitative—different sizes: there are minor and major seconds, minor and major thirds, for example. Returning to the keyboard with its white and black keys (Figure 4.2) will help explain this. Between any two adjacent keys there is a distance measured as a **half step**. Between F and the black key between F and G, there is a half step (**a**

FIGURE 4.2   *Keyboard with white keys named.*   *(Chart by Kin Hang Lam)*

minor second); between that black key and G, there is a half-step (**a minor second**). Between F and G, therefore, the distance is a **whole step** (**a major second**). A half step equals a minor second; a whole step equals a major second. Figure 4.3 charts the intervals in one **octave**, with the number of half steps within each.

Intervals in the European System

# of half steps	Interval name
0	Unison
1	Minor 2nd
2	Major 2nd
3	Minor 3nd
4	Major 3nd
5	Perfect 4th
6	Tritone
7	Perfect 5th
8	Minor 6th
9	Major 6th
10	Minor 7th
11	Major 7th
12	Perfect Octave

FIGURE 4.3   *Intervals in the European system.*   (*Chart by Kin Hang Lam*)

ACTIVITY 4.4

Step 1. To be sure you have this straight, in the middle of a sheet of paper make your own drawing of the span on the keyboard shown in Fig. 4.2. (Don't be lazy and photocopy the figure; you won't have sufficient space for the next steps.) Make the keys fairly wide and leave plenty of space above and below the keyboard.

Step 2. Above the keyboard, put a carot (^) marking every half step and write m2 for minor second; 2) in a first row below the key board, bracket (⌣) every interval of a major second (M2) and write M2.

Step 3. In a second row above, bracket every minor third and write m3.

Step 4. In a second row below, bracket every major third and write M3.

You can check yourself by counting half steps as enumerated for those intervals in Figure 4.4 and proceed to intervals beyond the major third, if you wish.

Major and minor thirds are crucial intervals for you to hear and feel. One way to do it is to sing the familiar melody of "Frère Jacques" (CD track 2-21): the melody on just those two first words of the song outlines a major third, first in ascent and then in descent. You might know this as "Are you sleeping?"; in that case, the major third occurs on "Are . . . sleeping." Sing it several times. Once you have that interval in your ears, try to lower the pitch on "Jac/sleep" by a half step; the melody will sound very different with a minor third.

Microtones.   Many musical systems use intervals smaller than the half step, the smallest named interval in Western music; resulting pitches at such intervals are sometimes called **microtones. Quarter tone** is another term that is frequently used in a rather loose manner to describe many different "types" of pitches that do not fall into the Western scale. For example, microtones/quarter tones are a feature of Arab music, which is based on a theoretical scale of twenty-four pitches per octave. The system includes all the twelve pitches per octave that coincide with those of Western music, but achieves its additional twelve notes per octave by subdividing the intervals into quarter steps. One obtains thereby "half-flat" intervals—a half-flat second, half-flat third, and the like. No musician would ever play the twenty-four notes in succession;

rather, the system just supplies a great variety of possible pitches from which scales may be derived. **Maqam Rast**, a melodic mode explored in depth in Scott Marcus's volume on the music of Egypt and the eastern Arab world in this series, features a half-flat third and a half-flat seventh (CD track 2-1).

ACTIVITY 4.5 *Listen to the beginning of CD track 2-3, the instrumental introduction to a song by the great Egyptian singer Umm Kulthum. In the melodic unit (phrase) that immediately follows the downbeat given by the double bass, the second note is a half-flat third. The penultimate note of that phrase is a half-flat seventh. The phrase repeats. Listen to the opening section several times, up to the beginning of the qanun (plucked frame zither) solo.*

Scale.   Theorists and practitioners in a number of musical systems think about melodic material in terms of pitch sets—groups of pitches. One clear way to articulate a set of pitches is to present them as a scale, in straight ascending or descending order. (Note: this is not appropriate for some types of pitch sets.) When one hears a scale, the focus can be on the pitches or on the intervals formed by the distances between the pitches. In Indian music theory, for instance, the focus is on the pitches, while in the European system the focus is on the intervals. I shall sample a few scale types and illustrate how scalar material might be used in melodic practice.

The Chromatic Scale.   Sounding all twelve pitches in an octave on the piano in ascending or descending order produces what in English is called a **chromatic scale**.

ACTIVITY 4.6 *Find a keyboard and use figure 4.2 (or your own drawing for Activity 4.4) to position a finger on pitch C in about the middle of the keyboard. Play each key in succession (both white and black) up to the next pitch C. You have sounded a chromatic scale of twelve pitches.*

A dramatic example of the chromatic scale in melody is the opening of the famous aria "L'amour est un oiseau rebelle," from *Carmen*, an opera by the French composer Georges Bizet (1838–75). Much of the first part of the aria consists of a descending chromatic scale. (This aria is more commonly called "Habañera," which is actually the Cuban song form that supposedly served as the stylistic basis for the aria.)

ACTIVITY 4.7 *At the point in the story of the opera* Carmen *that is recorded on CD track 1-28, a number of women factory workers mill about onstage, trying to attract the attention of soldiers who wait instead for the sensually flirtatious heroine, Carmen. The excerpt begins as she finally enters. Carmen is interested only in a soldier whom she does not see.*

First listen to CD track 1-28 all the way through, for the purpose of following the French text (even if you do not know French). The quick orchestral introduction to the aria begins at 1:02. In repeated listenings, focus on the chromatic scale at the beginning of the aria and through the selection. Occurrences of chromatic melody are underlined in the French text. You will hear it better if you try to sing along with the soloist. Keep listening, because that melody repeats.

(Carmen enters)

0: 05 All
La voilà!   *There she is!*

0:17 Men
Carmen, sur tes pas,   *Carmen, we're all at your feet!*
  nous nous pressons tous;
Carmen, sois gentille, au   *Carmen, be kind and at least*
  moins réponds-nous,   *answer us,*

Et dis-nous quel jour tu   *and say that one day you'll love us!*
  nous aimeras.
Carmen, dis-nous quel jour *Carmen, say which day you will*
  tu nous aimeras.   *love us!*

0:33 Carmen   *(after a quick glance at Don José)*
Quand je vous aimerai?   *When will I love you?*
Ma foi, je ne sais pas.   *Really, I don't know.*

Peut-être jamais,
peut-être demain,
Mais pas aujourd'hui,
c'est certain.

1:08
L'amour est un oiseau rebelle
que nul ne peut apprivoiser.
Et c'est bien en vain
qu'on l'appelle,
S'il lui convient de refuser.
Rien n'y fait; menace ou prière.
L'un parles bien, l'autre se tait;
Et c'est l'autre que je préfère.
Il n'a rien dit, mais il me plait.

1:36 Chorus
L'amour est un oiseau rebelle
que nul ne peut apprivoiser.
Et c'est bien en vain qu'on
l'appelle,
S'il lui convient de refuser.

1:37 Carmen
Amour, amour, amour, amour!
L'amour est enfant de Bohême,
Il n'a jamais, jamais
connu de loi.
Si tu ne m'aimes pas, je t'aime.
Et si je t'aime,
prend garde à toi!

2:05 Chorus
Prends garde à toi!
Continue to listen for repetition of the last three lines and the verse from
the beginning of the "Habañera."

Perhaps never, perhaps tomorrow,

but not today—that's certain.

Habañera
Love is a bird wild and free
whom no one can tame;
And it's useless to appeal to him,

if he's in the mood to refuse.
He heeds no threat or prayer.
One speaks well, the other is silent;
and it's the other whom I prefer.
He has said nothing; but he
pleases me.

Love is a bird wild and free
whom no one can tame;
and it's useless to appeal
to him,
if he's in the mood to refuse.

(first line overlapping with chorus)
Love, love, love, love!
Love is a gypsy child
who never, never heeds
any law.
If you don't love me, I love you;
And if I love you—
ah then, beware!

Ah then, beware!

Long chromatic descents and ascents and quick three-pitch chromatic motives comprise much of the melodic material in the contemporary piece "Mini Overture" by the Polish composer Witold Lutosławski

(1913–94) (CD track 2-2). This is a snappy fanfare for brass quintet. Within seconds of the start, the first trumpeter gives out a descending chromatic alarum, which is taken up in turn by the horn and trombone players. Immediately after, the trombonist initiates the idea of repeating three-pitch chromatic motives, answered very quickly by the second trumpeter and then the horn player. From that point you can hear rapid three-pitch chromatic motives that seem to be everywhere: 1:02 to 1:35 is thick with them, also at 1:55. The long chromatic line recurs at 2:35, recalling the beginning at the end.

Diatonic Scales. **Diatonic scales** are seven-note scales that comprise some arrangement of half steps and whole steps. If you have grown up hearing music in the European system, and you just sing the most natural scale that comes into your head, you will no doubt sing one of them—the **major scale**. You have learned it by osmosis. It is the scale you sing on the text syllables "Doe, ray, me, far, sew, la, and tea" in "Doe, a deer" (that is, the solfège syllables *do, re, mi, fa, sol, la,* and *ti* or *si*). The arrangement of whole steps and half steps within an octave of a major scale is W W H W W W H (CD track 2-22).

ACTIVITY 4.8 *Other CD tracks you have listened to thus far have melodies that use a Western major scale. Listen again to identify at least two of them. This is a good moment for you to be certain that you have added all the references to all the CD tracks thus far in your cumulative accounting for them (see Activity 1.5).*

Another important diatonic scale in the Western system is the **natural minor scale**. Its arrangement of whole steps and half steps is W H W W H W W. Major and minor thirds play the most significant part in distinguishing the major and minor scales.

The "Oriental" Scale. Perhaps you will immediately recognize CD track 2-23 as a Spanish flamenco song—by the vocal style perhaps, or by the guitar style. The scale in the melody might also sound familiar to you; Its intervals are as follows:

1	2		3	4	5	6		7	1
H	aug3		H	W	H		aug3		H

"Aug3" is another size of second—an **augmented second** comprised of three half steps. It distinguishes this scale from a diatonic scale and establishes its "difference." The music of the excerpt on CD track 2-23 is so particular to flamenco that the scale is strongly associated with the Roma, who developed the style. Linking the Roma (gypsies) and Spain and non-diatonic melody is logical. The Roma have a long history in Spain. So, too, did peoples of the Near East (more properly called "West Asia" now) of non-Christian faiths (Muslim and Jewish) until 1492, when Ferdinand and Isabella expelled them. Left behind were assimilated elements of those peoples' cultures—including music. Even today, some musics of southern Spain suggest some cultural retention through the centuries.

Non-Romani composers have used this and similar nondiatonic scales to suggest not only the Roma but also other exotic people and places in a fashion termed "orientalist" after literary theorist Edward Said (see Chapter 6). For that reason, this scale is sometimes called the "**Oriental scale**."

Number of Pitches in an Octave. To consider scales on a world-wide basis, it is useful to think in terms of the number of pitches that lie within an octave. There are numerous **heptatonic** (seven-tone) scales, of which the European major scale and the "Oriental" scale are two CD tracks 2-22, 2-23. From the perspective of the total number of pitches within an octave, Arab music scales, too, are all heptatonic—selections of seven pitches from the twenty-four possibilities mentioned under "Microtones." The scale on CD track 2-1 is an example. **Pentatonic** (five-tone) scales are also numerous, such as the scale of "Auld Lang Syne" (1, 2, 3, 5, 6), sung to mark the beginning of a new year.

ACTIVITY 4.9 *To experience music with two different pentatonic pitch selections, first sing "Auld Lang Syne." Then listen to CD track 1-7, a selection in a Javanese tuning system called* sléndro, *which is pentatonic. While the pentatonic scale of "Auld Lang Syne" has a clear "gap" between pitches 3 and 5, Javanese* sléndro *positions the five pitches more or less equidistantly within an octave.*

Rather than taking the span of an octave as the analytical frame for thinking about pitch selection, Arab and Turkish musics use the tetrachord as the basic analytical unit. A tetrachord is a four-note scalar segment whose first and fourth pitches are separated by the interval of a perfect fourth (for example, C to F, D to G). Within the span of an octave, there will be a lower and an upper tetrachord. Modern Arab music theorists usually recognize nine different tetrachords, each with a unique intervallic configuration, each named. On CD track 2-24, you hear the tetrachord named **rast** as both the lower and upper tetrachords. CD track 2-25 gives you *rast* and two others—**nahāwand** and **hijāz** for comparison.

Pitch Functions. Whether you have a set of five, six, twelve or some other number of pitches in a set, the idea of assigning some particular function to one or more of them is widespread. A South Indian classical *rāga* (**melodic mode**) is likely to have a beginning pitch, an ending pitch, and "life-giving tone(s)" on which the melody pauses and dwells.

In many musics, one pitch functions as what might be called a **tonal center**, or a fundamental pitch, or—thinking in terms of hierarchy—a primary pitch. One can often sense a fundamental pitch in listening to melody, perhaps because it occurs frequently or because the melody comes to an end on it. The best way to locate a fundamental pitch is simply to listen and let it emerge in your hearing—and not worry if you cannot sense it at first.

ACTIVITY 4.10 *Try feeling the fundamental pitch in these selections: CD track 1-15, Trinidadian steel drum; CD track 1-2, Chinese ensemble, "Moderate Tempo Six Beats"; CD track 1-5, "Ballad of César Chávez"; and CD track 2-21, "Frère Jacques" ("Are you sleeping").*

In the European tradition the fundamental pitch is called a **tonic**, and the system of music that is organized around having a functional tonic is called **tonal music**. It is appropriate to think of "tonic" as a "home pitch" because in tonal music aesthetics there is a definite sense of finality associated with returning to the tonic pitch to end a piece. You can feel this clearly on CD track 2-6, "West End Blues."

Hierarchy is so important in tonal music that three other pitches in a key are designated as more important functionally. The important pitch that is five pitches up from the tonic is called the **dominant**; as you have heard, in "Take Five" (CD track 1-32) the bass player articulates the metric structure by alternating between the tonic and dominant. The pitch located four pitches up from the tonic is the **subdominant**. Another important pitch is generally called the **leading tone**; located a half step below the tonic (or, in the less common case of the "upper leading tone," a half step above tonic), it is used to create a feeling of going toward the tonic.

Melodic Mode. Beyond the rather abstract idea of pitches and their functions, of intervals, and of scales is another way of thinking about what constitutes fundamental melodic material on which compositions and improvisation are based. That is **mode**, an idea about pitch and melody that encompasses both explicitly musical practice and extramusical associations. European major and minor scales are modes, in that there is sometimes a mood associated—a sense of major as "happy" and a sense of minor as "sad." "Association" is the operative word here. Tom Turino points out how, unlike in North America where the minor scale that begins with a minor third is associated with sad, somber, or serious emotions, it has no such emotional meanings for indigenous Andean people of South America. Rather, it is speed that bears an association with moods: slow tempos communicate more serious or profound sentiments, and fast pieces are associated with upbeat emotions (2007).

In addition to an expresive quality such as mood, it is musical practice that distinguishes modes. Rajna Klaser Ledoux has described the way she learned about mode in Turkish music, there termed **makam**.

> Every Tuesday morning I would meet my teacher, Yusuf Ömürlu Bey, for my lesson. Each time, he would have ready two identical binders containing select vocal and instrumental pieces in one *makam*. With these binders on his desk—one for him, the other for me—introduction of a new *makam* would commence. As he is browsing through the sheets deciding which tune we will start our lesson with, Yusuf Ömürlu Bey is humming in free rhythm a vocal improvisation, a *seyir* of a *makam* I am about to learn. This little ritual is followed by his explanation of the properties of the *makam*. He would write a scalar formation of a *makam*, clearly defining its tonic and dominant with whole notes, delineating its tetrachord and pentachord with arches, showing acoustical relationships between adjacent notes with standard symbols [letters] and also the general melodic progression of the *makam*.
>
> Up to this point, Yusuf Ömürlu Bey's instruction is very systematic and does not depart from the explanations one can find in

textbooks on Turkish music theory. His instruction is musically mute, my teacher never finding any reason to demonstrate either the scale or those nuances with his voice.

From that point, however, Yusuf Ömürlu Bey's instruction departs to the more illusive and poetic realm of "colors" [*renkler*] or "fragrances" [*kokular*] of the *makam* in question. This is where his passion for Turkish music and Turkish melody becomes obvious. As he demonstrates with his voice these *colors and fragrances in the form of characteristic motif, change in register, shift to important functional degrees, and melodic alterations that give particular identity* to the *makam*, his facial expressions depict *the emotional feel* of the *makam* that puts it into the realm of poetry. He frequently describes them with poetical tropes such as melancholy, happiness, and so forth. As a conclusion, Yusuf Ömürlu Bey hums another vocal improvisation demonstrating discussed features of the *makam* for that day, and segues into singing several vocal and instrumental compositions from the binder. (Klaser 2001: 62–4)

In the quote, I have italicized those characteristics—particular expressive qualities—that make mode a more encompassing idea about melodic material than even the composite of pitch and pitch function, interval, and scale.

To pursue *makam* (Turkish spelling) a bit with a musical illustration, I turn to *maqām* (Egyptian transliteration) Rast that is featured throughout Scott Marcus's book in this series on Egypt and the eastern Arab world. For pitch selection, *maqām* Rast will be performed with the *rast* tetrachord in the lower position, but with any of three tetrachords (CD track 2-25) in the upper position. It will take sharp listening to hear the quick shifts among them in the melody of CD track 2-1, but with a listening guide, you can at least get the principle of the melodic practice, with a focus on *hijāz* tetrachord.

0:05–0:11	The initial rubato phrase starts with the notes of a *hijāz* tetrachord (G-Ab-B-c),
0:33–0:38	The initial rubato phrase again.
0:55–	The *qānūn* solo reasserts the *hijāz* tetrachord.
1:26–1:30	With the entry of the percussion, a quick alternation, here *nahāwand* tetrachord
1:30–1:36	*hijāz*
1:36–1:37	*nahāwand*
1:37–1:39	*hijāz*, before falling to the tonic. A tonic pitch is a characteristic of modal practice in the *maqām* system.

Musicians in North India consider many of their melodic modes (*rāga*) bearers of special expressive capacity to communicate moods. Some historians explain that capacity by citing the ancient connection of music and drama, where the shifting moods in a play would be expressed musically. Other historians connect it with the shifting natural moods in a day, from meditative in the early morning hours, to energetic in midmorning, tantalizingly tentative at sunrise and sunset, and serious in the late night. Others explain it through the different contexts and functions of music in a complex court culture in which India's classical music was cultivated—music for religious worship, light after-dinner entertainment, serious discussion deep in the night. Perhaps it is a combination of nature and culture. Whatever the reason, meditative *Rāga Āsāvarī*, with all its particular modal characteristics, is best performed in early morning. The Malhar *rāga*s are best performed in the monsoon season, when, perhaps, they might relieve the oppressively humid atmosphere by causing a cloudburst (or by bringing a beloved, who is as awaited as the rain).

Rāga Jog, featured in CD tracks 1-11 and 1-12, is a relatively recent melodic mode, best played late at night, from midnight to 3:00 a.m.

Through Rāga Jog, two other possibilities for traits of a melodic mode can be illustrated—characteristic melodic phrases and particular ways of treating pitches melodically. These are exposed beautifully at the beginning of the first portion (*ālāp*) of an improvised instrumental selection performed by the illustrious sitārist Ravi Shankar.

ACTIVITY 4.11. *Listen to the first two minutes of CD track 1-11 in which Ravi Shankar presents the pitch selection and melodic nature of Rāga Jog in three ways.*

0–0:11 He gives you pitch Ṣa, the tonal center (Activity 4.3). Try to match it, get it in your head. In these initial seconds also he will run the nail of his little finger (right hand) quickly down the sympathetic strings that lie under the playing strings to cause the shimmering timbre on the sitār*. That is a Ravi Shankar signature moment.*

0:12–0:33 Shankar gives us the pitches of the rāga in short phrases—too quickly to catch them unless you really know what to listen for.

0:36–1:57 He begins improvisation in free rhythm and a slow speed. First he will improvise downward, until he reaches low pitch Sa. Try to hear some phrases that are characteristic of Rāga Jog, as follows.

A very short motive is used cadentially, that is, to end a melodic unit.

is a phrase that occurs several times.

Enjoyable in Jog is the inclusion of two forms of Ga (pitch 3, here Eᵇ and E♮). But you will not hear them in chromatic sequence (p. 114). The higher Ga (E♮) is used when the melody ascends upward—to the next pitch up—Ma (pitch 4) or higher. The lower Ga (Eᵇ) occurs when the melody descends from it—in the motive Sa-Gab-Sa, for instance.

The pitch Dha (6) does not occur at all in Rāga Jog.

SIMULTANEOUS PITCHES

In the discussion above, I focused on pitch as the fundamental material for melody. Here I shift to thinking about pitches that are heard simultaneously, bringing harmonic orientation into play. The amount of focus on harmonic relationships and the nature of them differs from music to music; no musical system cultivates "verticality" as much as does the European music system. In the discussion below, I present a few examples of ways in which musicians practice music with a harmonic orientation.

Naming "Vertical" Intervals. The term **interval** in harmonic think-ing has the same meaning as in melodic thinking: the distance between two pitches. You have already learned the names of those within an octave, but following figure 4.4 as you listen to CD track 2-26 will serve as a good reminder. Intervals that exceed the octave are called ninth (i.e., an octave plus a second), tenth, eleventh, and so forth. The vocal duo on CD track 1-5 are singing in a style that is characteristic of the Mexican *corrido*—in parallel thirds. Neither voice carries "the melody"; they sing pitches at the interval of a third apart—sometimes a minor third, sometimes a major third.

Dissonance and Consonance. The quality of the sound produced by a vertical interval is spoken of as **dissonant** or **consonant**. A widely held idea in European music theory has been that those intervals which are mathetically simple regarding the ratios of their frequencies (an octave is a simple 2:1 ratio) are "consonant." The consonant intervals are the first six of the natural overtone series: the octave, the fifth, the fourth, the major third, the minor third, and the major sixth. Complex intervals such as a major second, on the other hand are "dissonant." According to this theory, dissonance produces tension, whereas conso-nance offers relaxation, by release of tension.

ACTIVITY 4.12 *When a pitch is produced, we hear it as a sin-gle entity, but in actuality it is a composite of the fundamental fre-quency plus a set of mathematically related overtones—the **overtone series** shown in Fig 4.4 up to overtone twelve. Overtones can also be produced with the voice; this is demonstrated in "Western over-tone singing style" on CD track 2-27. The singer Robbie Beahrs presents two versions of the harmonic series, going from harmonic four up to harmonic 12 and back down, first slowly and then faster.*

Find a stringed instrument with which to experiment. (The strings inside a piano will do, or guitar or violin strings.) To obtain the first natural overtone of the pitch to which one string is set, sound the string while lightly touching it right in the middle of its length, producing a simple 2:1 ratio; do not press so hard that you touch the sounding board. Doing so should result in a ringing pitch an octave higher than the string's pitch when played normally. To get the second overtone, experiment with finding a spot where the string is divided into three equal parts. When you find it, the pitch a fifth higher than the first overtone (i.e., an octave and a fifth higher than the string's normal pitch) will result. To get the third overtone (a fourth higher than the second overtone and two octaves higher than the starting pitch), find the spot one-fourth the length of the string.

FIGURE 4.4   *(Overtone Series)*   *(Chart by Kin Hang Lam)*

Venturing beyond that mathematical concept of consonance and dissonance takes us into the subjective realm of musical aesthetics. For example, we find entirely different aesthetic ideas about the interval of a second: to Bulgarian women in the area of Sofia, the second is "pleasant and smooth"—in effect, consonant. In an example presented in Timothy Rice's volume on Bulgaria in this series, one woman sings the melody; another sings a part that zigzags between the tonic pitch and the note below it (CD track 2-28). They are striving to make their vertical intervals "ring like a bell" by narrowing them, especially on long-held notes, to somewhere between a major second and a minor second until they get the desired effect, an intense "beating" that is reminiscent of that produced on the paired Balinese instruments (CD track 2-19). The tension of singing is released at the end of a verse with a cry on the syllable "eee," leaping melodically up a seventh or an octave, and sliding down.

Nor is the idea about dissonant seconds and sevenths maintained in a good deal of contemporary composition, whether written in the tonal system or not. Lutosławski's "Mini Overture" abounds with minor seconds; they contribute part of the energy of the piece (CD track 2-2).

Western Functional Harmony. Intervals stacked vertically in tonal music are usually understood to form **chords**. A certain chord built on the pitch, designated as pitch, 1 (*do*) is the tonic chord (written in Roman numerals, I); likewise, a certain chord built on pitch 5 is the dominant chord (V), a certain chord built on pitch 4 is the subdominant chord (IV), and so forth. Not surprisingly, those chords constitute a hierarchy analogous to the pitch hierarchy discussed above: the tonic chord is all-important; the dominant chord and subdominant chords are important, in that order. This use of chords is called **functional harmony**.

Chords in the tonal system consist of three or more pitches. The most basic is a **triad**, so called because it consists of three pitches, the upper two of which are stacked a third and a fifth, respectively, above the bottom pitch or root of the chord.

> ACTIVITY 4.13 *To do this activity you need to gather at least two friends. Together count as you sing up from pitch 1 to 5 (starting anywhere that is comfortable for all of you), then sing just 1, 3, and 5 (leaving out 2 and 4). Sing 1–3–5–3–1 (ascent and descent) until it feels easy; those are the pitches of a triad. Then split up the pitches among you so that someone is singing each of the three pitches. When you sing them simultaneously, you are producing a triad. Build more triads, stacking thirds above any pitch.*

A sequence of chords is called a **chord progression**. In much tonal music a common practice guides which chord is likely to follow a given chord. The subdominant chord (IV) is likely to be followed by the dominant chord (V) or the tonic chord (I), for instance, and the dominant chord (V) is likely to lead to the tonic chord (I). Chord progressions of countless songs use just two or three of those chords.

> **ACTIVITY 4.14** *With the recording on CD track 2-29, sing this progression of these pitches:*
> *1 4 5 1 4 1 5 1 4 5 1*
> *If you were to build chords on each one of those pitches, your chord progression would be I IV V I IV I V I IV V I. (Roman numerals are used for naming chords.) The pitches are called the root pitches of the chords.*

The *corrido* "Ballad of César Chávez" (CD track 1-5) uses the tonic and dominant chords in a clear fashion. The guitar player anticipates the change with finger picking. Here I have rewritten the first two verses, with the chords indicated.

(Guitar intro settles on I.)

En un día siete de marzo, Jueves Santo en la mañana,

    I   V   V   I

Salió César de Delano, Componiendo una compaña.

    I   V   V   I

(Brief guitar interlude stays on I.)

Companeros campesinos   Este va a ser un ejemplo

    I   V   V   I

Esta marcha la llevamos   Hasta mero Sacramento.

    I   V   V   I

A genre of music that uses the I, IV, and V chords to the fullest is the blues. In most blues pieces, a chord progression that repeats in every verse provides stable underpinning for the flexible parts that swirl around it. Stripped to its simplest and earliest form, that chord progression is as follows.

I   I   I I

IV IV I I

V   V   I I(V)

ACTIVITY 4.15 *Listen to the* corrido *on CD track 1-5 and try to sing the tonic and dominant pitches that undergird the chord progression.*

If you succeed at that, proceed to CD track 2-6, "West End Blues," a 1928 Louis Armstrong hit. Try to follow the blues chord progression when the theme begins, just after Armstrong's famous introductory trumpet solo.

The first task is to feel the tonic. Listen through the selection until you are sure you have that. Then focus on chord changes. You should expect to get all the way through the blues chord progression in the length of one chorus.

0:15 Listen to the chords in the piano through the first chorus.
0:50 The second chorus features a solo by trombonist Fred Robinson.
1:24 Armstrong sings scat syllables through the third chorus, alternating with Jimmy Strong on clarinet.
1:59 The fourth chorus features a piano solo by Earl "Fatha" Hines.
2:33 The final chorus starts with a long-held high pitch on the trumpet before Armstrong takes off again.
The piece ends on a clear, comfortable tonic chord.

One of the effects of the global circulation of popular music, particularly from the Americas and the Caribbean region, is the widespread presence of functional harmony—or, in some cases, what seems to be functional harmony. On CD track 2-30, there are moments from a selection of new Egyptian music, featuring someone playing chords in rhythmic patterns that match the rhythmic modes played by the percussion

section. While these chords often match those of Western harmonic practice, they also frequently do not. Kadry Sorour said, "We generally don't
hear the chords as establishing a Western sense of harmony. Rather,
they add color to the *maqām* that is being played (personal communication to Scott Marcus, cited in Marcus 2007:173). In CD track 2-30, the
maqām is again Rast, with the *rast* upper tetrachord.

Tone Clusters. Complex tone clusters occur in Japanese *gagaku*
music, played on an aerophone called the **shō**. (It is the first instrument heard on CD track 1-9, and the players of *shō* sit at the rear
right in figure 1.8.) A **tone cluster** is a vertical set of pitches, without the functional implications of chords in the tonal system. In the
shō part in this musical tradition, the bottom pitch of the cluster and
the occasional single pitch correspond to melodic pitches. The effect
of the *shō* cluster is that of a complex chord played on an organ, sustained for several counts, and gradually changed to another cluster.
The *shō*'s part is important to the sound of the ensemble; without it
the texture becomes sparse, as you can hear in CD track 1-9 when
its part ceases.

INTERPLAY AMONG MELODIC
AND HARMONIC PARTS

Now I want to consider the interplay among musical parts when
groups of people make music together. The variety of melodic and
harmonic practices can be heard as lying along a continuum, at one
end of which is music with no harmonic dimension and at the other
is music in which the harmonic dimension is paramount. Musical relationships among the various parts result in what many music analysts
call **texture**. For a good deal of music in the European system, it is
possible to classify pieces according to categories of texture, and I refer
to those categories below. Many pieces, however, do not fit easily
within those categories, and when one considers musics outside of
Europe, the number of possibilities for ensemble relationships bur-
geons, causing many ethnomusicologists to avoid analyzing music in
terms of texture altogether. In this section I shall explore some of those
many possibilities, starting with ways a group of musicians might perform one melody.

Performing One Melody.

Solo and in Unison.   A musical texture consisting of a single melodic line and nothing else is **monophony**, literally "one voice." Melody is monophonic if sung or played by a single person alone (**solo**), as on CD track 1-8, the Native American "Blue Horse Special" and on CD track 1-18, a Japanese *syakuhati* solo (figure 1.2). The texture is still mono-   phonic if that single melodic line is sung by a group of people in **uni- son**, either on the same pitch or in octaves. (Note: singing pitches an octave apart is musically thought of as singing "the same" pitch.) For the first thirty-four seconds of CD track 2-31, the fourteenth-century song "Sumer is icumen in" ("Summer is a-coming in") is presented in unison by a mixed chorus. (The Middle English text is provided in fig- ure 4.5). Various signs of summer are noted—seeds growing, female animals with young, and the male animals restless—but the recurring reference is to the cuckoo, whose call is imitated melodically.

> *Sumer is icumen in.*
> *Lhude sing cucu,*
> *Groweth sed and bloweth med,*
> *and springth the wude nu.*
> *Sing cucu.*
> *Awe bletheth after lomb,*
> *Louth after calve cu;*
> *Bulloc sterteth, bucke verteth*
> *Murie sing cucu.*
> *Cucu, cucu.*
> *Wel singes thu cucu,*
> *Ne swik thu naver nu.*

FIGURE 4.5   *"Sumer is icumen in."*

Interlocking Parts.   Another way of performing a melody communally is to split it up among several musicians, assigning a single pitch or a few pitches only to each person. The melody is the sum of the parts. (This performance style was known as **hocket** in music of the late medieval period of Western history.) If you listen closely to the Peruvian panpipe selection (CD track 1-29), you can hear that two players com- bine pitches to make the melody in each part. This performance practice of **interlocking parts** occurs frequently in Balinese music also; on CD track 1-22, players of a group of *gangsas* create a single melodic line with pitches subdivided between them, interlocking in intricate rhythmic patterns, playing at rapid speed. From the beginning of the CD selection to 0:36 you can hear one of the two parts alone, from 0:36 to 1:03 the second part alone. From 1:03 to the end, the two parts join in a complete interlocking pattern (**kotekan**) to form the melody. These examples have demonstrated interlocking parts as melodic, but the same practice occurs in rhythm. On CD track 2-32, multiple players of bottles interlocked and alternated, together creating the resulting rhythm.

Rounds.   Along the continuum from horizontal to vertical orientation is the performance practice of singing a melody as a **round**. As you must know from singing rounds yourself, music makers begin the melody at systematically different spots, thereby overlapping. It is challenging, because you have to concentrate on singing the melody yourself—thinking "horizontally"—while at the same time hearing the combined voices "vertically." The total effect can be so busy that one must listen carefully to be sure that just one melody is being rendered. On CD track 2-31, "Sumer is icumen in" is sung as a round from 0:36 to 1:34; in this performance the women start the round and the men join.

A melody sung as a round is just one type of a texture called **polyphony** (literally "multiple voices") in European music terminology (see further discussion below). When each singer imitates the melody of other singers (rather than simultaneously singing a different melody), the result is **imitative polyphony**. In a round (also called **canon**) the imitation is strict; everyone sings the melody just alike.

ACTIVITY 4.16   *Reach back in your memory for a round you sang when you were young. Try to sing that melody or another that you remember with a friend or group of friends—first in unison, then in multiple parts. Perhaps "Frère Jacques" ("Are you sleeping?") is one of them; its melody is on CD track 2-21.*

Heterophony.   In **heterophony** (literally "different voices") multiple musicians perform one melody, but each musician might render the melody somewhat differently. In Arab music, for example, a lute player and a flute player might give slightly different renditions of a melody, in part because of the idiomatic capabilities of each instrument. The flute player might insert frequent trills, or the lute player might insert rapid and

repeated plucking of a single note. When played together, the two different renditions create a highly valued heterophonic texture (CD track 2-1).
Heterophony is widespread in Asian musical traditions. On CD track
2-33, the classical Japanese composition "Yaegoromo," the sung melody
at the beginning is self-accompanied on *koto* and further accompanied
on *syamisen* and *syakuhati* (figure 1.2). A heterophonic texture is created
by the somewhat different timing and pitches as the three instrumental parts and vocal combine to present "the melody."

ACTIVITY 4.17 *To test your hearing and understanding of
different practices for performing a single melody, listen to these
tracks on the CD and decide whether each is an example
of monophony or heterophony: tracks 1-3, 1-13, 1-14, 1-21,
1-26, 1-30, 1-34 and 2-1.*

Performing One Melody with Another Part. A single melody can
also be performed with one or more other parts that use pitch (as
opposed to a nonpitched drum, for instance) but whose function is not
melodic. Such a relationship among parts takes a number of forms in
music throughout the world; I mention only two here.

Melody and Drone. A widespread manner of performing a single
melody with a pitched but nonmelodic part is to put it over a **drone**—
sustained tone. A drone is usually thought of as being one pitch that
undergirds the melody by being sounded in a persistent fashion, as in
Scottish bagpipe music (CD track 2-34).
That a drone and melody can be produced vocally is demonstrated
by Tuvan throat-singing (**khöömei**), a solo-voice drone singing tradition practiced in the Republic of Tuva (part of the Russian Federation)
and surrounding regions, including Mongolia. Intimately connected
with the traditional nomadic lifestyle of herding animals on the Inner
Asian steppe, Tuvan throat-singing involves the production of a high-
tension guttural drone with one's voice accompanied by subtle manipulation of the mouth and tongue to shape the timbre of the sound
and create one or more melodies from the higher harmonics (CD track
2-35). The overall effect of Tuvan throat-singing is that of hearing multiple melodies (or voices) coming from just one singer.

ACTIVITY 4.18 *The Tuvan song called "Artii–Sayir" (CD track 2-35) is performed in a deep-voice throat-singing style called* kargyraa, *which means "to rasp" in Tuvan, a Turkic language. (There are several throat-singing styles cultivated in that geographic area.)*

As you listen to the track several times, be attentive to the whole sound and all of its nuances. How would you describe the timbre?

Do you hear a pentatonic melody produced from the higher harmonics? For this recording, Robbie Beahrs sings the melody three times with breaths performed traditionally; each time the melody is slightly different due to performance variation. Catch the timings when the melody begins to repeat.

Try to produce a visual transcription of the sounds you are hearing in whatever way you choose.

However, there are multiple varieties of drone. In Western classical music a temporary or short-term drone sometimes occurs; rather than "drone," it is called a "pedal point." On CD track 1-11 and 1-12, North Indian *sitār* (plucked lute figure 3.1) music, the pitch *sa* is sounded intermittently on a string designated on the instrument for a drone; while the sounding of *sa* on that string is far from constant, its function is heard as a drone. A drone might also consist of multiple pitches. When the drone in India's music is kept on **tānpūra**, a chordophone devoted solely to that role, it consists of multiple pitches that are sounded in succession constantly from the beginning to the end of a performance selection (CD track 2-36). The metal strings of the *tānpūra* provide a lush sound quality that contrasts with the vocal timbre.

Melody and Chords. Perhaps the most widespread practice of performing a single melody—thanks to the dissemination of American popular music worldwide—is to back it up with functional chords. The term for this texture is **homophony** (literally "same voice"). Chords undergird the melody, and the melody is conceived in terms of the harmony; in that sense, they are "the same voice." Because the term is so linked with tonal harmony, the label "homophony" is most applicable in such music. Examples can be heard on CD tracks, 1-5, 1-6, 1-28, 1-32 and others. In some homophonic music, such as choral renditions of hymns and patriotic songs, the harmonizing parts move in the same rhythm as the melody—another sense in which they are the "same voice."

Performing Multiple Melodies.

Polyphony. When multiple melodic parts are performed together, the texture is termed **polyphony** ("multiple voices"). The singing of rounds, the type of polyphony discussed above, is a musical practice in which one melody is taken up in turn by multiple musicians. Here, I discuss another type of polyphony: the texture achieved when multiple musicians perform different melodic parts simultaneously. But what constitutes a "melodic part"? Because they work with such a variety of musical traditions, ethnomusicologists who want to use the term "polyphony" consider any number of things to be a melodic part—anything from a short ostinato to a full tune. In his volume on Bulgarian music in this series, Rice considers a two-part woman's song to be an example of polyphony: one woman sings "a melody" while the other sings "a second melodic part," but not one he identifies as "a melody." Rice's idea of "melodic part" is typically flexible.

The line between homophonic texture and polyphonic can be fuzzy. Some scholars who work with western classical music would say that when the multiple melodic parts that are performed together move together rhythmically, that is a homophonic texture. To ethnomusicologist Jane Moulin, however, while the texture of a Polynesian *hīmene tārava* (CD track 2-37) that she contributed to this book sounds like chordal homophony, it is polyphony because the melodic simultaneity is not strictly chordal. *Hīmene tārava* are multipart compositions sung in Tahitian by large mixed choirs. *Hīmene* (from "hymn") denoting both "song" and "to sing," applies to all songs and contrasts singing with chanted rhythmic Polynesian recitations. *Tārava* ("extended; stretching out") describes the drawn-out tones on the vocable "e" at verse endings. Perpetuated as sacred Christian songs, *hīmene tārava* demonstrate how Islanders combine Tahitian ideas of song form, textual content, and polyphonic structure with melodic outlines and vocal part alignments based on Western-influenced chords. *Tārava* groups flock to the prolonged celebration in July in Pape'ete, the capital city of Tahiti, to represent their districts in a huge competition. Originally celebrated as La Fête Nationale with French colonial reference but since 1986 called by the traditional word Heiva, the celebration "validates a separate Tahitian identity that promotes indigenous language, highlights Polynesian ways of knowing and doing, and reconfigures colonial passivism as Islander agency" (Moulin, in Diettrich, Moulin, and Webb 2011: 60).

Melody and Ostinato.   Some scholars consider an **ostinato**—that is, a constantly recurring melodic, harmonic, or rhythmic motive—to be an extended form of drone.

A performance of "Sumer is icumen in" is not complete until the melody, which you have already heard performed in unison and as a round (CD track 2-31), is complemented by not one ostinato but two ostinati (called *pes* in medieval terminology). Each of them is a melodic motive. The text of ostinato 1 is "Sing cucu nu, sing cucu"; the text and melody of ostinato 2 reverse the two phrases: "Sing cucu, sing cucu nu." The two ostinati can be heard on CD track 2-31, from 1:28 to 1:57.

When all parts of "Sumer is icumen in" are performed together, a full polyphonic texture is created. From 2:01 to the end of CD track 2-31, you can hear the rich texture that results from the combination of the two ostinati and the melody performed as a three-part round. For performers and listeners, this piece demands simultaneous "horizontal" and "vertical" musical orientation.

In this chapter I have discussed pitch as the foundation for both melody and harmony, offering perspectives from music theory as well as practice. I also explored a variety of ways in which musical parts are made to relate. In the next chapter I shall discuss processes for structuring a musical selection.

Thinking about Structuring

The topic of musical structure has arisen several times in earlier chapters: from the perspective of instruments in chapter 2, in the section "Ideas about Ensemble"; from the perspective of the organization of time in the second half of chapter 3; and from the perspective of texture in chapter 4, in the section "Interplay among Melodic and Harmonic Parts." In this chapter I shall present several additional ideas about structures that musicians have found useful and meaningful.

Ethnomusicologists are interested in exploring not only *how* music is structured but also *why* it is structured the way it is. Accordingly, in this chapter, I consider a selection of structuring processes in composing and musicking that result in musical forms. It may help to think of musical **form** as architectural design in sonic form.

IMPROVISING AND COMPOSING

Pertinent to thinking about structuring as a process is the ongoing lively discussion regarding what is encompassed by the two terms "improvisation" and "composition." That discussion has been particularly crucial in ethnomusicological study for several reasons. Much of the music discussed in this book involves the process of interweaving musical material that is given with material that is being newly created even as one listens. That process is generally called "improvising"; ethnomusicologists understand it also as "composing."

There are two misconceptions about improvisation that we in ethnomusicology have to counter regularly. One is that improvisation is inevitably completely "free," implying that music being newly created during performance is not based on anything preexisting. Ethnomusicological research has not confirmed that idea. Rather, we usually see musicians using something musical that already exists—an idea about ensemble relationships, a rhythm pattern, the pitch selection in a mode, or something else—as the basis for new music.

The other misconception is that improvisation is not composition—or, put another way, that the process of creating music during performance is intrinsically different from the process of creating music before a performance. This distinction involves a bundle of assumptions. First is the idea that the timing of the creative activity is crucial—that composing necessarily precedes performing. However, it is widely recognized now that composing is a cognitive process that can be taking place in the mind at any time—including while performing.

The idea that composing must precede performing accompanies the supposition that composing means writing something down (or, conversely, that if music is not written, it must be improvised). This interpretation does not take us far when we consider that much music is created in the world, but relatively few people are interested in notating it. For example, writing is not required for Indonesian musicians to remember enormously complex, lengthy compositions. (See Brinner 1995). In addition, notation systems are invented to suit the purposes of a particular musical tradition and may have little to do with what happens to the notated item when it is performed. (See "Transmission of Musical Knowledge," in chapter 1.)

It is also sometimes assumed that the result of the compositional process is an item, a thing—a *piece*—which can be performed again and again in a relatively intact form. This idea about "a piece" is viable for a good deal of music, particularly if the modifier "relatively" is kept in mind: pieces in the European classical tradition, songs in the South Indian classical tradition, Irish dance tunes, Mexican American *corridos*, and many other repertoires are transmitted in a relatively intact form. However, the corollary—that composing has not taken place if the process of creating music does not result in a relatively fixed product—is an assumption that ethnomusicologists do not find viable. Improviser/composer Myra Melford suggests that we think of a continuum of ideals from thoroughly composed to thoroughly improvised—or, in reality, as free as possible (personal communication, 2007).

Beverley Diamond found a somewhat similar continuum among the Inuit. "In Nunavut, the songs are most often carefully composed and privately rehearsed before they are presented at a drum dance. The line between 'composition,' 'song reception,' and 'improvisation,' however, is not rigid. One singer whom I recorded in the 1970s improvised a verse about the visiting woman who was collecting songs. Some songs are received in dreams or in that half-awake state that one is in early in the morning after a night's sleep. Some songs may remain static, or composers may add to a song when new experiences warrant a new verse" (Diamond 2007: 39).

∞

The Ugandan musician Centurio Balikoowa, cited in Greg Barz's volume on East African music in this Global Music Series: "In most African musics we have this idea of the expectation and anticipation of the music always being developed *within a performance. There is that idea that listening would be boring if we didn't continue to add things into the performance. When we have an ensemble of three* endingidi, *two will play in contrasting keys, while the third player will be expected to improvise and put in something different so that they don't play the same thing."*

∞

More meaningful than defining in systematic ways what is "composed" and "improvised" is exploring the wide range of musical flexibility that exists in music around the world. The amount of flexibility and the nature of the flexibility that is exercised in the performance of given material varies widely from music to music. When an Irish dance tune (CD track 1-3, 1-23) or a Mexican American *corrido* (CD track 1-5) is performed, the community expects some degree of change—but not too much—to occur in each performance; this results in recognizable variants and is known as "the folk process of re-creation." Some flexibility—variations in phrasing, in speed, in dynamics perhaps—is expected in the performance of a good deal of notated music in the European classical tradition as well; this is called "interpretation." In a Middle Eastern ensemble performance, repetitions of precomposed music in the course of a performance are anticipated moments for variation, when the musicians are likely to add their own melodic ornaments or heterophonic realizations of the composed passages (CD track 2-1). In much music of Africa and the African diaspora, one primary structural principle assumes a particular form of flexibility—the contrast of something that varies with the more or less "fixed" patterns that make up a polyrhythmic texture (CD track 1-4).

Given these complexities, I suggest this. **Improvisation** is a compositional process in which a musician exercises relatively great flexibility with given material during a performance. The "given material" might be a tune, a chord progression, or a rhythm (twelve-bar blues or a drumming pattern), for example.

I have invited students to critique in writing my suggested definition of improvisation. Kirk Danielson responded to the assignment from his experience playing and listening to jazz, as follows:

I think this is a pretty accurate representation of improvisation. However, I think there might need to be a clause about how improvisation is already somewhat pre-thought, or previously constructed or practiced. Usually there is some kind of structure or arrangement or organization to the song, especially when many players are involved. Often in jazz, which is generally characterized by improvisation, there is a set of chord changes, a melody or "head," and a form, usually AABA or ABAB2 or twelve bar blues. The players will interpret the melody by playing in their own characteristic way. Perhaps the definition should be: Improvisation is the compositional process in which a musician exercises relatively great flexibility with given material during a performance, but often with a pre-construction notion of the structure or arrangement of the song, particularly when other players are involved. (2007)

ACTIVITY 5.1 *Search your personal collection for recordings of two versions of one popular tune—perhaps the one you chose for Activity 1.4. Use those performances to analyze the degree of flexibility in the particular style of your selections. Think about the expectation for flexibility and the musical results. How would you define "composed music" in this context? Would you be tempted to call anything in the selection "improvisation"?*

Consider, too, how you would define "an arrangement" and "a cover" fit in here, give it a try.

Responding to the question about covers in Activity 5.1, student Max Ghenis chose to focus the assignment on the Beatles' song "Norwegian Wood," which he had experienced in an arrangement for a marching band.

I choose this piece in awe of the value of instrumental covers, and as an advocate for the cover band as a unique and valuable musical category. Arrangements as intricate as Buddy Rich's "Norwegian Wood" show the extent to which covered material can be as original as any other music form. The reality is, cover bands and arrangers do the same thing all other musicians and composers do; they're just more overt about citing their sources. (2007)

Student Natasha Dagys made the point that different types of flexibility are expected in different contexts of performance of the same song. Her example was two versions of the song "When You Believe" on the soundtrack to the motion picture *The Prince of Egypt*. The first version was sung by the (cartoon) characters in the course of the movie, while the second plays during the credits sung by pop singers Whitney Houston and Mariah Carey.

> In the movie version of the song, the performance is more structured and sung similarly to an actor saying his lines; it follows strict cues, and the vocalists appear to be singing exactly what is written on a score. The pop version, however, exemplifies a more flexible style that begins very structured yet includes an improvised (or ad lib) section. The vocalists express emotion as well as showcase their vocal skills through variations in phrasing, timbre, and pitch. In this context, this type of flexibility is expected, since the attention is on the singers themselves, unlike the movie version, where the focus is on the lyrics and how they relate to the plot. (2007)

Persons who Compose. Thinking about the process of structuring music also brings up the matter of who is doing the composing. The question arises of just who a "composer" is in the eyes of a community. Is "a composer" necessarily a different person from "a performer"? In many musical traditions, composer-performers are commonplace. In Japanese music for traditional instruments, for instance, most of the traditional repertoire is by composer-performers. The composer of "Yaegoromo" on CD track 2-33 was a *syamisen* player, writing in 1804 for voice and *syamisen*; the other parts were probably added later by other composer-players. Recently, a new second-*koto* part for the instrumental section was composed by Keiko Nosaka, a contemporary koto artist. The practice of composers who are not *koto* and *syamisen* and *syakuhati* players writing for those instruments was introduced along with other Western practices.

Perhaps the prevalence in most European music since the eighteenth century of the custom of the composing person being a separate person from the performing person has contributed to thinking about composing and improvising as different processes. Think, for instance, of Johann Sebastian Bach (1685–1750), who was a master improviser even of complex polyphony, and of Wolfgang Amadeus Mozart (1756–1791), who improvised flashy piano solos within his compositions for piano and orchestra.

Think, too, about the number of composers at work on one musical selection; it is not always a single individual. The example of jazz presents a quintessential case of groups of persons composing "a selection" together. Tom Turino observed a different sort of communal compositional process in the Peruvian Andes (CD track 1-29):

> The night before most festivals in Conima, the core musicians of a given indigenous community ensemble come together to compose between one and three new tunes for that year's event. They do so within the established characteristics of a given genre which limit, and thus guide, the compositional process. . . . Pieces are composed collectively in a kind of "brainstorming" session. Sitting in a circle, the core [panpipe] musicians softly blow motives or sections of pieces simultaneously as they think of them. Musical ideas that do not seem promising are simply ignored. If someone comes up with an interesting musical idea others will listen and gradually join in playing it. At this point, if the original idea does not seem to have promise, individuals gradually stop playing it and go back to square one riffing new ideas. If the motive or section still seems promising the group will then brainstorm the next section of the AABBCC form based on this germinal idea. After an entire tune has been roughed out—by adding the additional sections bit by bit, playing them together, deciding whether they work, and brainstorming new ideas for portions not deemed attractive—group members will then fine tune the piece by suggesting small changes here and there and then playing through the piece with the new alterations. What was miraculous to me was that this whole process took place with hardly any discussion or even words being said. . . . By the end of the composition process the input of a number of people is combined into a finished piece and "the community" is considered the composer. Interestingly, group consensus decision making proceeds in much the same manner; verbal ideas are either simply ignored or are repeated by new speakers, perhaps with modifications or additions, until the contributions of a number of people are combined into a finished decision that the community fashions together. (2007)

Understanding that there are numerous ways in which music gets created, then, is one further consideration in thinking about what constitutes TMI—the music itself.

Now I turn to discussion of a selection of principles by which music has been structured. Priority is still given to why music may be structured the way it is, that is, structuring as a process in music making.

PUTTING SOMETHING SIGNIFICANT FIRST

In structuring a new musical selection, how might a composer or other musician(s) get it started? Easing gradually into a musical selection is a formal strategy that is preferred in a number of Asian musical genres. This is often achieved partially by leaving time relatively unorganized— as in the Egyptian ensemble example on CD track 2-1 and the *Thai pî phât* ensemble example on CD track 1-31. Putting something significant first is another oft-used formal strategy.

ACTIVITY 5.2 *In European classical music, an opening motive is often the primary* **theme** *or subject matter of the entire piece. Try to identify two of the best-known beginnings in European classical music on CD tracks 2-16 and 2-38. If you recognize them, assist a classmate who does not.*

Sonata Form. In the context of European court and theatrical music in the eighteenth century, a musical practice emerged that came to be called sonata form. As well as a formal structure, it is a compositional procedure or schema, involving as musical materials these components: one theme and possibly a second; a tonal center established at the beginning (the A section), with a shift to other(s) (a process called **modulation**) that resolves in a return to the original. Because the return to the original key occurs in the second section (B), the resulting form is binary. At some point, the form began to be described by some scholars as ternary, with the return to the original key taking place in the middle of the second section, so that it appeared to initiate a third (A'), with the structure shown in Figure 5.1. As you can see, thematic material is presented right away in the A section (that came to be called the exposition), is developed by detours to different keys in the B section, with a return to the original key; the A' section recapitulates the thematic material in the original key. A brief fourth section (the coda) is an optional way to reinforce the final cadence and end the movement. The formal procedure allows for great flexibility.

Explanation for the establishment of sonata form involves a number of factors. It originated with compositions in binary form (*sonata*)

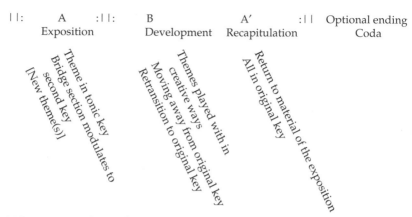

FIGURE 5.1   *Sonata form.*

for keyboard instruments by Italian composers such as Baldassare Galuppi (1706-1785) and Domenico Alberti (1710-1740)—the former associated with the comic opera and the latter a singer. The form was taken up by sons of the great German composer Johann Sebastian Bach and became particularly associated with Carl Philipp Emanuel Bach (1714-1788) and also Austrian composer Joseph Haydn (1732-1809). A second point of "origin" for sonata form was the orchestral overture (*sinfonia*) to Italian operas that also developed in the eighteenth century. Apart from the opera, *sinfonia* and keyboard *sonatas* were attractive genres for instrumental concerts— private concerts in the home of aristocratic patrons, but also in subscription concerts for the public that began to succeed as a performance venue in Paris from 1725, then burgeoned in Milan, Vienna and London. The sonata form made possible a kind of dramatic sequence such as one would have in an opera but independent from it. That is, a kind of dramatic progression from the beginning to end of an independent work or movement in sonata form is provided by the secure establishment of a primary tonality, then going away from it, and finally coming back.

Modulation, the shifting from one tonal center to another is a crucial characteristic of sonata form, and also constitutes an important practice in structuring a good deal of music created in the tonal pitch system. As its occurence in "Marieke" (CD track 2-8) shows, it can be used to dramatic effect.

> **ACTIVITY 5.3** *Listen to CD track 2-8, "Marieke." A mod-*
> *ulation occurs about three-quarters of the way through this per-*
> *formance. Try to catch the timing at the moment when it happens.*
> *It will help to try to hear the tonic pitch through most of the*
> *song, then listen for a shift. Once you identify where it happens,*
> *try to articulate why it occurs where it does.*

North Indian Instrumental Form. Just as sonata form puts significant thematic material first, the multi-sectioned instrumental sequence
of North Indian music (figure 5.2, *ālāp-jor-jhālā-gat-gat-jhala*) puts
significant material first. The beginning *ālāp* section asserts the pri-
macy of melodic mode in the Hindustani tradition as a performer
introduces the characteristics of the particular melodic mode (*rāga*)
that will provide the given melodic material for the entire performance
selection. Once the mode has been established, the procedure in the
sequence is to shift attention to other elements of music. Following the
ālāp, the instrumentalist begins to add pulsating rhythm to the melodic
improvisation (*jor*). Then, creating interesting rhythms with a combination of melody and drone pitches (*jhālā*), he or she accelerates the
speed of the playing. The first real break in the sequence occurs as the
drummer enters the selection; at that point a composition (*gat*) is presented, adding a metric cycle (*tāla*) and a tune in the *rāga* to the "given

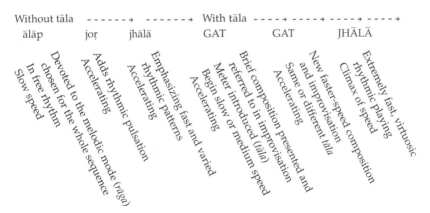

FIGURE 5.2   *Hindustani instrumental sequence.*

materials" that form the basis of further improvisation. The desire for gradual acceleration (see the section on speed in chapter 3) is turned into a structural principle when a composition in slow or medium speed is followed without break by a second composition in fast speed. This is a practice in Hindustani classical vocal music, as well. Indeed, this slow beginning and acceleration to a rapid conclusion is characteristic of Hindustani *rāga* development in general. The maintenance of the picture, feeling, and design of the slow and steady growth of the *rāga* is a highly prized and aesthetically satisfying aspect of the performance of mature musicians, one that suggests the growth of a plant from seed to full flowering.

ACTIVITY 5.4 *To demonstrate the Hindustani instrumental performance sequence, I chose moments from a nearly twenty-nine-minute recording in Rāga Jog. You have already become familiar with much of it, as I used CD track 1-11 to introduce you to the progression from free rhythm to pulsating (pp. 73) in the first three sections (**ā lā p, jor,** and **jhā lā**). I also used the beginning of CD track 1-12 to introduce you to Hindustani melodic mode (p. 119)—in this instance Rāga Jog. And, it provided the illustration of tāla, the North Indian system for organizing time metrically (pp. 84–87). Now it is time to listen through CD tracks 1-11 and 1-12, using the listening guides in Activities 3.10 and 4.12 for review.*

Next, it is time to listen again, with your attention to the aesthetic progression through both tracks. But take note: whereas Figure 5.2 indicates two compositions (gat), due to the short duration of this recorded performance, Ravi Shankar chose to play only one composition, without proceeding to a second composition and final jhālā. As you can see, this Hindustani performance sequence is extremely adjustable to such factors as time constraints
CD track 1-11
To 2:38 Ālāp (with short fade-out at 1:57)

The anticipated shape of a formal ālāp *is that the initial descent to a lower register will be followed by melody that ascends gradually through the middle register and up into a higher register. You hear a bit of that improvisatory climb in this short excerpt from 1:59 to 2:27.*

Short fade-out, then 2:31 to 2:38. The ālāp *has gone on for a while, but here you should perceive it coming to an end with the Ni̱ Ni̱ Sa motive.*

2.38 Jor

Pulsation gives a regularity to the rhythm, but, since there is still no drum being played, you know there is still no meter. The rhythm is still "free."

After a short fade-out, at 3:03, the jor̤ section becomes quite fast and the playing very excitingly virtuosic.

c. 3:40 jhālā

When you hear the constant strumming of Sa on a drone string, you are hearing jhālā. This ālāp-jor̤-jhālā *sequence ends with a melodic tihāī (see p. 145).*

CD track 1-12 Gat

This entire CD track gives you the leisure to listen for recurrences of the gat melody and of the short cadential melodic pattern introduced in Activity 4.1, for the trade-off in soloist role between sitārist *and* tablā *player, for the gradual acceleration that Hindustani performance aesthetics demand, and —if you have become a skilled listener—for variations from the* theka *pattern of tīntāl and the characterics of the melodic mode.*

Beyond 2:27–8, the cycle consists largely of a melodic and rhythmic tihāī to end the performance.

COMING TO AN END

The musical term for an ending is **cadence**. "Cadence" encompasses not only what happens at the very end but also how the ending is approached. The use of speed is another possible practice for coming to closure. Listening again to "Marieke" (figure 3.5, CD track 2-8), you can hear how acceleration is used to approach the ending. In a good deal of music, conversely slowing down occurs to mark the ending.

In most tonal music the ending is a matter of harmonic practice: we expect the last chord to be the tonic chord. The *corrido* and blues selections (CD tracks 1-5 and 2-6) demonstrate this cadential practice clearly. There is also a common practice in the choice of chords that lead up to the tonic and cause us to expect the ending. In the *corrido* and blues and in a great deal of other tonal music, the V (dominant) chord will immediately precede the tonic. Melodically, in tonal music pitch 7 (*ti*) or 2 (*re*) often functions as a lower or upper leading tone respectively, causing us to expect resolution to the tonic pitch.

Musical practice for creating an ending might involve rhythm and the metric structure. As was pointed out in Activity 3.11, in North Indian improvisational practice, musical units will usually end on a count 1. Because the improvising musician could decide to stop at any count 1 and needs to signal the accompanists to create an ending simultaneously, musical cues must be sounded leading up to that ending on count 1. One type of cue is a *tihāī*—a melodic or rhythmic pattern that is performed three times, with the last repetition ending on the cadential count 1. A *tihāī* brings the performance on CD track 1-12 to an end.

ACTIVITY 5.5 *On CD tracks 2-39 and 2-40, George Ruckert demonstrates two* tihāī *that can be created, for example, from the drumming stroking phrase: Tete kata gadi gena dha. In the first one (CD track 2-39), he chooses to put one count between the first two repetitions; that becomes part of the pattern. Played (or spoken) three times, then, it consumes 17 counts (including the final count 1). Speak the pattern several times, saying "rest" for the counts after dhas. The* tihāī *comes to an end on the final dha, so you don't need to repeat "rest" there.*

Tete kata gadi gena dha -
Tete kata gadi gena dha -
Tete kata gadi gena dha

Tihāī *occur within a* tāla *cycle, and Ruckert chooses to put his into* tīntāl, *the cycle of 16 counts that you spoke while studying Chapter 3 (see p. 85, CD track 2-14). To fit this first* tihāī *into* tīntāl *and come to an end on count 1, he needs to begin it on a count 1. On CD track 2-39, he begins the recitation by speaking the* tīntāl *theka and then goes right into the* tihāī. *Listen to this several times and then speak it all with him.*

To *create the* tihāī *on CD track 2-40, Ruckert chooses to speak the pattern right through without any count between the repetitions. That consumes only 15 counts—not a full cycle of* tīntāl. *So he has fun with it: he puts two counts after the third dha and makes that the pattern. He keeps on going with the principle of three times through until the final dha comes out on a count 1. Speak that three times (without thinking about* tīntāl*), saying "rest rest" for the two-count separations.*

Tete kata gadi gena dha/ Tete kata gadi gena dha/
Tete kata gadi gena dha —Tete kata gadi gena dha/
Tete kata gadi gena dha/ Tete kata gadi gena dha —
Tete kata gadi gena dha/ Tete kata gadi gena dha/
Tete kata gadi gena dha

On *CD track 2-40, Ruckert again starts with the theka and then recites the whole* tihāī. *Listen to this several times and then speak it all with him. Enjoy!*

Finally, if you want really to struggle, try speaking both tihāīs *with Ruckert while doing the hand motions of the* tāla. *(See p. 87.) Good luck!*

Especially when music is structured in response to a fluid context, consideration of cadential practice (i.e., how something ends) needs to be complemented by considering why the music is brought to an end. The story is finished, the performance time runs out, the artist is ready to quit, the audience loses interest, the person in trance returns to consciousness—all these and more can bring about musical ending.

TELLING THE STORY

In many instances the demands of telling a story musically are significant factors in the structuring process. In this section I offer a few examples of different responses to those demands.

Music for the Moment. As a *dalang* (puppeteer) in Indonesia weaves his story with shadow puppets, he sends cues to musicians who instantly respond with music appropriate for the moment—battle music, walking music, meditating music (figure 1.5). While the music with which they respond is pre-composed, the musicians cannot know in advance what will be called for when. In any given performance, the plot is usually not the main focus. Rather, the elaborations, digressions, and manner of execution of well-known stories take precedence.

Through-composed Music. In "telling" the story of the battle in 202 B.C.E. between the monarch of the Ch'u dynasty and his challenger from what would become the Han dynasty in China, the music in "The Great Ambush" (CD track 2-41) continually changes. Because the musical content changes from beginning to end—no musical section in this selection is repeated i.e., because, the form is called **through-composed**. Also, this particular example is programmatic, that is, an instrumental rendering of "a text." The piece opens with the *pipa* (figure 5.3) imitating the powerful and martial sound of drums in the high register; that is followed by highly dramatic effects produced by means of different playing techniques, speeds, **dynamics** (use of volume), and the like. Some of the music imitates sounds of a battlefield, while other passages only suggest thematic content.

ACTIVITY 5.6 *Listen to CD track 2-40, the first two minutes of "The Great Ambush" performed by Tsun-yuen Lui.*

Several versions of the program have been published, each listing the events of the battle. This one suggests eighteen sections: massing of troops, the line up, drum beats, the signals, artillery barrage, bugle calls to open a gate, calling the generals, taking battle stations, the dispatch, the ambush, the skirmish, the cannonade, shouts, the charge, the siege, the call to retreat, the Ch'u army routed, the suicide of the Ch'u leader.

Plot on a timing chart where the programmatic sections come in the piece in order to answer this question: Is the program clear, or not?

Contrasting Instrumentation.   In forms of music drama in numerous cultures, shifting instrumentation (including voices) is exploited fully. In the short section from the opera *Carmen* on CD track 1-28, the interplay among instruments, men's chorus, women's chorus, and heroine (Carmen) provides a kind of structure by instrumentation that heightens the sense of the text and moves the drama along.

ACTIVITY 5.7   *Make a photocopy of the text given in Activity 4.7 and follow it as you listen again to CD track 1-28 to refresh your memory of the scene (p.112).*

This activity focuses on the instrumentation. Listen to the whole selection to identify and list as many of the instruments as you can—remembering to include voices in your list—a male solo voice, a female solo voice, a male chorus, a female chorus, a mixed chorus, if you hear those. Each constitutes a musical part in the instrumentation. On the photocopied text, mark what you hear in terms of shifting instrumentation. Note who sings, with whom or alone, unaccompanied or accompanied, with what instrument, and the like.

When you have completed your listening, write an analytical summary of the way Bizet uses instrumentation in structuring the scene. For example, think about how changes in instrumentation heighten the sense of the text and, even when the text repeats, create a kind of dramatic motion.

Strophic Form.   **Strophic form** provides an excellent design for telling a story. The word "strophe" (stanza or verse) usually refers to the text, but it has been adapted in musical terminology to refer to a song tune that is repeated while the text changes. That is the form chosen for *corridos*. The melody of "The Ballad of César Chávez" (CD track 1-5; figure 1.4) is strophic: the same melody is repeated for each stanza of text. Often, when there is considerable musical repetition, you need to focus on what is changing.

	Text lines	Melody lines
Verse 1	A B C D	A B C D
Verse 2	E F G H	A B C D
Verse 3	I J K L, etc.	A B C D, etc.

ACTIVITY 5.8 *The selections on CD track 1-32 "Take Five," and CD track 2-6 "West End Blues," are both in strophic form, though their "verses" or "stanzas" are called "choruses." Make a listening chart for each, in which you articulate what changes and what stays the same. Go to your cumulative record of information for some guidance.*

It is Sunday morning at the Power of Jesus Around the World Church located along the outskirts of Kisumu, Kenya.... The congregation is invited to begin the service by laying their hands on a group of members who recently lost a family member. Before long, one of the service's leaders begins to speak in tongues. The bereaved members all fall to the ground as they too begin proclaiming in unintelligible statements. Within minutes a large portion of the congregation is swept up in the spirit and the emotion of the moment. . . . After an extended period of time one of the pastors begins the call of a well-known chorus known in North America as "Kumbaya" [CD track 2-42], singing into a generator-powered microphone. The give and take between the soloist and the congregation builds up gradually. The spirit healing session "cools" down after a half hour or so, and the performance of "Kumbaya" reunites the community, giving them back "language" while at the same time bringing them back to their seats. (Greg Barz, in the volume on East Africa in this series)

RESPONDING TO THE CONTEXT

In many instances, musical selections are structured in response to something in the context, broadly conceived—from sacred to secular, from ritual to concert, from formal to casual, and the like. Limitations or opportunities provided by technologies are a sort of context; the short time available on early recordings, for instance, caused musicians to curtail what would have been longer selections. In addition, aesthetic values are a sort of context to which musicians may respond in the structuring of music. Composing for a particular opera diva causes a score to have more arias for one character than others. If a cathedral has balconies on either side from which choirs might sing or instrumentalists might play, a composer might write interactive music to surround the worshipers with affective sound. Below, I sample a few contexts to demonstrate this point further.

Audience-Performer Interaction. In a number of contexts, an expectation prevails for interaction between audience and performer—not just as a matter of expressing appreciation but as a means for interactive shaping of what is performed. Here examples are given from a small ensemble tradition, a larger ensemble practice, and in a storytelling context.

In an improvised performance such as the Hindustani performance sequence described in figure 5.2 (CD tracks 1-11 and 1-12), audience response can play a big part in how the soloing musician proportions the music he or she is creating. If the audience notes approval with "wah! wah!" or with a shake of the head, then the musical idea that drew the response might get prolonged, repeated with subtle changes.

Audience-performer interaction can also shape performances by some larger groups, such as the Arab-American ensemble shown in Figure 2.16. Arab audiences react in the moment, participating in a shared performer-audience feedback system. The lively interaction can be heard at several points even in the short portion of a selection reproduced in CD track 2-1 (see figure 5.3) at the beginning, during the *rubato* **muqaddima** section (to 1:27), and beyond. This audience reaction reveals an aesthetic value in eastern Arab music whereby a premium is often given to musicians and listeners alike achieving an ecstatic state, **tarab**, during performances. A number of musical features facilitate the creation of *tarab* in art music contexts, including the focus on one *maqām* (melodic mode) at a time, which allows the mood of the *maqām* to reign over the occasion.

Here is where the *tarab* aesthetic comes into structuring: while aspects of overall progression are worked out in advance, much is typically left to be decided as the performance unfolds. Repetitions (when and how many) are often determined in the moment, allowing the performers to react to the existing mood and energy. Furthermore, a song or instrumental composition can be stopped at any number of points in response to the urge to shift to one of several improvisatory genres.

Muqaddima (Ensemble introduction) - - - → - - - - - - → - - - - - → - - - - - - -Song

Rubato section - - - - → - - - - - → - - -Section in rhythmic mode - → - - -Song
    (rhythmic ebb & flow)   (from 1:28)   (at 3:02)
Full ensemble, followed by   Full ensemble
Qanun solo with ensemble   Melody played 5 times, at
     responses (from 0:58)   1:27, 1:46, 2:02, 2:19,
                             2:35
                    Ending phrase repeated
                      quietly as transition

FIGURE 5.3   *Egyptian performance structure.*

To help build the overall mood, audience members are supposed to show their immediate reactions to the music by gesturing in a variety of ways and by calling out any of a number of traditional phrases (Marcus 2007: 115).

The eastern Arab aesthetic feedback system invokes a different behavioral expectation than the internalized individual aesthetic reactions by audience members that characterize practices in some Western concert-going contexts—that is, remaining silent and unmoving, revealing reaction only at the end of a piece. (Exceptions to this are rife, of course, such as opera performances). Balinese audiences, too, recognize the desired inner state of divine inspiration that may overcome a *dalang* (master puppeteer) during a ***wayang kulit*** performance (Gold 2005: 90). While the Western audience practices will not affect the structuring of the music being listened to, the eastern Arab and Balinese audience practices may affect the shaping of the drama.

The Liberian Kpelle "epic pourer" is completely in charge as he narrates the story of the hero Womi, a superhuman ritual specialist (CD track 2-32), but interaction with the audience is crucial to the telling. Ruth Stone sets the stage from her fieldnotes:

> In a backyard, not too distant from the market street, Kulung, an epic singer was preparing to begin his performance of the Woi epic, a story that is familiar to Kpelle people because in earlier years it was routinely performed in Gbeyilataa and other village communities around Liberia. A soft mat had been placed on the ground, and he knelt there as he made sure that his supporting performers were in place. The people from Gbeyilataa, some eight miles from Totota, formed the bulk of the crowd. One man agreed to be

the questioner, while two young men began to tap the bottles to form the interlocking background rhythm for the performance. Four more young men and women from the assemblage sat together on a bench where they formed the chorus that, together with the instrumentalists, created the backdrop for the epic performance (2005: 22–23).

The "epic pourer" voices all the characters in the story, sings, responds to a volunteer questioner from the crowd, and directs a group of supporting listeners who also provide the musical backdrop. The structuring process within which he works is **part-counterpart**, in which one or more supporting parts interact. In the Kpelle epic genre, that structuring process is played out in several ways simultaneously. Repeating what could have been one rhythmic part, two musical supporters tap bottles to form an interlocking rhythm. Another four or more young people form a chorus; what could have been one extended choral phrase is segmented between the two groups. The narrator and all the musicians together articulate a form in which the narrator's part is flexible, while the supporting group's parts are fixed. In addition, the narrator and the questioner articulate a form; in that case, both parts are flexible.

When an Indian or Pakistani *qawwālīyā* sings in a Muslim Sufi gathering, he watches the participants for signs of going into trance in order to encourage it musically. In this instance, the "performer-audience interation" is enacted within a ritual process and a devotional response structures the music (Qureshi 1987). The shaping of music in response to a ritual situation happens all over the world.

In the case of several Korean performance genres, the single most important structuring principle—progression through a series of *changdan* (see chapter 3)—originated in the highly interactive context of shamanistic ritual. Though the context has changed to concert presentation, the gradual build up of tension that is reminiscent of the progress of a ritualized séance (*kut*) remains in a structure wherein the rhythm patterns change in a series of sections.

Revealing their origin in shamanistic ritual, several concert performance genres of Korean music use a progression through a series of *changdan* as the single most important structuring principle (see chapter 3). Effecting a gradual buildup of tension that is reminiscent of the progress of a ritualized seance (*kut*), the rhythm patterns change in a series of sections. That is the structure of the important solo instrumental genre of **sanjo** (CD track 1-21). Not only does the rhythm pattern change, but the speed of the basic beats also gets gradually faster from the beginning to the end of a piece.

ACTIVITY 5.9   *Track the succession of* changdan *through the selection on CD track 1-21, portions of a solo instrumental performance genre called* sanjo. *Here it is played on* komŭngo *(figure 2.11) by Han Kap-deuk and, on* changgo *(figure 3.2) by Hwang Deuk-ju.*

In the timing chart, a dot/asterisk indicates a drumstroke, but only as a way to represent the changdan—*not as a transcription of all that you hear. Note the gradual increase in speed.*

0:00–2:39: Chinyangjo *(six pulses divided into three subunits each)*

    • - - | - - - | - - - | - - - | • - - | • - - •   *(16 cycles)*

2:40–5:46: Chungmori *(4 pulses divided into three subunits each)*

    • - • | • - • •• | • - • • | • - - •   *(17 cycles)*

5:47–fade out: Chungjungmori *(4 pulses divided intro three subunits each)*

    • - - • | • - - • | • - - • | • - - •   *(5 cycles)*

Intra-ensemble Interaction.   Interaction among members of an ensemble are at play in the Egyptian selection on CD track 2-1 from 1:28, when the full ensemble launches into a melody in rhythmic mode. The number of repetitions of that melody will depend on the context; in this instance it is played five times. As the ensemble performs this precomposed introduction, the singer, Umm Kulthum, would traditionally be sitting in a chair in the center of the ensemble semicircle. When she is ready to sing, she stands up; on CD track 2-1, that happens during the fourth time through the melody (between 2:19 and 2:35), and you can hear the audience responding with applause. Her ensemble, understanding her signal that it is time to move on in the composition, responds by softening its sound a little. But in this performance, she must not have been quite ready to start singing. Seeing her signal that unreadiness with her hand, the *qanun* player (the leader of her ensemble) must have signaled to everyone else because we hear the ensemble energized. It repeats the melody again. The whole intro-duction (*muqaddima, p.150*) ends with a small phrase played quietly over and over so that focus shifts fully to the singer. Everyone waits, as she decides when the moment is right to begin singing.

Now the audience-performer interaction intersects with intra-ensemble interaction. Umm Kulthum sings the first phrase of the song "Aruh li min" (at 3:02), and the audience responds with a huge wave of applause. So strong is the applause that she stops singing. She has stopped for at least two reasons: she needs to acknowledge the applause, and she also needs to make sure that she does not lose control of the crowd. Toward her audience she was respectful and appreciative but always in control. Whenever the audience response would get "over the top," Umm Kulthum would stop and politely wait for the audience's energy to dissipate. What would the ensemble players do? They would keep playing, but at this point in this particular performance, they have not yet figured out what to do. Their interaction with the singer con-tinues as they await the signal to proceed (Scott Marcus, personal com-munication, 2001). This stirring performance is by an artiste who held an extraordinary position as a female singer in the Arab world.

In this one selection of Egyptian music, then, we see that the pre-composed piece has a set form (a *rubato* section that includes space for an elaborating *qanun* solo, a full ensemble section in rhythmic mode, and a song), but the execution of that form in performance is shaped by the musicians, responding in a flexible manner to cues from the audience and from each other.

The part-counterpart relationship spoken to earlier between the per-former and the audience comes into play in interaction between mem-bers of an ensemble as well. One type is **call and response**, with which you may be familiar. Call and response is sometimes taken generally to imply the juxtaposition of solo with group, sometimes more point-edly referring to a musical repartee among parts. In either case, it is deeply significant in African music, for example. Almost as soon as they could talk, the Liberian Kpelle children heard in CD track 2-43 would sing in ways they had heard adults sing; this counting song is a clear instance of the call and response structuring process. As they had heard adults in their context, the child soloist varied her line, while the others performed without fundamentally changing their part. The words are "One, two, three, try it again. Fence two, three, try it again." ("Fence" is a term that often refers to ritual, since many rituals are per-formed within an enclosure that is fenced in to keep noninitiates out

(Stone 2005:66). The same intra-ensemble interaction is at play as the master drummer or singer creates one part to which an ensemble of instrumentalists or singers responds, when one player in a xylophone duo leads and the other responds, when listeners encourage a praise singer with a response. Transported to North America in the era of slavery, that structuring process could be heard as one worker led in song, with fellow workers responding. In contemporary gospel, a lead singer embellishes a solo with support from the choir; in the blues, there is the same sort of interplay between singer and instrumentalists as well as among the instrumentalists.

ACTIVITY 5.10   *The structuring process of solo-group instrumentation and part-counterpart musical interaction are heard in music all over the world. With that idea as a focus, review the variety of musical practices that are offered on the CDs. Listen to each selection again, for the purpose of finding those structures. This is a good time for you to double-check to be sure that you are up-to-date on your cumulative record of all the references to the tracks on the CDs.*

Music and Movement.   So very often, music and movement are inextricably interrelated. Here is offered a few examples that range over sport, a game, dance, and Christian worship. Straddling the boundaries of dance, music, and sport is Brazilian *capoeira*, a "blurred genre" that can be described as a game or martial art with music, a form of dance with vocal and instrumental accompaniment, as a drama, and as mentioned in Chapter 2, a philosophy and worldview that emphasizes liberation and embodies reciprocity (Murphy 2006: 55). The capoeira ensemble typically comprises a singer and chorus who interact with call and response; this can be heard on CD track 1-16. In addition, there are three *berimbaus* (musical bows, at three different pitch levels), *pandeiro* (tambourine), *agogô* (double metal bell), *reco-reco* (notched bamboo scraper), and *atabaque* (large drum resembling a conga). The ensemble forms the polyrhythmic backdrop. Competing within a circle of spectators, two contestants use athletic leg thrusts to throw each other off balance. As physical play changes, the music should change accordingly, and if the music changes, the contestants should respond in kind. *Capoeira* players depend on the lowest-pitched *berimbau* for specific melodic-rhythmic patterns, called **toque** for the tempo of play, and for specific phrases that suggest the timing for movements. During a long period of apprenticeship, players learn to integrate their movements with the sound and rhythms of the *berimbau*, using what could be described as full-body hearing. Players use the groove established by the *berimbau* to choose unexpected moments in which to launch an attack on their opponent (Murphy 2006). "The musicians [all *capoeristas* themselves] create the atmosphere within which the game comes to life; they make the game possible, and the game, in turn, gives meaning to the music" (Lewis 1992: 134).

In Inuit communities across the whole of Arctic Canada and Alaska, women and children in particular have created games that bring joy and laughter to indoor space. A widely known example is juggling games, in which the changing meters of a song "counterpoint" the steady rhythm of juggling three or more balls. The rhythm of juggling must be consistent. The action of tossing a ball with one hand and catching it in the other creates a 1-2 pattern. In Figure 5.4, a partial transcription of a juggling game on CD track 2-44, however, you can see how the word rhythms create groupings that constantly shift from 3 to 2 to 5 or 7. While the jugglers would not think of these different word groupings as changing "meters," this European convention can be useful to represent the song. To sing the changing patterns and juggle in a consistent duple one at the same time is a challenge (Diamond 2008).

Rather than working "against" the text as the Inuit polyrhythmic game does, Polynesians use the integration of movement and music as a means for complementing texts, to the extent that Islanders view performance as embodied aural poetry. In Polynesian dance, emphasis is on the hands whose primary function is to illuminate selected words so that listeners can understand and enjoy the poetry more fully (Moulin, in Diettrich, Moulin, and Webb 2011:13).

When music is meant for regularly-structured dance, it is important to coordinate the form of the music and the dance. Thousands of Irish dance tunes have a **binary form**—A and B sections (CD track 1-3). Each section is eight measures long. The two sections are usually repeated in performance, creating a tune that is thirty-two measures long.

qu-luk-pa qu-luq-qu-luq-pa   tu-nit tu-nit tu-nit___   a-ya-ya

a-ja-ju-ni   a-ja-ja___   a-ja-ju-ni   ka - mang-u-kua ka-

mi-u-taa-li   puq-ta-llaq-si-ruq-tik   au-mik

au-mik   qa-nung-mik   tak-ta-lat-ti-vuq

a-liq-qang-ma u-na ti-vu-a-li u-na   a-na-ngni-tu-a-luq-ju-aq

va-ta-li va-ta-va-ta-li   a-li-qat-tia-nga u-va-nga-lu *etc.*

FIGURE 5.4

ACTIVITY 5.11   *On CD track 1-3, "Tar Road to Sligo" is played for one minute and thirty-one seconds before the musicians move on to the second jig ("Paddy Clancy's") in a medley. The band consists of fiddle (Becky Tracy), mandolin (Stan Scott), and whistle (Dora Hast). The tunes move in compound duple meter at a fast clip. The first section (A) is repeated exactly. The B section varies the pattern a bit: In the repeat, the first four measures are retained exactly, but the last four measures are slightly different (B'). The total structure is: A A B B' A A B B' A A B B', with each segment taking about eight seconds.*

Listen to CD track 1-3 and identify what changes, in the midst of so much repetition.

The bipartite structure of dance tunes in the British Isles and in associated traditions in North America is closely linked to the designs of the dances. Many Irish, Scottish, and English set formation dances feature a setting section (dancers remaining in place) followed by a traveling part. Anyone who has participated in North American square dances will recognize this form; one section of the tune is used when the active couple dances a figure with another couple in the square, then returns to place; the second section corresponds with the promenade or traveling part. The influence of dance design on the performance of dance tunes can still be heard when the tunes are played in a listening context such as a concert or a *seisun* (session) like those described in the Scott-Hast volume on Irish music in this series (figure 5.5). The form of tunes remains the same, but the tunes are grouped in different kinds of medleys, as in CD track 1-23, to

FIGURE 5.5   *Session at Gleeson's of Coore, near Miltown Malbay Co. Clare. The session has been a feature for decades, catering to musicians and dancers alike. In this photo the musicians are Ita Crehan (keyboard), Eamonn McGivney (fiddle), Conor Keane (accordion), Michael Downes (fiddle), P. J. Crotty (flute, mostly hidden), Angela Crotty-Crehan (concertina). The set dancers include singer Peggy McMahon and singer/concertina player Kitty Hayes. Musicians Junior Crehan and Annette Munelly are having a break at the bar.   (© Peter Laban, Miltown Malbay Co. Clare)*

maintain musical interest without the dance (Peggy Duesenberry, personal communication, 2001).

In the small community of the Maskelyne Islands, Vanuatu, in the Pacific region of Melanesia, a Presbyterian genre known as *salvesen ami* (Salvation Army) combines hymnody with movement structured from elements of both ceremonial dance and military drill indigenized from the Victorian-era Christian culture of paramilitarism. In CD track 2-45, the hymn "O brother, stay awake" coordinates with movement in three formal sections. It begins as many *salvesan* hymns do, with a *rubato* section, during which the singers simply walk around the dance circle in "free" time. When the clapping starts, the whole group engages in a kind of vigorous marching. In the third section, when the pulse is further subdivided, some younger men improvise dance steps. Villagers are singing at the uppermost limits of their vocal range, creating bursts of choral intensity. Individual voices, together with the group, weave a multipart choral texture (Webb, in Diettrich, Moulin, and Webb 2011: p. 92).

Close coordination between movement and music occurs also in the Balinese dance form of *topeng*; the best illustration of the necessity for extremely tight coordination is the element of sudden interruptions (*angsel*) in the flow (CD track 2-46). Short *angsels* are usually only one- or two-beat interruptions and are always syncopated. The long *angsels* consist of a sequence of events. The dancer cues the drummer with a movement particular to long *angsel*. This occurs immediately following a short *angsel*. The drummer then responds by playing louder, filling in the space following the short *angsel* (otherwise empty). The rest of the musicians know to reenter instantly, rather than wait until midway through the metric cycle as they would in following a short *angsel*. There are short *angsels* at 0:28, 0:34, 0:52, 1:15, 1:38, and 1:44. They are immediately followed by a series of swelling dynamics: the melody is continuous, becoming soft and loud several times until the dancer cues the final *angsel*, at which point the musicians break, as in the short one. The music and movement are tightly coordinated: as the dancer bends his knees, swaying from side to side, the music becomes softer. He straightens his knees and raises his arms high, and the music becomes loud. He jerks his hand suddenly, elbow high and bent, and freezes as the music abruptly stops. As he does this, the drummer makes the *plak* stroke with his left hand, so that the dancer appears to have made the sound (Gold 2005: 108.) This is all easy to imagine as you listen to CD track 2-46.

SOCIAL VALUES

In this chapter, I have taken the ethnomusicological approach of exploring not only *how* music is structured but also *why* it might be structured the way it is. As a further example, I shall demonstrate how one social value held by different groups of people is played out musically in different ways. The shared value is this: the conduct of cooperative, supportive social relationships within a group is prized above individual achievement.

As observed by Santosa and cited in chapter 2, the Central Javanese tradition of *gamelan* music (CD track 1-7) is a practice that conserves relations not only among patrons and the musicians but also among members of the community; it is a communal practice in which no one individual stands out. This can be heard in the homogeneous nature of the sound ideal. Furthermore, no one instrumental part stands out from the others in any sustained manner; the marking of the important colotomic structure on multiple instruments is embedded in the ensemble melody. Even in the modal introduction, the one section of a piece in which a single "voice" might be heard as an individual, the constraints of brevity and conventional instrumental patterns keep the expression of individual musicality in check. The music expresses community.

Jazz, in comparison, is a musical practice that, above all others, symbolizes throughout the world the African American identity that emerged from difficult human circumstances. Even when jazz is practiced by people of other groups—as it is, all over the globe—its meaning is remembered and resignified (CD track 1-32). Performance practice in jazz is of a group, for a group, expressing a cause held in common or remembering that cause. Rather than submerging the individual musicians within the group in the musical structure, however, individual creativity is featured in two ways—cooperatively, in that individual players take the spotlight in turn, and competitively, as musicians engage in fierce cutting contests that display and stretch their explicitly jazz-style musicianship. Through musical practice, a global musical community is created even as the historical and culturally-specific senses of community continue.

In this chapter I have discussed how and why the structuring of music contributes to making music meaningful and useful in people's lives. Aspects of earlier discussions—of instruments in ensembles, of rhythmic, of melodic and harmonic practice—have been recycled, to put the pieces together, in a manner of speaking. In the final two chapters, I shift the focus explicitly to ethnomusicology as an intellectual field and research practice.

ACTIVITY 5.12 *You have now been introduced to a few ways in which music is structured, ranging from crucial moments, such as beginnings and endings to entire aesthetic structures from beginning to end of a selection. You have also considered reasons why some music is structured as it is, ranging from the demands of storytelling and the desire for integration with movement, to interactions among musicians or between musicians and audience.*

To put your favorite music into the picture, work with a few selections by a favorite artist or group—perhaps something you have thought about earlier for a different purpose, to address the following questions.

- *Putting yourself in the position of the performers (or other affecting agents), what do you imagine might have been the intended use(s) of what they created? Easy listening while doing something like studying or chilling? Dancing or exercising? Causing you to think?*
- *What musical form do you hear from the beginning to end of the selections? Is there constant change or do you hear repetition of some sort? If repetition, what is repeating— melody? text? Can you catch patterns? Conversely, can you hear what changes?*
- *Can you discern any causal connections between the imagined intended use of the selections and musical form?*
- *How does one of your selections begin? Do the other selections by the same artist(s) begin in the same approximate way?*
- *How do your selections end? In the same approximate way?*
- *Finally, do you find your artist or group utilizing consistency of form as a musical characteristic of their style, or do you find them exploring variety?*

Thinking Critically about Issues

When the moment came to write this chapter, I was in French Polynesia, following the lure of the South Pacific to celebrate a significant birthday. In this beautiful place, I wondered, how can I concentrate on writing about the topics that unify the case studies in this series—such matters as globalization, identity, and authenticity? I need not have worried, for the issues were all around me. Globalization, for instance: the music that newly made Polynesian friends wanted me to send them upon my return home was American—ranging from rock 'n' roll and rhythm and blues to the latest styles. By no means, they said, was American popular music meant to replace "their own" music; it was just that the global availability of American music presented a range of choices. I, on the other hand, especially wanted to experience "their music," something different that would permit me a glimpse even as a tourist of another culture. And, frankly, as an ethnomusicologist with a historical bent, I wanted to reassure myself that the cries of alarm heard for years over inevitable "gray-out," or homogenization, of the world's cultures in the face of unmitigated global flow had not erased the beautiful Polynesian music that is audible on recordings distributed in the United States. I need not have been so concerned; "the local" thrives as an element of global cultural flows into and among the Pacific Ocean areas of Melanesia and Micronesia as well as Polynesia.

What I had not really focused on before I got to Tahiti was that it is *French* Polynesia. French Polynesia is not a nation-state; its residents have voted to continue its status as a territory although it is thousands of miles from France. Tahiti's political status serves as a reminder of the long era of colonialism, when European nations (and relatively more recently, the United States and Japan) asserted claims over a substantial portion of the earth. Colonialism forms the backdrop for numerous new nation-states and the sense of nationalism therein. Here around me, I now realized, were the ever lively topics of the nature and effects of culture contact and the formation of senses of identity and relations of power—all topics important in the study of music. It was not at all surprising when, in 2011, the book *Music in Pacific Island Cultures* (2011) was completed for this series with these very issues selected as themes.

In this chapter I shall discuss a selection of those topics, but first a commentary on two rubrics is needed: "music in global culture" and "world music." "Global culture" suggests that there are ideas, systems of production, and products circulating among peoples to the extent that something is widely shared but nothing is truly global, i.e., used, consumed, produced or understood in the same way. Even those 'things' that are most universally human are understood in different ways. Nothing is only local and nothing is totally global.

The rubric "world music" was first coined (as far as I know) by ethnomusicologists in the early 1960s to categorize instruction in traditions other than those of European classical music. It became an industry-sponsored term, a convenient label for the marketing of those traditional musics. "The most exhaustive guide to them, *World Music: The Rough Guide*, looks at 'ethnic' musics in particular places; here, the editors are concerned mainly with what they perceive to be 'indigenous,' 'authentic' musics. And they are marketing their book primarily to those western consumers who want to buy what they believe to be the authentic, the real" (Taylor 1997: 16). Read on for a discussion of authenticity.

In time, "world music" came to include popular music produced around the world. The term had always carried the sense of "Other," and the rubric "world beat" took on the same connotation. In his 1997 book *Global Pop*, Tim Taylor points out that while "world music" and "world beat" are putatively labels for musics, they are more often used to label musicians: "If it seems that the world beat category refers to music that is somehow exotic, different, fresh, and North American/British pop/rock oriented, it is also true that musicians who make this—or any—music that sounds mainstream will be categorized by their ethnicity rather than music" (16–17). Writing for *Time*, Christopher Farley asserts: "The old-school term world music is a joke, a wedge, a way of separating English-language performers from the rest of the planet. But there has always been crossover . . . in 1967 Frank Sinatra recorded an album of songs by Brazilian composer Antonio Carlos (Tom) Jobim. . . . Such music became world music only when darker-skinned folks sang it" (2001: 7).

It is, I think, time for us to move on from the term "world music." The title "Global Music Series" for this set of textbooks is intended to encompass the study of music as it flourishes in some places in the globalized contemporary world—whether that music springs from a particular long tradition or results from global flows.

Throughout this book, in the course of introducing you to numerous ways of thinking about basic elements of music (instruments, organization of time and pitch, and structuring), I linked the concepts and practices to ways in which people make music meaningful and useful in their lives. In so doing, a number of perspectives arose—for example, the ways in which cultural and social status and value come into play with regard to music, the relationship of music with senses of community, the importance of context, roles and responsibilities of those involved with musicking as well as their relationships with their communities, the effects of colonialism and globalization, and many others. All these have had to do with fairly broad ways of understanding what "the music" is; they are all core in the ethnomusicological study of "music" (see chapter 1).

In ethnomusicological parlance, however, the word "perspective" is likely to be replaced with the word "issue." "Perspective" implies a viewing point, whereas "issue" is more like the word "topic." More than the rather neutral word "topic," however, "issue" implies something that is important to debate or discuss. Discussion of an issue assumes the likely deliberation of multiple perspectives—experiences and observation of multiple people, practices, and histories, for example. The word "issue" also assumes possible disagreements and some degree of complexity. In this chapter, I invite you to think about the perspectives offered earlier, but within the framework of issues.

The choice of issues pursued in this chapter has been guided by three criteria. The most significant criterion is the aim of deepening your thinking about the material presented in chapters 1–5. Whereas I presented most of it on a musical practice-by-musical practice basis (as in "here is this and there is that"), the issues approach provides more potentially connective tissue. The second criterion is the purpose of this book as a framing volume for case studies in the Global Music Series; each of them is conceived around three or four themes that the author considers to be significant for the musical communities and their practices. The issues featured here lay the groundwork for many of those themes. The third criterion is a desire to divulge something of the intellectual history of the field of ethnomusicology when it is pertinent. The resulting discussion provides, I hope, a backdrop for thinking about the conditions of music and the study of it in the twenty-first century.

ENCOUNTERS AND IDENTITIES

From the earliest days of ethnomusicology in American universities, music has been studied through the lives of people. Numerous scholars have written about the processes of and responses to contact between groups with different music.

A Focus on Influences. Having witnessed considerable change in the musical traditions of the groups they studied, anthropologists in the 1930s developed a theory of change, termed "**acculturation**." In 1961 a statement of the theory was carefully crafted by the International Musicological Society: "Acculturation comprehends those phenomena which result when groups of individuals having different cultures come into sustained first-hand contact, with subsequent changes in the original culture patterns of either or both groups" ("Criteria for Acculturation," 1961). Specific elements of that statement should be noted: individuals within groups are credited; the nature of the contact being considered is first-hand (i.e., not mediated) and sustained; and change might result for either one or both groups. Unfortunately, the term "acculturation" became applied to studies that skewed this theory: Groups became lumps of people (whole tribes or immigrant groups, for instance). Furthermore, the change that was noted in acculturation studies was primarily in the culture of dominated groups, as the theorists belonged to what was perceived as and was in reality a dominating group (as in "the West" and "the rest"). A habit developed of essentializing the culture of whole groups—that is, citing one or a set of traits that one can easily forget are enormous generalizations, sometimes with historical political roots, such as the biologically racialized assertion that all Africans have a good sense of rhythm.

ACTIVITY 6.1 *Essentializing is something all of us are prone to doing; sometimes it is useful for generalizing about something. A related word for making such generalizations is "stereotyping"; the word "essentialize," however, implies the process of reducing, even of minimalizing, whatever one is thinking about. All too often that can be very misleading and have negative effects.*

To prepare for a class discussion, write down at least one essentialist statement that you (or others) might be in the habit of making.

A Focus on Boundaries. The introduction by Fredrick Barth to a collection of essays titled *Ethnic Groups and Boundaries: The Social Organisation of Culture Difference* (1969) contributed to a shift of scholarly focus from acculturation—the influence of one group on another—to the construction and maintenance of boundaries between people. The term "ethnic group" was introduced, reflecting the anthropological concern with classification (Stokes 1994: 6). Significantly, this meant a shift to greater inclusiveness: rather than viewing culture mostly from the perspective of a dominant group, all groups were potentially given voices by analysis of social action, called "social performance" by the French theorists Pierre Bourdieu (1977) and M. de Certeau (1984). Ethnomusicologists began exploring musical practices as evidence of people's using music in the construction and maintenance of boundaries between themselves and other groups—boundaries of nationality, ethnicity, race, religion, language, class, and gender for examples.

Whether the Other is a dominating group or another dominated group, a large proportion of these studies focus on relations of power among peoples. Many studies have appeared under the rubric of "identity study," that is, the examination of musical practices that express, if not assert, difference through the construction of an identity of some sort.

The National Community. A great deal of attention has been focused on expressions of national identity, with music playing important roles. In the geopolitical sense, the term "nation" is applied to an independent political area with geographic boundaries. Some stateless ethnicities reside across geopolitical boundaries and assert strong determination to establish their own national territories. Prominent among these at present are the Kurds and the Palestinians.

The term "nation-state" adds "state" to the sense of nation as political area with geographic boundaries. The state is an apparatus for management, a mechanism for the maintenance of an internal community and the conduct of relations with other nations. The modern nation-state as a political reality came into being in Europe in the eighteenth century and gathered momentum with world events in the nineteenth and early twentieth centuries.

The word "nation" is, however, used in two senses. In the sense of culture, the term "nation" is applied to some subgroups within a geopolitical nation—an African American nation and American Indian nations being two examples. In Canada, the term "nation" is the norm with reference to First People (the rubric preferred to "American Indian" or "Native American") because of the important long-term goal of parity of governments. (The word "tribe" is generally regarded as derogatory north of the border, but acceptable in the United States.)

Nation-states developed as the site for processes of modernization, wherein the growth of the capitalist economic system spawned urbanization, commercialization of culture, and the intensified use of technology as in industrialization and in print culture. To consolidate and communicate changing values, public school systems were instituted, and the use of multiple mass media for communication expanded as a basic tool. European and then North American processes of modernization then became synonymous with "progress." To put it succinctly, modernizing was and is "a euphemism for adopting capitalist ethics and worldview" (Turino 2008: 98). To put it another way, to modernize, meant for all intents and purposes "to westernize."

A basic component of the economic success of the modern European nation-states (and then of the United States and Japan) was the extension of their geographical boundaries for political control of a substantial amount of the world's land and population. As the tools of modernization were applied in colonized areas, they became coupled with the inexorable influence of Western culture on Others. In the cultural sphere this could mean, for instance, instruction in European music in new public school systems and the transmission of music through the media of the new music industries. The case study by Marcus on music in the Middle East considers westernization and modernization in relation to contexts for music making, instruments and ensembles, attitudes toward music, music in the schools, and pedagogy.

Another set of words is worth thinking about. Cultural encounters in the course of colonizing the Middle East and India had given rise to a discourse about "the Occident" and "the Orient," adhering to a rationale that Edward Said termed "orientalism." In Said's words, orientalism is "a system of knowledge about the Orient, an accepted grid for filtering through the Orient into Western consciousness" (1978: 6), a "cultural enterprise, a project whose dimensions take in such disparate realms as the imagination itself . . . the spice trade, colonial armies . . . a complex array of 'Oriental' ideas (Oriental despotism, Oriental splendor, cruelty, sensuality), many Eastern sects, philosophies, and wisdoms domesticated for local European use" (1978: 4).

In the European imagination in the period of world exploration, "the Orient" meant—not Asia as a totality as one may think—but particularly the "Near East," as lands of Arab and Indian cultures were called in reference to their location relative to the colonial powers to "the West."

Lest we associate this discourse only with the British and French who dominated "the Orient" from the early nineteenth century until the end of World War II, Said reminds us that since that time America has dominated the Middle East and approaches it (and East Asia also) as France and Britain once did. Because the word "Oriental" now connotes derogatory colonialist attitudes, English speakers today use the term with caution.

In chapter 4 I examined a microscopic manifestation of orientalism—"the Oriental scale," with its lingering reference to sensual Otherness. That one musical scale heard in CD track 2-22 in particular continues to suggest the generalized "exotic other," and the use of it may outlast the use of the word "oriental." I recently heard it employed in Ken Burns's documentary series, *The War*—first a soulful violin line based on that scale over a vague "harmonic" steadiness behind the telling of the bombing of Pearl Harbor, a musical underlining of the otherness of the Japanese to Americans, and then again as the genocide of the Polish Jews—Hitler's other—is narrated. From the earlier discussion of microtones/quarter tones, you can realize what an essentializing connotation has clung to that particular scale. However, many types of nondiatonic scales exist and in many musical systems around the world.

"The West," too, is a rubric that is so all-encompassing as to be incautious, unclear, and potentially misleading. Thinking geographically, what is "the West" taken to include? Europe, surely, but all of Europe? For the Bulgarians in Eastern Europe until the late nineteenth century, for instance, "the West" did not include themselves but meant Central Europe owing to the Bulgarian political situation as part of the Turkish Ottoman Empire for three hundred years. Not until the end of World War II and the establishment of a communist government in Bulgaria in 1944 did modernization (read "westernization"), in the form of urbanization, massive industrialization, and widespread high school education, become the norm there (Rice 2004: 7).

ACTIVITY 6.2 *With good maps of the world handy to you, answer these questions. Thinking geographically, what is "west" of China, Japan, India, the Philippines? Where does Asia end and Europe begin in that enormous, continuous landmass? Where do the demarcations into western and eastern hemisphere lie? Within the hemispheres, where does the continent of Africa fit?*

Thinking culturally about "the West," what does the rubric mean? Even just the European cultures are very different from each other, and the encounters of other cultures with them differed accordingly. Historians of European musics are likely to be careful to write about the various repertoires in terms of a single country or city or court— Italian opera as opposed to German, for instance, madrigal at the court of Ferrara, the Viennese symphony, and the like. To what do you refer when you say "the West"?

"The West" is a rubric that is likely to be used (often unintentionally) geopolitically. Categorizing African American, Caribbean, and Latin American musics as "non-Western" musics as often happens is a habit of speech that suggests marginality with respect to structures of power. When Asian scholars write "the West," they are usually implicating the hegemonic wielders of political, economic, and therefore cultural power in the colonial era, as well as the musical practices of particular peoples and institutions who bore and still bear that power. I have been careful about the rubric of "the West" in this book. However you choose to use the rubric, "the West," I hope that you will be careful, too. Words are very important.

Embedded in discourses of both Orientalism and modernity was the assertion of the superiority of "the West." In dealing with the power of "the West" in the nineteenth century, Japanese leaders invested in the belief in the superiority of European music—a legacy of the colonial era—in their process of modernization. And the Japanese transmitted it to Koreans, whom they colonized in the early twentieth century. The dilemma this assertion has caused for musicians of indigenous traditions in those countries is serious and ongoing (CD tracks 1-18, 1-21, and others). The situation in Japan and Korea is quite striking when compared to that of India: political leaders and musicians alike in that former jewel in the crown of the British empire have been unswervingly confident of the superiority of their classical music, with its long history, intellectuality, and spirituality (CD tracks 1-11, 1-12, 1-19, 2-40, and others).

World War II (1941–45) effectively disrupted the paradigm of global (imperial) colonialism; a number of new nations came into being in the ensuing decades. Several independent nations also emerged near the end of the twentieth century from the dissolution of the Soviet Union. Not surprisingly, nation building—and therefore music and nationalism—is a topic that persists in ethnomusicological study.

Processes other than modernization and westernization also are at work in nation building. Among them are the construction of a united community, the choosing of emblems of representation that all citizens may share, and the assertion of some sort of difference by which one nation-state can be distinguished from others. Music can be important in each of them. To demonstrate these processes, I shall continue to move between historical and present time and continue to draw on case studies in this series for examples.

One of the first tasks in building a new nation-state is to create a united community even when the population is heterogeneous in some way. In French Polynesia the diversity is ethnic, with Tahitians and multigenerational resident Chinese, Japanese, Europeans, and Americans. In addition, occupants of the territory's several islands have long traditions of distinguishing themselves from each other. They would all have to perceive themselves as part of a socially constructed national group—an **"imagined community"** (Anderson, 1991). Furthermore, if French Polynesia were to become a nation-state, it would need to deal with the inevitable claims of multiple groups and construct a national identity that would unite them somehow.

For colonial Americans of the eighteenth century, the new identity could not be an outgrowth of shared language, beliefs, customs, traditions, and norms the way it was in European nation-states. Americanists point out that the United States may be the only nation in the world that was invented from an idea, lacking any foundation in a defined territory, a religious authority, a common culture, or a single people. Indeed, the Indian tribes, the country's earliest inhabitants, were themselves separate nations, each with a language and culture of its own. Until 1871, when congressional action ended the practice, those nations, their sovereignty recognized, could separately negotiate treaties with the U.S. government. These political conditions, without anything unified on which to build, made it highly unlikely that support for an overall American national identity might have been constructed on an Indian tribal base.

The creation of even an "imagined" united community in the United States (as in *e pluribus unum*) has been and always will be extremely challenging. (Look at the unfinished pyramid on the one-dollar bill, suggests Adelaida Reyes.) Declaring independence from British colonial power was just one major step. As Reyes eloquently discussed in her volume on America in this series (2005), for more than a hundred and fifty years after the nation declared its independence, power—social and aesthetic—stood firmly on a Europe-derived base. Even to the 1950s, 80 percent of those who immigrated to the United States were of European ancestry. Americans had to travel a long road through two world wars and earn status as a superpower before they could take their independence from Europe as a *psychological* reality. Only then could they break free of their habitual deference to Europe. This was due in no small part to the resistance of the new Americans to assigning otherness to those to whom they were still bound by deep historical, cultural, and personal ties. America thus chafed against, but nonetheless emulated, those whose cultural hegemony it found difficult to escape. And even as those ties were loosened by time, the fact remained that the principal threat to identity is not what one differs from most obviously but what one resembles enough to be mistaken for. Reform of immigration laws in the 1960s widened the range of diversity throughout the country as nothing had before. In that decade also, the black power and civil rights movements laid the groundwork for the rise of ethnic pride among African Americans, Native Americans, Latinos, and other groups. With the influx of Asians and formerly locked-out populations, diversity built up enough of a critical mass to mount a multiculturalist challenge to the then-dominant Anglo-European melting-pot assimilationist ideal. The recognition of a boundary that distinguishes America's music from other musics, Europe's in particular, was the necessary prelude to formulating an American musical identity (Reyes 2005: pp. 68, 30, 63–64).

From the 1870s the Japanese government found European music useful for nation building. Once they made the decision to follow the European and American models for including music in their new public education system (established expressly as a tool in the modernization process), they faced a dilemma: the various indigenous traditional genres had such deep class and other type of group associations that none could satisfy the community-building task for which music was needed. The solution was to adopt a different (i.e., non-Japanese) music that could be transmitted in such a way that it would be shared by all Japanese. As a result of the continuing emphasis on European music for over 140 years, Japan's traditional music has become exotic to most of its citizens. To counteract that, national cultural policy enters the picture again. Among the steps taken, the government's National Theater fosters the preservation of those forms deemed most important. (Wade 2005).

In time, governments around the world have established a variety of national cultural policies to meet the challenges posed by both internal heterogeneity and the forces of westernization. The approach in China has been multi-directional. Frederick Lau (2008) discusses such nationwide institutions as the symphonicized Modern Chinese Orchestra and the music conservatory. On the other hand, he notes that regional and local musical styles are widely appreciated. Interchange, dialogue, even confrontations between those national institutions and local traditions have produced many of the new developments in Chinese music.

"Music nationalism" is the use of music specifically to assert the all-important sense of united community within a nation-state, and also to assert some sense of difference to citizens of other nation-states. The national anthem is the most obvious example of the powerful medium that music can be. Think of broadcasts you have seen of the Olympics and consider the sight of the gold medal winners, standing under their nation's flag, listening to their national anthem. That focused moment of music nationalism is meant to announce the winner with a musical signal, to set the victor apart from the other contestants, and also to engender a sense of pride among citizens of the medalist's nation.

New nation-states have a flag and an anthem; many of them also have an emblem. The emblem may be anything—something from nature such as an eagle, something material such as an airline, something cultural such as a musical instrument, or even a composer. Frédéric Chopin (1810–49) is a case in point: the great Polish composer (CD track 2-11) and pianist was successfully redefined by the Polish intelligentsia in terms of the changing contexts of Polish nationalism. Chopin had little experience of his country's folk music; rather, he was an international composer in the European tradition, stranded in Paris by political circumstances and personal choice. His late romantic style came to denote revolution and the struggle of the individual against the world. By the early twentieth century he had posthumously become a cult "Pole" in Paris, which, in turn, was part of what made him valued in Poland, a genius representing a distinctly Polish contribution to Europe's international culture. In socialist Poland, however, Chopin was celebrated for his adherence to his roots and his refusal to conform to the bourgeois aesthetics of romanticism. One way or another, he remained emblematic of the Polish nation.

One type of music that has been crucial historically in the construction of new nation-states is folk music. Its connection with nationalism and national identity is discussed below in the section on authenticity.

ACTIVITY 6.3   *Anthems provide the quintessential musical assertion of nationalism. To think about them as a musical statement, do three things.*

1) *Look into the history of the anthem of your country: when, why, and by whom did it come to be composed and adopted?*

2) *Make a list of the occasions on which you hear the anthem of your country and consider why it is invoked on those particular occasions and whether or not it always sounds the same. If not, why not?*

3) *Select any two other nations in contrasting parts of the world and find performances of their national anthems. Drawing on the analytical skills you have developed through using this book, analyze the two and compare them musically with the anthem of your country for this purpose: formulate at least two questions about why they are what they are.*

Regional Identity.   Another sense of boundary expressed through music that emerges as significant in several of the Global Music Series volumes is the layer of regional identity within national identity. In Fred Lau's *Music in China*, where identity is one of the overarching themes, we get a sense of the importance of the meaning of regional musics in that nation. In one sense, Chinese music is made up of many regional genres, and one usually needs to identify the region from which a music originates; for instance, CD track 1-2, **jiangnan sizhu** ensemble music is from the area south of the Yangtze River around the city of Shanghai and CD track 1-27 is opera from the Gwangzhou (Canton) region. In a similar vein, a person's identity is invariably defined in terms of ancestral place of origin—not the nation but the region—and social class. Regardless of where one lives, the sense of identification with the place of one's origin and not one's birthplace is an important notion that grounds an individual. This tie to a specific region is manifested in multiple ways, such as dialects, cultural practice, food, and music, that, as a complex of practices, become emblems of a regional identity. However, in the modern context, regional music is often used as one of the necessary ingredients that make up what is generally called "Chinese music," a collective category that is tied to the emergence of modern nationalism. Regional versus national music turns out to be a complex issue.

So important is it in Brazil (another huge country geographically) that John Murphy organized his volume through it (2006); CD track 2-10 gives you a taste of music from Northeast Brazil. Such music has been crucial for articulating the nostalgia felt by northeastern migrants to the large cities of the south and, indeed, in the 1940s played a crucial part in the very invention of the concept of the northeastern region of Brazil, even to the point of becoming a symbol of an "authentic."

Gender. Another kind of identity that has been explored in the case study volumes and in ethnomusicology in general is that of gender. Studies that focus on gender are about the ways maleness and femaleness are constructed. (Gender is a cultural category, while sex is a biological category.) Concerning gender, you can find observations scattered throughout this book; in chapter 2, for instance, I explore the gendering of some musical instruments.

Historically in ethnomusicological writing, as in other scholarly disciplines, gender has usually gone unnoted unless the musical practice being studied is particularly associated with females. Otherwise, maleness is taken for granted, and male spheres of cultural action have received the lion's share of attention.

Focus on women and their musical practices is burgeoning, however. In the volume on South India, for example, Vishwanathan and Allen remark that despite women's participation in artistic life from time immemorial there, written accounts of South Indian music and literary history have tended to concentrate on the contributions of men. When work by or about women musicians, authors, or composers has been published, in some cases it has been deliberately altered, in effect erased and suppressed (2004: 74). Unfortunately, the same could be said for women musicians in many places.

A variety of perspectives are being taken—woman musicians as symbols of a nation, as players of gendered roles in a community, as forces for social or cultural change, as political spokespersons, as inter-cultural negotiators, and as individual artists. Relating directly to a cultural icon featured in this book, for instance, is Virginia Danielson's excellent ethnographic biography of the great Egyptian singer, Umm Kulthum (CD track 2-1). I think also of Carol Muller's *Rituals of Fertility and the Sacrifice of Desire: Nazarite Women's Performance in South Africa* (1999) and Ellen Koskoff's study of a Jewish community in New York City (2001), for other instances. Ideally, whether the focus of our study is musicking by males or females, and particularly when the focus is on both, we should remark on gender because of its many implications for understanding musical practice.

Performance in public, as opposed to private, spheres has been a thorny issue in many places. Women who brave the possible consequences of having their music received as performed sexuality rather than expressive artistry have been pioneers. In some cultures, for instance, the respectability of a female performer must be carefully negotiated; the stardom of a singer such as Umm Kulthum in Egypt is quite remarkable in light of that reality (CD track 2-1). In both South and North India female vocalists of classical genres have in the past found the refusal to accept payment for performance as a means of maintaining unquestionable respectability.

In so many instances, the performance of a particular musical genre is a gender role. Exploring the reasons for that can reveal much about the culture and its history. In Japan, for instance, the musico-dramatic form *kabuki* has been performed exclusively by males for several centuries, although it originated with female performance. In America women instrumentalists still find it difficult to break into the predominantly male world of jazz instrumental performance.

The control of musical knowledge is another arena where gender considerations often arise. In India, whether the learners are male or female, most teachers have been men. In contemporary Japan, while there are a few famous male performers of *koto*, instruction on the instrument has passed almost entirely into the purview of women (Figure 1.3).

Likewise, the authoritative role of leader in musical ensembles is often subject to gender considerations. North American women are making their way increasingly into the ranks of professional choral conductors (figure 1.1). In the orchestral world, however, the gender barriers are tall and thick; there are still few professional women conductors.

ACTIVITY 6.4 *Use the Internet and search for professional orchestras, orchestra choruses, opera companies, and opera choruses. They usually bear the name of the city in which they are located. Some websites give a historical list of their conductors as well as information on the present individual; check that as well.*

Select one organization with particularly good documentation on the internet, to consider questions such as these. Do the performers appear to be of multiple ethnicities/races or homogeneous in that regard? How many men and how many women do you see performing, and what roles do they have? In photos used for promotion of the organization, how are conductors and soloists presented? Are there distinctions between the presentations of gender in such photos? How are the various performers dressed? Is there any overt representation of class? What are the ticket prices, and what does that suggest to you? Feel free to raise further questions yourself.

Ideas about masculinity and femininity can be understood by considering the matter of performance style. In her book, *Engendering Song*, Jane Sugarman explores social and musical practices among the Préspa Albanian community. She writes:

Throughout a wedding celebration, men and women gather to sing in ways that strongly differentiate them by gender. . . . While women sing softly and "thinly" of courtship and marriage, sitting with great composure deep within the host family's house, men sing loudly and "thickly" of heroism and romance, drinking and toasting boisterously in the family's courtyard. (1997: 252)

Social attitudes in South India early in the twentieth century also provide a good example of this, with gendered style affecting "the music" as well. Concerts by women singers stressed harmonious ensemble performance, rather than the jousting improvisational back-and-forth affiliated with improvisation and gendered as male musical behavior (Vishwanathan and Allen 2004).

Conversely, it is important to note when the gender of a performer is explicitly not the point. In some traditional Japanese vocal music, it is difficult to tell whether a man or a woman is singing, so ungendered is the style; an expressive rendering of the text is the most important criterion for performance style. In Chinese opera, the way gender is represented in musical drama is more important than the sex of the performer (CD track 1-27). The dramatic role of a refined woman, for instance, may be played by a woman or a man; either will meet the expectations for sound quality and presentation that are "given" for the role. Star singers of the Turkish urban art music genre *fasıl* include both men and women, and due to the fact that the Turkish language is ungendered (the pronoun "o" means either "he" or "she"), any song can be sung by a man or a woman. However, *fasıl* performance often involves considerable gender ambiguity, particularly since many noted singers have been either transgender or, more recently, transsexual (Bates 2011: 42).

ACTIVITY 6.5 *If you were to launch a research project on gender and music, what might it be? Would you, for instance, be interested in culture change that is reflected in music? Or the performance of gender by your favorite musicians? Or the ways in which texts of a set of songs express something about gender or gender relations? Pick a potential topic and investigate it sufficiently enough that you know it is a viable one (if not, pick another!). Write up a 50 to 75 word project proposal that states the topic, raises questions you would pursue, and suggests the sources you would use.*

Multiple Identities.   The focus on boundaries in ethnomusicological study has led us to understand "identity" in a number of ways—not only "types of identity" such as national, regional and gender, but from many perspectives. Tom Turino reminds us: It is generally understood that social identities are always multiple and situationally relative. The same person can identify with her family, community, school, region, with others of the same gender or social class, as well as with an 'ethnic' designation or country depending on the goals and salient nodes of identity within a particular situation (2008: 4). To demonstrate this, I invoke the steelband, or pan (CD track 1-15, Figure 2.17), which was officially proclaimed the national instrument of Trinidad and Tobago. The emergence of the steelband as a symbol of national identity draws us into stories of other types of identity—social class, ethnicity, race, gender (Dudley 2004). An instrument of the lower class originally, pan began as an ingenious creation of poor people who made the most of meager resources; around 1940 people began to tune different pitches on the surface of metal containers such as paint cans. Untrained musicians took pride in mastering the musical language of the educated class. When, in the nationalist movement of the 1940s and 1950s, the collection and promotion of folk music and dance was considered important, some intellectuals in Trinidad held up the steelband as an example of "urban folk" creativity. Its cultural status gradually ascended, and middle-class youth began to play in bands; by the 1960s women even began to play. During the 1970s schools all over Trinidad began to include steelband in the curriculum. When the prime minister declared it the national instrument in 1992, some Trinidadians of East Indian descent protested that such a symbol favored the status of Afro-Trinidadian culture over Indo-Trinidadian culture. But proponents of pan countered that the steelbands had come to include people of diverse ethnicities and classes. Regardless, Trinidadians could claim to have developed the instrument entirely on their own, and furthermore, because it had achieved international recognition, it was an ideal emblem for a unified national community.

As people have multiple sensibilities, musical practices can have multiple "identities" as well. For those of Mexican heritage, for whom the connections among race, ethnicity, and social hierarchy result in social alienation in United States society, mariachi music takes on a dimension of value that is necessarily different from that in Mexican society (CD track 1-6). Emerging from its rural roots in several states of western Mexico, the music of mariachi ensembles was seized upon in the early twentieth century by Mexican media and officialdom as an important expression of Mexican national identity. Mariachis appear with campaigning politicians, as "folkloric" entertainment for tourists, and in government-sponsored representations of Mexico to the international community. Mariachi musicians, however, often are quick to express the disjuncture between being glorified by officials as a source of national identity and pride on the one hand and being neglected or victimized by class prejudice on the other.

In the United States, the Mexican American movement beginning in the 1960s and the emergence of mariachi-in-schools programs heightened the position of mariachi music as a positive signifier of cultural identity. Mariachi music's social value increased dramatically among Mexican Americans when popular singer Linda Ronstadt, of Mexican American background, launched her national tour and *Canciones de Mi Padre* album in 1987. Ronstadt brought a new spotlight of public attention to the music and made it "cool" to like mariachi music. Her promotion of the music put it in a new social light—it was worthy of the American popular mainstream, not marginal, and it was contemporary, not outmoded—and Mexican Americans flocked to it. Thousands of young Mexican Americans enthusiastically have taken up mariachi music as a closely held badge of personal and group identity. As discussed in Daniel Sheehy's volume in this series, Mexican-born mariachi musicians point to the respect and appreciation shown to them by American audiences.

ACTIVITY 6.6 *Pursuing the idea of multiple identities, turn your thoughts to yourself, the identities you embody by birth or have chosen to construct. How do these identities enter into the way you live your life? Do you keep them more or less separate, for instance, or do they overlap and shift rather seamlessly? Think as well about how you express these identities—through clothing, through forms and styles of speech or movement, by choice of associates and activities—and most important here, through music and dance.*

AUTHENTICITY

The association of music with national, ethnic, and other types of identity gives rise to one issue that just does not go away. In fact, concern with it is due largely to nationalism. As observed by Peter Wade in his *Music, Race, and Nation* on music in Colombia:

The notion of the modern homogeneous nation in Latin America owes a great deal to European models, not just for the structures of the nation-state, but for the basic cultural values of "civilization" espoused by elites. This has led to debates within Latin American political and intellectual elites about "imitation" and "authenticity": some nationalist currents have felt that a "proper" nation cannot simply be a copy of some other (notionally original) societies and cultures; there must be some authentic cultural traditions to create originality, difference, and hence identity. (2000: 11–12)

The linking of authenticity to music came about through the thinking of the Prussian preacher Johann Herder from the late eighteenth century. Herder argued as follows (as summarized in Taruskin 2001): Language makes humans human, but it must be learned socially, in a community. Since thought is based on language, human thought is a community product. Each language manifests unique values and ideas. When the concept of language was extended to learned behavior or expressive culture—customs, music, and so on—they too were seen as essential constituents of a precious collective spirit. Expression of the collective spirit became an explicit goal of the arts. Distinctive culture could serve both as a marker of difference in external relations and a symbol behind which the citizenry could rally as a community. Thus was born the concept of authenticity as faithfulness to one's essential nature.

Authenticity became an object thing as well as a quality. Where was it to be found and in what forms? Herder placed authenticity with the folk: folklore was authentic wisdom, folk music the true music of a people. With folklore elevated in value, its appropriation by elite culture to express national identity began to flourish.

The ambitious collecting of items of folk expressive culture began with Herder himself. The collecting of folk music—songs particularly, due to the value accorded to language—became an important activity of prominent figures in the history of ethnomusicology and of European music such as the Hungarian composers Béla Bartók (1881–1945) and Zoltán Kodály (1882–1967). Post–World War II socialist nations' collecting was and is state-sponsored, with the focus on archiving songs as items—the possessions of a nation, or of a region within a nation, or some other distinguishable group. Composers also collected in order to have new material for their creative work.

Questions of authenticity and folk music remained closely linked, and aspects of Herder's thinking resonated still in the publications of Maude Karpeles, an important figure in folk music research in the first half of the twentieth century. In the *Journal of the International Folk Music Council* in 1951, Karpeles defined authenticity in folk music: developing unconsciously, evolving through a process of continuity, variation, and selection, and transmitted orally. While the word "authenticity" does not appear, and her "developing unconsciously" became "springing from the creative impulse," Karpeles's hand can be seen in a resolution of the IFMC in 1953, in which folk music is defined as a "thing" that exists owing to certain creative processes:

> Folk music is the product of a musical tradition that has been evolved through the process of oral transmission. The factors that shape it are: (i) continuity which links the present to the past; (ii) variation which springs from the creative impulse of the individual or the group; and (iii) selection by the community, which determines the form or forms in which the music survives. (*Journal of the IFMC* 5 [1953]: 23)

Even very recently, where the words "authenticity" and "authentic" appear in writing about music, they are likely to refer to one or more elements in that definition of folk music. I shall focus on each of those elements in turn.

The idea of a product occurs twice in the IFMC definition: "Folk music is [a] product," and then "the form or forms in which the music survives." Whether one calls them "objects," "items," or "forms," "products" are thought of as possessing (or lacking) authenticity. In the flurry of 1980s research and argument about authentic performance practice of European music before 1750, for example, the aim was to perform as authentic an object (a piece of music) as possible—using period instruments or new instruments modeled after them, trying to learn from written sources how ornaments would have been produced, and the like.

In this way of thinking about authenticity, the act of performing also becomes an object (or, as Taruskin puts it, a text). It is happening, for instance, when, in the interest of "authentic performance," a conscientious conductor of a non-Bulgarian choral group works with the singers to achieve a sound as close as possible to that of a traditional Bulgarian chorus (CD track 2-28). Whereas the authenticity movement in musicology was a historical project, contemporary multicultural projects are more likely to try to produce "authentic performances" modeled after performance as it is heard in recent times.

Authenticity is also thought of as residing in a person who has acquired the knowledge that permits him or her to perform authentically or to evaluate "authenticity" as a critic. Here, "authenticity" resembles "authority." As Taruskin states it: "Authenticity . . . is knowing what you mean and whence comes that knowledge. And more than that, authenticity is knowing what you are, and acting in accordance with that knowledge" (1995: 56). Taruskin's "you" puts the emphasis on a person's individual identity. The matter of authenticity's residing in a person emerges for ethnomusicologists who seriously pursue the practice of a contemporary music as a means of doing research. A lively debate persists with regard to those persons' "authenticity" as performers if the music is not one they grew up knowing. Often the debate is about whether it is "really" possible to be bimusical or multimusical (equally "authentic" in more than one tradition of musical practice), or whether someone who is not native to a culture can possibly be an authentic culture bearer of the music of another culture—knowing something inside out, in a manner of speaking. The debate usually arises because some individuals consider themselves to be authoritative in a non-native musical practice, while others doubt the authenticity of that identity. You can pose the same question about performers of early European music who did not live at the time and therefore in the culture of the music they are performing.

> **ACTIVITY 6.7** *Discuss these questions with your friends: Do you think a non-native musician can be an "authentic" performer of Indian classical music? Can a Japanese musician be an "authentic" performer of jazz or European classical music? Can a white person be an "authentic" performer of black music? Can a black person be an "authentic" performer in the European operatic tradition?*

"Authenticity" becomes easily paired with the idea of "tradition" as in the IFMC definition: "Folk music is the product of a musical tradition." Even in this definition, however, "tradition" is difficult to define. It appears to be a style of performance, or a musical genre—something within which items evolve. David Coplan defines tradition as "dependent upon a symbolically constituted past whose horizons extend into the present" (1990: 40). For the purposes of this discussion, the key idea is that a tradition links the present with the past.

The nature of "the past" to which tradition is linked has been a subject of much discussion in the humanities in recent years. In her study of the American genre of country music, Joli Jensen found that enthusiasts locate "the past" in whatever they believe to be disappearing in modern life and find the expression of nostalgia in country music to be useful in facing the realities of the present:

> I believe that we ratify the conflicts of modernity by ascribing to country music the authenticity we see evaporating in the present. . . . Country music, and its burden of maintained authenticity, is a way to address, obliquely but intensely, unresolvable conflicts in modern life. . . . Various markers designate country music's "realness": natural origins, spontaneous production, communal performance, heartfelt lyrics, sincere performers, and loyal fans are among the aspects invoked to prove that country music is more real than other forms. (1998: 160–61)

"Natural origins [if she means creative impulse], spontaneous production, communal performance"—these phrases resonate with the ideas in the IFMC definition of folk music.

Nostalgia pervades the sense of the past of youth in Bulgaria, who conceive "traditional experiences" as those that precede modern experiences (Rice 2004). They yearn for music that does not use the most obvious devices of modern popular and classical music such as loud electronic instruments and percussion. I will return to other ideas about "the past" below.

Commercialization and the media are two realities of modern life that emerge in discussions of "authenticity." Often it is in the context of the consideration of change, or "variation," as it is put in the IFMC definition of folk music. That folk music changes is not at issue: change or variation is taken to be natural and is still generally accepted as part of the folk music process. It is the reason for the change that causes concern about authenticity. Karpeles argued in 1968 that "genuine folk song" is not possible in modern industrialized society ([10]), and that idea still lingers, with commercialization, mass media, and other characteristics of modern life being regarded as negative forces.

In fact, commercialization is part of the reality of a good deal of music that is considered to be "traditional." In his volume on Mexican and

Mexican American music in this series, Dan Sheehy explores this with regard to mariachi music, (CD track 1-6), at once a music rooted in over 150 years of tradition, a commodity governed by market considerations, and a dynamic, evolving musical stream of activity. In Mexico it is shaped and expanded by tributaries of musical innovation and social meaning from the American side of the border. According to Sheehy, a key to knowing mariachi music "from the inside out" is understanding mariachi musicians as a community linked by their common occupation (2006).

The community, or group, is another element that obviously emerges in discussion of authenticity. It appears in the IFMC definition of folk music in two ways that resonate with Sheehy's remark about mariachi: the group as a source of musical creativity and an agent for selection of what will endure. Joli Jensen and many other scholars have looked at it from the opposite perspective: music constructing community, and musical change disrupting community.

> When a new genre's authenticity is challenged it is an acknowledgement that culture constructs social groups. In displacing the honky-tonk sound as the dominant kind of country music, the Nashville Sound abandoned, even betrayed, those fans who loved the sound of steel and fiddle. Social groups—call them fans, audiences, markets, or communities—are constructed in and through cultural genre. Changes in the genre change the ways people in these groups can define themselves and their relationship to each other. (1998: 163)

Here, a musical genre is an "authentic" item, in that it is expected to adhere to a model on which there is consensus and bears meaning around which a group can form. This notion is familiar from discussion above of the process of community building in nation-states.

The roots of an idea called "authenticity," then, lie in the modern Western world and in cultural politics. Ideas about authenticity emerged in relation to folk culture, and even when they develop about something without that connection, they generally involve a link to tradition or at least to some idea about "the past." Notions of authenticity in music are generally held to be constructed: "Claims about authenticity . . . are involved in a power struggle over the ownership of value in which tradition and modernity are key terms" (Wade 2000: 25). Many of us, I would guess, would agree with Australian Tony Mitchell that "notions of musical purity and authenticity are an idealistic form of colonialist nostalgia" (1993: 335).

But at the same time, we ethnomusicologists balance a profound respect for traditional [indigenous knowledge], including dance and song, with an admiration for the creative projects of innovative contemporary artists" (Diamond 2008: 34). While the sociologist George Lipsitz suggests that "concepts of cultural practice that privilege autonomous, 'authentic,' and non-commercial culture as the only path to emancipation do not reflect adequately the complexities of culture and commerce in the contemporary world" (1994:16), we still find notions of authenticity proclaimed, as people make music meaningful and useful in their lives. As Tim Rice put it, if authenticity is to retain any meaning at all, it has to mean that music is authentic when it responds in some meaningful way to the culture and society around it, as it virtually always does (2004).

A number of wonderful cases in point are included in the chapter on music, performance, and representation in *Music in Pacific Island Cultures* (2011). Jane Moulin writes, for instance:

> Since the opening of the international airport in 1960, Tahitian tourism officials have worked vigorously to market the islands of French Polynesia as a destination of distinction, one in which the performing arts are integral to the overall tourist experience . . . .
> As a former professional dancer who performed regularly in Tahitian hotels I am surprised by travelers who are immediately skeptical of hotel performances. Perhaps scared off by the artificial packaging of commodified culture that is typical of tourist destinations around the world, they assume that the hotel show by definition is merely a cheapened and unrealistic version of the "real" thing.
>
> However, tourism in French Polynesia has been of tremendous benefit to music and dance . . . . Tahiti's major hotels actively support regularly scheduled evenings of dinner entertainment by Tahiti's best dance troupes and are the most active venues for the performance of traditional music and dance. These performances provide an income to musicians and dancers but, more important, they offer a place for performers to hone their skills through repeated presentation while allowing local residents to see outstanding music and dance throughout the year. In fact, one major hotel estimates that local diners are up to 70 percent of the audience

at its three weekly shows . . . . Local clients are vital to these performances because they will not settle for an atypical or incompetent presentation.

Unfortunately, the tourist industry also negatively affects the presentation of music and dance in many places—in the major hotels worldwide and on tourist ships to name just two types of venues. When you are in a situation to observe shows that cater almost solely to tourists, you are in a good context to think back about the complicated issue of authenticity; if opportunity to do so presents itself, you might discuss this with the performers, to get their perspectives.

ACTIVITY 6.8 *Do you think of some music perform or you consume in terms of "authenticity?" If so, articulate your ideas about what makes it "authentic." Then consider the points above, relative to your ideas.*

TRANSCENDING BOUNDARIES

Ethnomusicologists are now vitally interested in the transcendence of boundaries by both people and music. This was greatly spurred by the burgeoning attention to popular music from the 1980s—musics that have been circulated and are circulating across just about every imaginable boundary. Indeed, music can be useful where people desire or need for boundaries to be transcended. In East Africa, for instance, where a number of ethnic groups with different value systems reside together, musical contexts provide important opportunities for negotiating differences. Negotiation takes the form of friendly competition, as popular entertainment events include musical performances such as song duels, choir competitions, drumming, and dance contests (see Barz's volume on East Africa in this series).

"Trans" is the operative prefix in "transcending boundaries." "Trans" is attached to terms for process, for instance. "Transculturation" has been espoused by the ethnomusicologist Margaret Kartomi to replace the term "acculturation" (1981: 234). Kartomi defines "transculturation" as "a process of cultural transformation marked by the influx of new culture elements and the loss or alteration of existing ones." Originally proposed by the Cuban anthropologist Fernando Ortiz, the term "transculturation" was intended to avoid the connotation of political hegemony implied by the older term, but it does more than that. It causes us to reconsider the matter of cultural encounter in the process of musical change. The term "transculturation" neither specifies nor even implies a physical location where the cultural transformation occurs. No people are specified, as in the "groups of individuals" in the definition of "acculturation" above. No circumstance of transmission is specified, as in "sustained first-hand contact." What is more or less specified is a sense of time, suggested by that contested word "culture." "Culture" usually implies some kind of history, some kind of continuity, some kind of "tradition." With the exception of that last factor, the term "transculturation" would seem appropriate to cover the circumstances of the circulation of musics worldwide.

ACTIVITY 6.9 *Since place, people, and circumstances of "influx" are not specified, you may find the idea of "transculturation" applicable to music that has been created within a diasporic group. Taking a music you are familiar with—salsa, gospel, Asian-American jazz, country-style polka, for instance—as a case study, write a brief essay arguing for or against the utility of the term "transculturation" as defined by Kartomi to guide your thinking about that music.*

"Trans" is the operative prefix again in terms that describe the transcending of boundaries of place, as in "transnational" and "translocal." This takes us to the lively issue of globalization, to which I shall return below.

The Mass Media. Circulation of knowledge—and its corollary, access to knowledge—without the necessity of a personal encounter has been the hallmark of the mass media—print; radio, and television; the various audio and visual formats that have been developed through time from cylinders to vinyls and on to possibilities of downloading from websites, filesharing, streaming services and digital media stores—all of which are important means for transcending boundaries. This was first approached in chapter 1 in the section on transmission by aural/oral, tactile, and visual means. The use of mass media is usually an element mentioned as key in the process of modernization that I discussed earlier in this chapter. Now, of course, the mass media are a potent force in the lives of just about everyone on the planet.

Many scholars share the opinion that the mass media's effects on musical cultures are neither positive nor negative in themselves; the effects depend on the uses to which they are put and the responses they engender. In a thought-provoking introduction to *Ethnicity, Identity and Music*, Martin Stokes suggests that the control of media systems by states, through ownership of the technology and its ability to exclude rival systems through censorship, is a tool of social control that few authoritarian states have overlooked. But media are not a sure means of enacting social control. A consumer can turn off a radio or television set, or tune to some other station.

Indeed, the media can be used by artists to undermine social control. Using song as a medium for speaking out about the suffering of the Tunisian people, twenty-two year old Tunisian rapper Hamada Ben-Amor ("El General") released his *"rais al-bled"* on YouTube early in the accelerating citizen protests that led ultimately to the downfall of President Zine al-Abedine Ben Ali in January 2011 (see *"el general, the voice of Tunisia," English subtitles*). Circulated among youth and students throughout the country via YouTube and perhaps other sites, *"rais al-bled"* is credited with contributing to the energy of the revolution. In early 2011 in Egypt as well, amid the first protests against President Hosni Mubarak, a number of rap songs celebrating and supporting the Egyptian revolution came out featuring Egyptian, UK, American and other rappers—one for instance on YouTube at *#Jan25Egypt—Omar Offendum*, another by Master Mimz, a woman of Moroccan descent living in Britain, who wrote "Back Down Mubarak" (http://www.youtube.com/watch?v=Hw0pxk_hFhY).

For musicians and their audiences, issues of the effects of media have never been simple. Changes in technology have had tangible effect even on TMI—"the music itself." The revolutionary, if de facto, privileging of one fixed rendition of a song—mistakes and all—frozen on a 78 RPM disc, as "the" authoritative version, confronted musicians in India and elsewhere with one of the most profound conceptual changes in the history of music. When recording of early discs began in India, the leading male musicians who had been given their *guru*'s repertoire during a long and arduous period of musical apprenticeship took to it slowly and reluctantly. A strong reason for their reluctance either to record or to broadcast their intellectual property was an intuitive apprehension that these unknown new technologies could reduce their direct control over the reception and consumption of their art—who could listen to it, under what circumstances, and what listeners could do with that music. They would, in effect, transcend the boundaries of the artists' authority (Vishwanathan and Allen 2004).

When scholars began to study music on a global basis and faced the tremendous power of the current Euro-America capitalist colonialism, the predictions of impending cultural "gray-out" forecast a dire future for music. However, new technologies no longer imply anywhere near the same kind of dependence upon large companies, and local industries all over the world are fostering local musical productions. Tiny niche markets can be catered to because it costs virtually nothing to store the music and make it available for download via the Internet (Anderson 2006). The issues involved here are huge. This takes me to the topic of globalization.

Globalization.   Globalization is the quintessential path to and result of transcending boundaries. "Globalization" suggests increasing connectivity around the world with respect to many spheres of life and the taking up of values and practices in multiple locations simultaneously. An early term for it in music scholarship was a "trans" word: "transnationalization." "The notion of globalization understood as transnationalization— taken often as a synonym for universalization, meaning Americanization for some, Japanization for others, and neo-colonialization for yet others— takes for granted the erasure of geopolitical boundaries and the transcendence of space through mass-mediated communication . . . instantly shifting population groups and their reconstituting of space relations in tandem with the intense trafficking of ideas and goods and the networking of people" (Guilbault: 2005, Vol. 5 p. 149). The term "translocal" has been useful for the ethnomusicologist Tom Turino as he suggests an analytical possibility for narrowing the often unrestricted use of the term "global." He reserves the term "global" to describe phenomena such as the contemporary system of nation-states that "literally or very nearly encompass the totality of the earth" (2000: 6).

For us ethnomusicologists who are Asianists particularly, the circumstances of global connectivity with integrated global markets, exchange of technology, values, and practices seem nothing recent. The limitation of the idea of "globalization" to the contemporary condition is short-sighted. We think of what is now called the Silk Road—which took goods and ideas in organized ways between the Mediterranean and the Pacific from the late second century BCE (until the late nineteenth century CE)—that was a significant factor in the flourishing of the great civilizations of China, Egypt, Mesopotamia, Persia, India, and Rome and helped to lay the foundations for the modern world. Religious beliefs of Christianity, Buddhism, and Islam, paper and silk manufacturing—and musical instruments—were carried back and forth across the landmass of the known world (as opposed to the whole world known now). One result was the dissemination of a type of plucked lute—the *oud* in West Asia, its successor *pipa* in China (CD track 2-41) and *biwa* in Japan (CD track 1-9), as well as its successor lutes of European musical practices.

Other great empires (little mentioned in Western tellings of history) have existed since, facilitating widespread connectivity with integrated markets over great geographic expanses. The Turkish Ottoman Empire (1299 to 1922 CE) is a case in point, as Rice discusses in his volume on Bulgaria, Marcus does in his volume on Egypt and the eastern Arab world, and Bates does in *Music in Turkey*. The Ottoman Empire caused cultural connections through the sharing of instruments, musical and poetic forms, concepts and practices. Colonial formations did the same in the nineteenth and twentieth centuries, causing the dissemination of European and Europe-derived instruments, musical and poetic forms, repertoire, concepts, and practices that are spoken to in the volumes on Trinidad, Mexico, Egypt, First Nations, Java, China, Japan, Korea and more. The Soviet bloc caused the same over enormous geographic expanses, including establishing models that would be followed by the communist government in China (see Lau 2008). The process of globalization is both historical and ongoing.

Covering over one-third of the earth's surface, the Pacific Ocean is the site of one of the most awe-inspiring migrations of human existence, a migration that resulted in wide cultural diversity but still managed connectivity sufficiently widespread to permit retention of perceived similarities and a sense of shared heritage as Pacific Islanders—a sense of "Pacificness" restricted neither by time nor place. That Pacificness is now shared around the world through diasporic communities and the forces of globalization (Diettrich, Moulin, and Webb 2011).

Worldwide integration through technology and market exchange is the hallmark of globalization, and we are beginning to understand that many, if not most, musics have emerged from processes of hybridization or fusion.

To stay in the Pacific Island region for a moment longer, a quintessential example of the circulation of technologies and goods and also musical practices is afforded by a "Welcome Song" from Moch Island, the smallest island in Chuuk State in Micronesia (CD track 2-47, fig. 6.1).

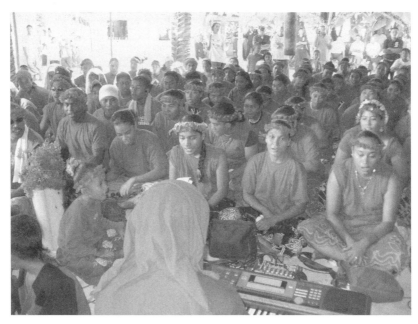

FIGURE 6.1   *Village group from Moch Island, Mortlock Islands (Chuuk State, Federated States of Micronesia), singing at a 2006 celebration.*   *(Photo courtesy of Brian Diettrich)*

On the occasion in 2006 when Brian Diettrich recorded this song, a day-long government inauguration was being held, with feasting and performances of new songs (text and music) specially prepared by villages. As you can hear, electronic keyboards are prominent in the song, along with the vibrant logogenic choral homophony so favored through the region.

In his *Subcultural Sounds: Micromusics of the West*, the ethnomusicologist Mark Slobin has commented on fusion while noting the diversity of styles in the music of the *klezmer* musician Andy Statman. A leading mandolinist in bluegrass/newgrass music in the 1970s, Statman helped to found a fledgling *klezmer* movement, "a drive by younger Jewish-American musicians of differing pasts and persuasions to forge a new 'ethnic' style based on their neglected 'Jewish' roots." In the next fifteen years Statman's music branched out past the older *klezmer* sound to include not only his old favorite, bluegrass, but beyond. He explained to a reporter from the *New York Times* that "the orchestra plays traditional Jewish European music, but we also flow freely into bits and pieces of what we like. . . . It's our own form of improvisation, and folk music and the bluegrass influence is right there"; Statman calls the result "Moroccan African Mongolian klezmer music" (12 April 1992). Slobin rejoins: "In figuring out this stance, remember that the 'traditional Jewish European music' itself was a blend of styles including Moldavian, Ukrainian, and shades of Balkan, all transformed in New York in the 1920s and 30s" (1993: x).

In addition to fusion, then, a preference for eclecticism can result from "intense trafficking of goods and ideas." For another example, the folklorist's definition of "folk song" is an artificial construction of no particular importance to traditional Irish singers themselves. These folksingers' repertoire includes music hall song, locally composed songs, country music, rock, rhythm and blues, rap, fusion styles, and others (Scott and Hast, 2004). Needless to say, this challenges notions of authenticity.

In addition to hybridity/fusion and eclecticism, the widespread "intense trafficking of goods and ideas" sometimes gives rise to a weakening or even loss of their original association with a sense of place. Scholars speak of a process of indigenization by which new cultural ideas or expressive objects may be adopted but made or used as something that functions within the existing structures, institutions, or values of a society. The Japanese genre of imperial court music (*gagaku*, CD track 1-9) is a case in point. Brought to Japan between the fifth and eighth centuries of the Common Era, when influences were strong from China and other Asian musics, a process of indigenization of the ensemble and its music from the ninth century was so effective that its foreignness has faded in the minds of most Japanese (Wade 2005). Indigenized in a much shorter period were social dances performed in square formation, first brought to Ireland by French dancing masters in the mid- to late nineteenth century; they were quickly indigenized in Ireland by the composition of new choreography and the use of Irish dance tunes for the accompanying music (Scott and Hast 2004: 5). In Ireland, too, the bouzouki has become a favorite instrument, so popular that an indigenized Irish variant is in regular production and general use. Christian choral music is another case in point wherever it is found (CD tracks 2-37, 2-42, 2-45). Finally, is not American jazz a quintessential product of a process of indigenization!

In addition, the intense trafficking of intellectual property challenges concepts of the ownership of "culture" (the right to intellectual property). Questions with far-reaching implications are being raised. Should you or should you not be able to download music from the Internet without worrying about who owns it? Should the composer of the national anthem of a new nation-state be paid royalties on the song, as one individual recently asserted to his government? Should DJs be able to sample copyrighted materials without permission? Should poorer, economically dependent nations be forced by the United States and other powerhouses in the entertainment industry to change their local copyright conventions to conform to international copyright conventions that clearly work to the advantage of the powerhouses (a process seen by scholars of popular music such as Jocelyne Guilbault as a new form of colonialism)?

ACTIVITY 6.10   *To think about the issues of intellectual property rights, write a quick summary of your own practices for acquiring the music you want to hear. Then use the Internet to find at least three commentaries by musicians on access to their music and at least three on the part of "the industry" or the legal profession to glimpse what it sees as the issues. Finally, analyze where your practices and concerns lie within those opinions.*

As transnational corporations these days create integrated global markets and change the nature of our cultural encounters, the importance of the nation-state and ethnic groupings as sources of identity and identification recedes somewhat. Individuals grow more cognizant of their multiple, shifting identities (multiple subjectivities) as they think in terms of their nationality as well as their ethnicity, their affiliation with others in a transnational diasporic "community" (Clifford 1994), or gender or religious affiliation or something else that supersedes localized boundaries. For ethnomusicologists, this has meant looking at the ways people are making music meaningful and useful as they situate themselves in a globally oriented world—transcending old boundaries with a sense of freedom or erecting new ones to gain some sense of control, as they explore multiple musical practices made available and visible through the media and make aesthetic choices for themselves.

The Local. Yet "the local" endures, in several senses of the word. For some transnational music, the original place associations of the music remain intact, however widely the musical style circulates and is played with creatively. Tango is Argentinian no matter where it is found; Irish music is Irish, no matter where it is made or who makes it; mariachi played in Los Angeles is recognized by everyone to be Mexican. The cultural space each occupies is linked to, but no longer dependent on, place.

The ways in which "the local" intersect with "the global" are myriad. Historians and other scholars see, for instance, a particularly urban cultural formation—a sense of shared "cosmopolitan" habits of belief, thought, technology use, practices, and the like—that can be found among particular groups of people across borders of different countries around the world. Ethnomusicologist Tom Turino has found a valuable analytic with which to look at Andean (particularly Peruvian) musical traditions and practices; see his book in the Global Music Series. He uses the term "cosmopolitan" to refer to objects, ideas, and cultural posi tions that are widely diffused throughout the world. Through the lens of music of Zimbabwe, in East Africa, however, he sees cosmopolitanism as always localized and always shaped by and somewhat distinct in each locale. "Cosmopolitan cultural formations are therefore always simultaneously local and translocal, i.e., situated in many sites which are not necessarily in geographical proximity; rather, they are connected by different forms of media, contact, and interchanges"— what he calls "cosmopolitan loops" (2000: 7–8). A "translocal music" refers to a particular music such as a repertoire or a genre, around which an affective community has formed in multiple local spots. Tango is a good example: a national craze in its native Argentina, it is also locally significant in locales as disparate as Istanbul, Tokyo, Helsinki, and Berlin. For scholars such as Turino who think about translocal music, connectivity among the communities is emphasized as well as local scenes themselves.

Whether global or cosmopolitan, global-local or local-translocal, musicians at the present time negotiate complex sets of relationships. The example of a Haitian group, Boukman Eksperyans, is given by the sociologist George Lipsitz in his important book *Dangerous Crossroads*:

> Ever since their recording debut in 1989, the members of Boukman Eksperyans have been making music rendering them both dangerous and endangered. . . . Their 1990 carnival song, "Ke'-m Pa Sote" ("My Heart Doesn't Leap, You Don't Scare me") played a part in the

popular revitalization of voudou, helping to spark [an insurgent movement]. By connecting the dance hall with the voudou temple, "Ke'-m Pa Sote" also united town dwellers and rural peasants in opposition to the corruption that permeates Haitian politics. . . . Through its music, Boukman Eksperyans inverted, subverted, and reappropriated for revolutionary ends the rituals and symbols long employed by the [Haitian paramilitary forces] to preserve tyrannical rule. By the same token, they attempted to use the commodity culture brought to Haiti over centuries by foreign investment and foreign invasion as a focal point of resistance to the exploitation and oppression perpetrated on the people by outside powers and the country's own comprador elite. . . . The same circuits of investment and commerce that bring low-wage jobs to Haiti's factories and fields carry the music of Boukman Eksperyans to a wider world audience. The same connections between U.S. multinationals and Haitian poverty that insures a perpetual presence on the island by the American security state also makes the visibility of Boukman Eksperyans in the U.S.A. a strategic resource for the group as they try to criticize their government and still stay alive. (1994: 8–10)

Boukman Eksperyans make music meaningful and useful not only in their lives, but in the lives of many others for whom they sing.

ACTIVITY 6.11 *Explore just how "global" your "local" musical choices are by making a systematic inventory. Visit the largest recording store in your location and make a catalog of the types of music available for purchase. Tune in to every radio station you can receive. Investigate all the explicitly artistic channels available through your TV. (Leave aside the Internet for this one.) Then situate yourself with regard to those choices, thinking about the perspectives discussed in this chapter.*

I have focused here on only a few of the lively issues that unify the case studies in this Global Music Series. My approach has been to contextualize them, to put them in the broader perspective of the intellectual work of the field of ethnomusicology. I now direct you to those case studies, where you can see the issues addressed in a "local" context.

CHAPTER 7

Thinking about Fieldwork

Study through fieldwork is a particular hallmark of ethnomusicology, and this chapter guides you in experiencing that for yourself. Basically, doing fieldwork is the process of learning about something directly from people. Fieldwork provides an opportunity to learn how people experience music and express culture.

Where is the field and what is the work? Historically, "the field" meant any place other than a library (where materials recorded in some form are the primary source). And because most ethnomusicologists worked someplace other than in their own culture, "the field" meant somewhere distant. In reality, however, "the field" encompasses the library and the Internet as well, because the best way to start is to find what has already been reported on the subject. In the broadest and most pragmatic terms, the "field" is anywhere we can learn about a topic, including with our own family and friends. Our home communities offer abundant field locations.

The "work" in fieldwork has always meant any kind of activity that contributes to learning about music. Take the process of locating sources, for instance: early recordings of calypso that were important for Shannon Dudley's book on carnival music in Trinidad (2004) were none too easy to find, but necessary for his tracking of the sociocultural meanings of steelband (chapter 6 herein: p. 177). Collecting of tunes has been hugely important to most everyone who has worked on Irish music (CD tracks 1-3, 1-23). Meeting musicians and audience members is another kind of locating of sources, as Ruth Stone did in order to learn what Liberian musicians and audiences valued in performance (chapter 3: p. 94). Beverley Diamond was fortunate to locate Inuit and First Nations peoples who would welcome her into their communities for fieldwork, including the indoor spaces where she could observe the juggling game (CD track 2-44).

Doing a lot of observing is another aspect of the work in fieldwork. (Remember visual learning that was discussed in chapter 1.) Attending numerous concerts provided Scott Marcus a window into the dynamics of the performer-audience relationship in Egyptian music (Chapter 5: p. 149).

A third example of activity in fieldwork—and one that most ethno-musicologists treasure—is making music; you can learn a great deal by being a participant observer. Perhaps more importantly, when we put ourselves in the position of being a student of music along with other music makers, our experience is one of sharing rather than staring, and our relationships become less distant.

Even casual conversation about music turns into "work" whenever we begin to think about it systematically rather than in random fashion and to keep a record of what we have learned. Another term for hanging out at that point is "field research." You read of Rajna Klaser LeDoux's experience with her vocal teacher in Turkey (Chapter 4: p. 117), and you tried experiencing Korean rhythm as Donna Kwon did in her study of the percussion ensemble practice that is pictured in figure 3.2. If George Ruckert and Matthew Allen had not studied North Indian and South Indian musics as practitioners, they could not have become so comfortable with those formidable (to me) rhythmic practices (CD tracks 2-7, 2-14, 2-39, and 2-40). Lisa Gold could explain the challenge of coordinating sudden stops of *angsel* because she has years of experience as a participant observer playing Balinese gamelan (Chapter 5: p. 158, CD track 2-46).

Learning from people can be fruitful and fun if three guiding principles are followed:

1. Keep focusing on the purpose of your project, while being open-minded to change.

2. Remember that you are seeking to learn from others, not seeking to prove something you have already decided is the case.

3. Imagine yourself in the position of any person with whom you are consulting. What kinds of questions would you enjoy (or not enjoy) being asked, for instance? Here the "golden rule" really applies: treat others as you want them to treat you! This is a matter of the ethics of fieldwork.

PICKING A PROJECT

WORD OF ADVICE: *For your project choose something you can easily manage to do. It does not need to be a complicated topic; it should be a straightforward starting point. A broad topic should be narrowed. That is, your project should be small scale and short term.*

Anticipating that you may wonder what I mean by "a complicated project," I picked just one from this book as an illustration. In Chapter 1 (p. 16), I cited Tim Rice's reading of the politics of wedding music in communist-period Bulgaria. For Rice to have gained that understanding took considerable field research, i.e., it was a very complicated project. He had to have investigated the history of Bulgarian Muslim communities and their musical repertoires. He had to learn about government policies, how they were enforced, and what the effects were. He also had to gain knowledge of the nonminority Bulgarians who were the clients of the Roma musicians in order to sense the hopes for freedom they harbored and explore why music other than their own "folk music" served better to express them. All that took years.

The project you pick can be almost anything, as long as you keep it small scale and short term. A project could be derived, for example, from any number of points made in this book that particularly interest you. Activity 3.1 (p. 71) is intended to point you in that direction. For another example, relating to the section on dissemination of musical knowledge, if you take or have taken instruction on an instrument or voice, you might shape a project around your teacher's pedagogy. How were or are you taught? What materials does your teacher use, and why were they chosen? Does your teacher teach other students the way she or he teaches you? What has been your teacher's learning experience, and what is its relation to the present teaching methods? To do this project, you would draw on your own participant observation, interview your teacher and other students, and perhaps observe lessons of other students (with permission of both the teacher and the students, of course).

Thinking from the people point of view, a good place to start might be doing a life history, to learn about someone's musical experience and the meaning of music in his or her life. Activity 1.1 could be the basis for such a project, for instance.

- Is there a member of your family who loves music, with whom you have never talked about it? This might be a good way to get to know a grandparent or aunt or uncle better.

- What is the musical experience of someone you know from another culture?

- Is music meaningful and useful to them, and if so, in what ways?

Thinking from the topical point of view, identify something having to do with music that you are really interested in and build a project around it. For example:

- If you play in a band or sing in a chorus, explore the history of the group: When and why was it founded? What sort of people have belonged to it, and why? Who has supported it financially? Where has it performed? How does it fit into the general music scene in the area?

- Consider the same sort of project, but with a group on campus that you do not participate in. This presents a greater challenge with regard to locating sources.

- If there is a kind of music you really love, learn if there is a local group that performs it and find out about "living that music" from the music makers' perspectives. One of my students studied the reasons why other students play in pickup bands. She looked into points raised in this book—choice of music to play, ideas about skill level, their motivation for making the music, their intended audience and what relationship they envisage with that audience in their musicking, and the like.

- If you like instruments, look for an instrument maker or repairer in your vicinity and learn about them from that perspective. One of my students found a local luthier to interview and observe at work. First, however, he studied about the construction of lutes in printed sources, so he could build on a body of information and therefore ask better questions. He followed up on such questions as what could affect the sound of the instrument, how the pitch was set, the specifications an intended buyer (if any) might have made, the economics of instrument production, and other questions.

- If you are interested in another field of study, try a topic that combines it with music. One of my students investigated the correlation of abilities in math and music.

- Propose a hypothesis to test. One of my students hypothesized that studying music helps improve concentration.

- If you have become interested in any music unfamiliar to you before studying with this book, design a project that will take you into it more deeply. This is a good opportunity to learn more about a culture other than your own, for example.

WORD OF ADVICE: *Dedicate a notebook or computer file or some other repository to this project right from this early stage. I prefer something easily portable because I find that I need to use it at unexpected as well as anticipated times—when an idea suddenly occurs to me or someone makes a good suggestion that I might pursue, for instance.*

WORD OF ADVICE: *Make a list in your journal of several possible projects. Many things can happen, so you need a backup idea.*

WORD OF ADVICE: *Keep a record in your journal of all ideas and activities, with entries dated. Note even things you try that do not work, such as effort to connect with a consultant.*

PLANNING THE PROJECT

Once you have an idea for a project, you should plan how to carry it out. Asking yourself some questions is a good way to test the viability of your project—whether or not you can manage to do it. If it becomes clear that one project is not easily doable, repeat this questioning process for other projects on your list until you find the right one for your interests and circumstances.

What: What sorts of activities will I need to carry out to do this project? Will it be sufficient to interview persons, or will I need to attend performances as well, or just hang out?

Who: Who will I need to speak to—one person or several? If one, is that person likely to welcome my questions and have time for me? If several, how many and why? Do I want to ask the same questions of each one, or do I want to learn about something different from each one?

When: Will it be easy to arrange a time to see the people I need to see? Where is the flexibility in my schedule? Can I adjust to their schedule, since they are doing me a favor? If they can meet only at night, for instance, can I manage that? If hanging out or volunteering to help with something in return is important, how much time can I allow for that?

Where: Where will I need to go to carry out this project? If it is at some distance, how will I get there? How much time will it take to get there and back? How far is too far?

How: What kind of technology will I need? A camera or a phone with photo capability or even video? Should I have a recorder of some sort to document interviews or to have something to play back to someone for stimulating discussion or double-checking what I think I heard?

WORD OF ADVICE: *If you will need to use technological devices, be sure to think ahead. There's nothing worse than a dead battery at a crucial moment. And don't forget to ask permission in advance to use any technology. If someone does not want you to use it, be ready to accept that cheerfully and go to Plan B.*

Cost: Is this going to cost something monetarily? Do I need to make toll calls to speak with people? Do I have to pay mass transit fares or buy gas or cross a toll bridge to get somewhere? Do I need to purchase a hosting gift if I visit someone's home? Pay for tickets for a performance or two? Have equipment such as recorders and cameras and supplies for them?

DOING THE PROJECT

WORD OF ADVICE: *In your journal, make a tentative schedule for doing the project—by when you need to have done what. It's a good idea to work backward from whatever deadline you may have.*

One caveat: *If you have any plan to publish a written report or research essay (see "Finishing the Project"), it may be required on your campus to get the approval of your institution's review board (IRB) before you do the project. You, as the principal investigator, and your teacher, as the faculty adviser, must acknowledge responsibility for the conduct of the study and the protection of the rights and welfare of the human subjects who are directly or indirectly involved in the project. The requirement to get approval and the nature of the application clearly relate mostly to scientific research, but the concerns raised are appropriate for some ethnomusicological research as well. If approval of your project is required, you need to allot time in your tentative schedule for the approval process.*

The application will cause you to consider something very important—the possible ramifications of your "field research" on the lives of other people. This you need to have thought through thoroughly before beginning the project. You also need to consider the matter of reciprocity—"giving back" in some way appropriate to your means and to the situation. Sometimes the very fact that you are paying attention to something valued is a kind of reciprocity. This, you need to work out both sensitively and pragmatically.

Sometimes the most time-consuming part of a project is establishing the contact with the person or persons you need to speak with. Figure out before you call just how you are going to introduce yourself. Be ready to say who you are and why you are calling (see guiding principle 1 on p. 196). Do not forget to keep a record of each call you make or message you write—even if you do not reach the person or get a response. Be persistent: after waiting a reasonable length of time (being considerate of your consultant and having decided how much time you can afford to wait, given your schedule), call again; try several times within two weeks. If you try several times within two weeks and never connect, then you know you had probably better not count on meeting that person. If you do connect, and the person really does not seem to want to meet with you, follow guiding principle 3 and graciously say, "Thank you for your time anyway." Move on to Plan B.

> **WORD OF ADVICE:** *Call or write or—even better—go to the research location* now! *Do not put it off. Begin making contacts even before you have taken some of the steps suggested below.*

Here is where "the field" is located in the library. (I hope you resist the temptation to completely replace the library with the Internet.) Search for studies already published that might guide you in your project. If, for instance, you are going to do a life history, find some published life histories that are based on interviews to get the flavor of such research; jazz history offers many such accounts, for instance. If you are going to learn about a musical organization, find a published history of a musical organization and analyze what questions were asked in order to write that history. If you are going to interview someone from another culture, do some basic reading about that culture and listening to its music. You will learn much more if you build on something. Keep notes on it all in your journal with clear citations of where you found the information and full information on the sources. For assistance with the format for bibliographic information, use as a guide the entries in my References section for this book.

Creating a survey questionnaire is one way to conduct research; conducting an interview is another. Before you meet with anyone, make a tentative list of questions you will work into the conversation. Formulate questions so that you are not leading the respondent to an answer. Practice interview or survey questions on a friend. You may discover that they are too general, too detailed, too personal, unclear, or drawing answers that are not the sort you were looking for. Keep honing the questions as you do the research; you need good questions to get good answers.

Think ahead about how you are going to capture what you hear in a conversation. Do you hope to record the conversation? Ethics dictate that you must not assume that it is OK and, besides, if your consultant is nervous about it, that could affect the quality of the conversation. If you or the person you are meeting prefers it, be satisfied with your note-taking; jot down as much as you can manage. Have the machine and any supplies ready, however, in case you prefer and are permitted to record. Do not depend on plugging anything in; also, insert batteries and test the machine before you need to use it. (Take extra ones, too!)

You'll find it useful to jot quick notes even while recording, to cue your follow-up questions.

The same ethics pertain for making a visual record of some sort. Get permission first. I find that most consultants do not mind having their photograph taken, at least as a kind of documentation, and appreciate receiving a copy as a follow-up thank you (and an element of reciprocity). Before you end your meeting, show your consultant what you have written and get signed permission to use it in your final project.

For further guidence, a list is the best help.

- Make a checklist of everything you need to take when you go to meet with someone. It is very useful if you have a sudden opportunity.

- When you are interviewing someone, listen carefully. Follow up on things they say, as well as asking your planned questions.

- In all your relationships with people, imagine yourself in their places. Show sensitivity in your interactions. Act with others as you want them to act with you!

- Label and date your recordings. Be sure to get people's names right. Keep a list of them in your notebook.

- Keep a list of the photographs you take.

- As soon as possible after meeting with someone, add to the notes you took during the interview anything you forgot or did not have time to record. Also, summarize in your journal the most important things you learned. Then write up your impressions of that person as an informant—were they knowledgeable, vague, helpful, reluctant, and so on—as a guide for using the information they gave you. Discerning whether a person is a relative "insider" or "outsider" can be helpful (but you must define what you mean by those two statuses). If you try to do your project on the Internet, you will not be able to do the same sort of evaluating of your source that you can do in person.

In the case study volumes of this Global Music Series, you will find the authors situating themselves with regard to their insider-outsider status. Sometimes that status is utterly clear on everyone's part, as in "We, Dora Hast and Stan Scott, are outsiders here, American musicians with a long-standing passion for Irish traditional music. Jerry's invitation [to the session] on this night in early June, 1997 is a pleasant surprise" (2004: 1). Sometimes it is less clear: "At a village dance I attended in the Pirin region in 1973, I noticed a man staring at me. . . . He demanded gruffly, "Who are you?" I explained that I was an American student spending the year in Bulgaria researching traditional music. He thought about this a minute before exclaiming, "You lie! . . . You speak Bulgarian and you dance Bulgarian dances. Therefore you are a Bulgarian" (Rice 2004: 44). The question of who is an insider, who an outsider, is sometimes related to the issue of authenticity, as in Activity 6.4. It can be quite political and a matter of some sensitivity to which you need to be attuned.

- Figure out some way to double-check information you receive—by asking a second person the same question or checking a newspaper article perhaps.
- Reread this chapter periodically to keep you on track.
- Enjoy yourself.

FINISHING THE PROJECT

To finish your project, plan some kind of oral or written presentation. Your journal, summaries and further notes, tapes, photos, questionnaires, and double checks are your resources for this. Do not forget to articulate some sense of your experience, as well as the results of your study.

- Organize an oral presentation.
- Create some kind of art: a long poem or series of poems, a song, a visual essay, a painting or a video, a theater piece.
- Write a report on your project or essay on the research project. Sending a write-up to the people with whom you worked is a good and ethical thing to do.
- However you decide to do it, be sure to follow up with your consultants to thank them.

In addition to having learned about something that interests you, by carrying out your fieldwork project you will have learned more about how people make music meaningful and useful in their lives. Ideally, your project will bring some benefit to the persons with whom you collaborated.

Glossary of Musical Terms

Acceleration   Speeding up the pace of the basic beats.

Acculturation   A theory of change in the process of cultural encounters.

Ādi tāla   South Indian meter of 8 counts subdivided 4 + 2 + 2.

Aerophone   Instrument whose primary sound-producing medium is vibrating air.

Aesthetics   Artistic values.

Accompanist   Person performing a supporting musical part.

Affect   Expressive capacity

Ālāp-joṛ-jhālā-gat   North Indian instrumental form.

Alto   Lower female voice; instrumental range below soprano.

Angsel   In Balinese music, a cue, sign, or articulation of a dance movement and music marked by a sudden rhythmic break or accent.

Arpeggio   Pitches of a chord sounded sequentially.

Assymetrical meter   Rhythmic grouping with subgroups of irregular numbers of counts.

Atsimevu   Lead drum in West African *gahu* ensemble

Aural transmission   Learning by hearing.

Axatse   Shaker in West African *gahu* ensemble

Ballad   In folk music terminology, a narrative song.

Bar   In Western meter and notation, one metric group of beats (also called MEASURE).

Bass   Lowest vocal or instrumental range.

Ba yin   Ancient Chinese classification system for instruments.

Beat In rhythm, consistent equal-length durations, in some systems long or short subgroups of a rhythm; in pitch, periodic variations in amptitude due to the interference between two sound waves with different frequencies.

Berimbau Brazilian musical bow used in *capoeira*.

Binary form Musical form of two different sections (AB).

Bridge On a chordophone, a component that holds the string up from the main body of the instrument.

Cadence Musical term for an ending.

Call and response Generally, the juxtaposition of solo with group; more specifically, a musical repartee between parts.

Canon Strict imitative polyphony, with the identical melody appearing in each voice but at staggered intervals (*see* ROUND).

Capoeira Brazilian dance/martial art/game with musical accompaniment.

Changdan In Korean music, rhythmic cycle or rhythmic grouping of accented and unaccented beats.

Changgo A Korean two-headed hour glass-shaped drum.

Chungmori changdan A Korean rhythmic pattern.

Chord In tonal music, three or more pitches sounding together in a functional way; intervals stacked vertically.

Chordophone Instrument whose primary sound-producing medium is a vibrating string.

Chord progression A sequence of chords that structure the music.

Chorus In musical structure, long refrain added to song verse; main section of a popular song.

Chromatic scale Scale using all twelve Western pitches within an octave.

Classification A category with clear criteria.

Clave In Caribbean and Latin American music, a rhythmic pattern repeated without change as a rhythmic foundation for a musical selection.

Colotomic meter Articulation of the metric grouping by one or more instruments in a Southeast Asian ensemble.

Composing Creating music, whether in the mind or in writing, whether to be repeated in the same form or subject to variation.

Concertina A free-reed type of aerophone popular in Irish music

Concertmaster/Concertmistress Male or female leader of the violin section of a European orchestra who functions as assistant to the conductor.

Consonant From medieval European thought, intervals or chords that sound relatively stable and free of tension; generally, an aesthetically pleasing interval or chord.

Corpophone One's body used as a musical instrument.

Corrido Mexican and Mexican American narrative song genre.

Culture (musical) Ways in which people make music meaningful and useful in their lives.

Dalang In Indonesian theater, a puppet master.

Dapu In Chinese music, the process of a musician realizing a prescriptive notation in sound.

Deceleration Slowing down the pace of the basic beats.

Descriptive notation Notation intended to document how the music should "sound".

Diatonic scale Scale comprising some arrangement of half and whole steps.

Didjeridu Australian aborigine aerophone.

Dissonant From medieval European thought, intervals or chords that sound relatively tense and unstable; generally, a discordant interval or chord.

Di-tze Chinese flute-type aerophone.

Dominant In tonal music, the fifth pitch up from a tonic; root of a dominant chord (V).

Downbeat In Western meter, count 1.

Drone One or more pitches sounding persistently.

Dumm In Arab music, a mnemonic syllable for the deepest or lowest sound a drum can produce.

Dynamics The volume of sound.

Electronophone Instrument whose primary sound-producing medium is electricity.

Enharmonic pitches In tonal music, two names for the same pitch.

Ensemble Musical group.

Fasil   Turkish urban art music genre

Filulu   A Tanzanian flute-type aerophone.

Flat   In notation, a sign indicating that the note to which it is attached is to be played or sung a half step lower.

Form   The design of a musical selection.

Forró   Northeast Brazilian dance genre.

Frequency (pitch)   In acoustics, rate of vibration (cycles per second) in a string, column of air, or other sound-producing body.

Fret   On a lute-type of cordophone, a raised appendage on the neck of an instrument that ensures precise pitch production when the string makes contact with it.

Functional harmony   Chords as used in the Western tonal system.

Gagaku   Japanese court instrumental ensemble and repertoire.

Gahu   West African secular dance drumming practice.

Gamelan   In Indonesian music, "ensemble".

Gankogui   Double bell in West African *gahu* ensemble.

Gender   Cultural constructions of maleness and femaleness.

Genre   A type of music.

Gong ageng   Largest gong in Indonesian *gamelan*.

Groove   The way ensemble musicians interact during performance.

Guitarrón   Mexican bass-sized chordophone in guitar family.

Half step   Interval of a MINOR SECOND.

Harmony   Pitches heard together; in tonal music, system of functional chords.

Heptatonic   Systematic set of seven pitches.

Hertz   The SI unit of frequency defined as the number of cycles per second of a periodic phenomenon.

Heterogeneous ensemble sound   Combining instruments with different timbres.

Heterophony   "Different voices"; musical texture of one melody performed almost simultaneously and somewhat differently by multiple musicians.

Hichiriki   Double reed aerophone in the Japanese *gagaku* ensemble.

Hijāz   A particular tetrachord used in Egyptian modes, and the name of a melodic mode.

Hīmen tārava   Multi-part compositions sung in Tahiti by large choirs.

Hocket   *See* INTERLOCKING PARTS.

Homogeneous ensemble sound   Combining instruments with similar timbres.

Homophony   "Same voice"; musical texture of block chords, or melody with chords.

Idiomaticity   Musical material resulting partially from an instrument's capability.

Idiophone   Instrument whose primary sound-producing medium is the body of the instrument itself.

Imagined community   A socially-constructed community.

Imitative polyphony   Musical texture of one instrument or voice "imitating" the material of another part.

Improvisation   Result of a musician exercising relatively great flexibility with given material.

Instrumentation   Instruments (including voice) used in a musical selection.

Interlocking parts   Texture of one musical part subdivided among several musicians; in a polyrhythmic texture, coordination among multiple musical parts.

Interval   Distance spanned between two pitches.

Intonation   Sense of pitch placement.

Īqā   Arabic term for "rhythmic mode."

Jiangnan sizhu   Chinese ensemble music from the area south of the Yangtze River around the city of Shanghai.

Jig   Irish dance genre.

Kabuki   Popularist type of traditional Japanese theater.

Kaganu   Support drum in West African *gahu* ensemble.

Kalimba   South African Nsenga idiophone, commonly called "thumb piano."

Kargyraa   Deep voice style of Tuvan throat-singing.

Kempul   Hanging gong in Central Javanese *gamelan*.

Kenong   Large kettle gong in Central Javanese *gamelan*.

Ketawang   A colotomic form in Central Javanese music.

Kethuk   Small, relatively low-pitched gong in Central Javanese *gamelan*.

Key   In tonal music, a tonality named after the main pitch.

Khoomei   Tuvan solo-voice throat-singing tradition.

Kidi   Support drum in West African *gahu* ensemble.

Klezmer   Term invented c. 1980 for largely instrumental music animating celebrations of eastern European Jews.

Kompak   Balinese ensemble music aesthetic.

Komungo   Korean zither-type chordophone.

Kotekan   In Balinese music, term for interlocking parts.

Koto   Japanese zither-type chordophone.

Kutkŏri changdan   A korean rhythmic grouping of twelve counts in moderately fast tempo.

Leading tone   In tonal music, the pitch a half step above or below the tonic.

Logogenic   Orientation to word rather than to melody in texted music.

Major scale   Western scale with whole steps and half steps arranged W W H W W W H within an octave.

Major second   Western whole step; interval spanning two half steps.

Makam   See *Maqām*.

Maqām   (Turkish, *makam*) Term for melodic mode in the Arabic language.

Maqām Rast   A melodic mode of Egypt and the eastern Arab world.

Maqsum   An Egyptian rhythmic mode.

Mariachi   Mexican and Mexican American ensemble.

Measure   In Western meter and notation, one metric group of beats (also called BAR).

Melodic mode   Generally, pitch material for melody bearing particular expressive qualities; in Western music, one of several species of the diatonic scale.

Melody   Any selection of pitches in succession. "A melody" is a particular succession of pitches, see motive, tune.

Membranophone   Instrument whose primary sound-producing medium is a vibrating skin.

Metallophone   Xylophone-type idiophone with metal keys.

Meter   Regular grouping of beats.

Metric cycle   Repeating articulation of a grouping of beats.

Microtone   Term for an interval smaller than the Western half step.

Minor second   Smallest interval in Western music; also called *half step*.

Mnemonic   Formula (in music, usually syllable) to aid in memorizing.

Modulation   In a piece of tonal music, shifting from one tonal center to another.

Monophony   "One voice"; musical texture of a single melodic line and nothing else.

Motive   Melodic or rhythmic fragment used to construct a larger musical entity; THEME.

Mṛdaṅgam   In South Indian music, a barrel-shaped drum.

Muqaddima   Term for the pre-composed instrumental introduction that is part of the formal structure in some song forms of Arab music.

Musician   A person who experiences music as a practice.

Musiqa   Term in Arabic language for secular music.

Nahāwand   A particular tetrachord used in Egyptian melodic modes, and the name of a melodic mode.

Netori   Term for a prelude in Japanese *gagaku* music.

Ney   In Arab music, a flute-type aerophone.

Nonmetrical rhythm   Not organized in regular rhythmic groupings.

Octave   In Western music, interval spanning eight pitches, the highest duplicating the pitch name of the lowest; generally, the distance between two pitches in which the frequency of the second pitch is twice that of the first.

Oral transmission   Teaching by sounding—speaking, singing, or playing.

Orientalism   System of European discourse about the Middle East (West Asia) and India (South Asia) (Edward Said).

"Oriental" scale   Nondiatonic scale with major, minor, and augmented seconds arranged in the pattern m A m M m A m.

Ostinato   Constantly recurring melodic, rhythmic, or harmonic motive.

Overtone series   Like "harmonic series," referring to the constituent frequencies of sounds but numbered differently, the first overtone being the second harmonic.

Parlando rubato   Nonmetrical rhythm.

Part-counterpart   Form in which one part is responded to by one or more supporting parts.

Pedal point   In Western classical music, a temporary or short-term drone.

Pentatonic   Systematic set of five pitches.

Perfect pitch   Exceptional aural memory for pitch intonation.

Phrase   Usually, melodic unit; a musical thought.

Pipa   Chinese lute-type chordophone.

Pî phât   Thai instrumental ensemble.

Pitch   The quality of "highness" or "lowness" of sound; a sound produced at a certain number of cycles per second.

Pitch area   Acceptable range of intonation for a pitch.

Pitch hierarchy   Some pitch(es) in a pitch set given more importance.

Pitch register   An area in a pitch range.

Polyphony   "Multiple voices"; musical texture of two or more melodic parts performed together.

Polyrhythm   Musical texture of multiple rhythmic patterns performed simultaneously.

Prescriptive notation   Minimalist notation that gives instruction on how to sound out the music (see also tablature).

Program music   Instrumental selection associated with a story or other extramusical idea.

Pulse   Consistent equal-length durations.

Qānūn   In Middle Eastern music, a struck box-zither type of chordophone.

Qawwālīyā   North Indian or Pakistani singer of Muslim Sufi music.

Quarter tone   Term used loosely to refer to pitches at an interval smaller or larger than those in the Western scale in Arab music, half-flat.

Qur'ān Sacred text revealed to the Prophet Muhammad.

Rāga Term for melodic mode in India's music.

Range A total span; the distance from the highest to the lowest pitch.

Rast A particular tetrachord used in Egyptian melodic mode, and the name of a melodic mode.

Recitative Singing that imitates and emphasizes in both pitch and rhythm the natural flow of speech.

Reel Irish dance genre in duple meter.

Refrain Repeating text and melody added to a verse.

Repertoire Group of pieces that are linked in some way.

Rest A momentary silence in music; in notation, a sign indicating momentary silence.

Rhythm Any succession of durations. "A rhythm" is a particular succession of durations.

Rhythmic mode Rhythmic grouping bearing particular expressive qualities.

Riqq In Middle Eastern music, a frame-drum (tambourine) type of membranophone.

Ritardando (or *ritard*, Italian) Gradual slowing of the pace of the basic beats.

Roma Peoples formerly referred to as gypsies.

Round Tune designed to be performed as a CANON.

Rubato Ebb and flow in the pace of the basic beat.

Salsa Popular Caribbean dance music genre.

Salvesein ami Melanesian presbyterian hymnody with movement.

Samba Brazilian popular music genre.

Sanjo A Korean solo instrumental form.

Saron Indonesian metallophone-type idiophone.

Scale Pitch set (and therefore intervals) presented in straight ascending or descending order.

Scat syllables Vocables used by jazz singers.

Selection A piece or performance.

Sharp In musical notation, a sign indicating that the note it precedes is to be played a half step higher.

Shō   A Japanese free-reed type aerophone

Siku   Peruvian panpipe (flute-type) aerophone.

Sikuri   Peruvian ensemble of three sizes of *siku*.

Sitār   North Indian lute-type chordophone

Sizhu   Chinese ensemble of stringed and wind instruments.

Sogo   Support drum in West African *gahu* ensemble

Solfège   Syllables used to name pitches; sometimes, mnemonic drum syllables.

Solo   Performance by one person; a musical part meant to stand out.

Soundscape   Sound(s) that form or arise from an environment.

Sonata form   A tripartite musical form of Viennese origin.

Soprano   Highest vocal or instrumental pitch range.

Speed   The rate of the basic beats.

Staff notation   Western system of notating music on a five-line staff.

Steelband   Trinidadian ensemble featuring tuned metal pans.

Strophic form   Form consisting of an entire melody repeated.

Style   The combination of qualities that create distinctiveness.

Subdominant   In tonal music, the fourth pitch up from a tonic; root of a subdominant chord (IV).

Syakuhati   (*shakuhachi*) Japanese flute-type aerophone.

Syamisen   (*shamisen*) Japanese lute-type chordophone.

Syncopation   In terms of beat, stress between the beats, offbeat; in terms of meter, accenting a beat where stress is not expected.

Tablā   In North Indian music, a drum

Tablature   Type of notation that gives technical performing instructions.

Tactile transmission   Teaching by touch.

Takk   In Arab music, the mnemonic syllable for the high-pitched sound produced when striking a drum where the head meets the rim of the instrument.

Tāla   Term for India's system for organizing measured musical time.

Tambura   A Bulgarian lute-type chordophone.

Tānpūra A hybrid lute-zither-type chordophone used to produce a drone in India's music.

Tarab In Arab music, the aesthetic goal of an ecstatic state.

Tempo *See* SPEED.

Tenor Higher pitch range of a male singer or instrumental pitch range below alto.

Tetrachord Four-note scalar segment with first and fourth pitches separated by the interval of a fourth.

Texture Musical relationships among ensemble parts.

Theka A one-cycle-long stroking pattern by which drummers articulate a North Indian metric grouping.

Theme The basic subject matter of a piece of music.

Through-composed Form in which musical content changes from beginning to end of a selection.

Tihāī A North Indian cadential practice.

Timbre Particular quality of sound; tone color.

Tīntāl A North Indian meter of sixteen counts.

Tonal center Some pitch in a pitch set given most importance in melody; key note, fundamental, primary pitch, tonic.

Tonal music The system organized around having a functional tonic.

Tone *See* PITCH.

Tone cluster A vertical set of pitches, without the functional implications of chords in the tonal system.

Tonic A tonal center; in Western music, the fundamental pitch of a scale or key; root of a tonic chord (I).

Topeng A Balinese dance form.

Toque A rhythm pattern played on *berimbau* in Brazilian *capoeira*.

Triad In tonal music, a simultaneous sounding of pitches a third and a fifth above the root of a chord; generally, a simultaneous sound of three pitches.

Transculturation Term for a process of change in cultural encounters.

Tune A relatively singable, fairly short, complete melody.

Tuning Pitch(es) to which an instrument is set.

Unison   All performing the same part.

Vihuela   (Mexican *mariachi*) Five-stringed lute in guitar family, always strummed for rhythm.

Vocables   Song text syllables that are not linguistically meaningful.

Visual transmission   Teaching and learning by visual means including music notation, graphical, film, and the like.

Waltz   Dance in triple meter.

Whole step   Interval of a MAJOR SECOND.

References

Anderson, Benedict. 1991. *Imagined Communities: Reflections on the Origin and Spread of Nationalism.* Rev. ed. London: Verso.

Anderson, Chris. 2006. Newyork: Hyperion.

Baily, John. 1985. "Music Structure and Human Movement." In *Musical Structure and Cognition*, 237–58. London: Academic Press.

Baines, Anthony, and Klaus Wachsmann, trans. 1961. "Erich M. Von Hornbostel and Curt Sachs Classification of Musical Instruments." *Galpin Society Journal* 14(3):3–29.

Barth, Frederick, ed. 1969. *Ethnic Groups and Boundaries: The Social Organisation of Culture Difference.* London: Allen and Unwin.

Barz, Greogory. 2004. *Music in East Africa: Experiencing Music, Expressing Culture.* New York: Oxford University Press.

Bates, Eliot. 2011. *Music in Turkey: Experiencing Music, Expressing Culture.* New York: Oxford University Press.

Berliner, Paul. 1978. *The Soul of Mbira.* Berkeley and Los Angeles: University of California Press.

———. 1994. *Thinking in Jazz: The Infinite Art of Improvisation.* Chicago: University of Chicago Press.

Berrios-Miranda, Marisol. 1999. "The Significance of *Salsa* Music to National and Pan-Latino Identity." Ph.D. diss. University of California, Berkeley.

Blacking, John. 1955. "Eight Flute Tunes from Butembo, East Belgian Congo." *African Music* 1(2):24–52.

———. 1961. "Patterns of Nsenga *kalimba* music." *African Music* 2(4):3–20.

———. 1997. *How Musical is Man?* Seattle: University of Washington Press.

Bordieu, Pierre. 1977. *Outline of a Theory of Practice.* Cambridge: Cambridge University Press.

Brinner, Benjamin. 1995. *Knowing Music, Making Music.* Chicago: University of Chicago Press.

———. 2008. *Music in Central Java: Experiencing Music, Expressing Culture.* New York: Oxford University Press.

Browner, Tara. 2002. *Heartbeat of the People: Music and Dance of the Northern Pow-Wow.* Urbana: Universal of Illinois Press.

Buia, Carole. 2001. "Best of Both Worlds." *Time*, special issue, *Music Goes Global*, 158(14) (fall):10–12.

Certeau, M. de. 1984. *The Practice of Everyday Life.* Berkeley and Los Angeles: University of California Press.

Clifford, James. 1988. *Predicament of Culture: Twentieth Century Ethnography, Literature and Art.* Cambridge, Mass.: Harvard University Press.

————. 1994. "Diasporas." *Cultural Anthropology* 9(3):302–38.

Coplan, David. 1990. "Ethnomusicology and the Meaning of Tradition." In *Ethnomusicology and Modern Music History*, edited by Stephen Blum et al. 35–48. Urbana: University of Illinois Press.

"Criteria for Acculturation." 1961. In *Report of the Eighth Congress of the International Musicological Society*, 139–49. Kassel: Bärenreiter.

Danielson, Virginia. 1997. *The Voice of Egypt: Umm Kulthûm, Arabic Song, and Egyptian Society in the Twentieth Century.* Chicago: University of Chicago Press.

Diamond, Beverley. 2008. *Native American Music in Eastern North America: Experiencing Music, Expressing Culture.* New York: Oxford University Press.

Diettrich, Brian, Jane Freeman Moulin, and Michael Webb. 2011. *Music in Pacific Island Cultures: Experiencing Music, Expressing Culture.* New York: Oxford University Press.

Douglas, Gavin. 2010. *Music in Mainland Southeast Asia: Experiencing Music, Expressing Culture.* New York: Oxford University Press.

Dudley, Shannon. 2004. *Carnival Music in Trinidad: Experiencing Music, Expressing Culture.* New York: Oxford University Press.

Eyre, Banning, interviewer. 2011. "Michael Frishkopf & Kristina Nelson on Koranic Recitation." Cairo, Egypt. http://www.afropop.org/multi/interview/ID/212 accessed October 29, 2011.

Gold, Lisa. 2005. *Music in Bali: Experiencing Music, Expressing Culture.* New York: Oxford University Press.

Guilbault, Jocelyne. 2005. "Globalization and Localism" in *Enciclopedia della Musica*, Vol. 5. Torino: Einaudi. pp. 138–156

Handler, Richard. 1986. "Authenticity." In *Anthropology Today* 2(1) (February):2–4.

Hast, Dorothea E. and Stanley Scott. 2004. *Music in Ireland: Experiencing Music, Expressing Culture.* New York: Oxford University Press.

Herrera-Sobek, Maria. 1993. *Northward Bound: The Mexican Immigrant Experience in Ballad and Song.* Bloomington: Indiana University Press.

Hobsbawm, Eric, and Terence Ranger, eds. 1983. *The Invention of Tradition.* Cambridge: Cambridge University Press.

Hornbostel, E. M. von. 1928. "African Negro Music." *Africa* 1:30–61.

Jameson, Fredric. 1991. *Postmodernism, or The Cultural Logic of Late Capitalism.* Durham, N.C.: Duke University Press.

Jensen, Joli. 1998. *Nashville Sound: Authenticity, Commercialization, and Country Music.* Nashville: Country Music Foundation Press and Vanderbilt University Press.

Karpeles, Maude. 1951. "Some Reflections on Authenticity in Folk Music." *Journal of the International Folk Music Council* 3:10–16.

————. 1968. "The Distinction between Folk and Popular Music." *Journal of the International Folk Music Council* 20:9–12.

Kartomi, Margaret J. 1981. "The Processes and Results of Musical Culture Contact: A Discussion of Terminology and Concepts." *Ethnomusicology* 25(2)(May):227–49.

————. 1990. *On Concepts and Classifications of Musical Instruments.* Chicago: University of Chicago Press.

Kingsbury, Henry. 1988. *Music, Talent, and Performance: A Conservatory Cultural System.* Philadelphia: Temple University Press.

Klaser, Rajna. 2001. "From an Imagined Paradise to an Imagined Nation: Interpreting *Sarki* as a Cultural Play." Ph.D. diss. University of California, Berkeley.

Koskoff, Ellen. 2001. *Music in Lubavitcher Life.* Urbana: University of Illinois Press.

Kubik, Gerhard. 1979. "Pattern Perception and Recognition in African Music." In *The Performing Arts*, edited by John Blacking and J. W. Kealiinohomoku, 221–49. The Hague: Mouton.

Kwon, Donna. 2011. *Music in Korea: Experiencing Music, Expressing Culture.* New York: Oxford University Press.

Lau, Frederick. 2008. *Music in China: Experiencing Music, Expressing Culture.* New York: Oxford University Press.

Lerdahl, Fred, and Ray Jackendoff. 1983. *A Generative Theory of Tonal Music.* Cambridge, Mass.: MIT Press.

Levin, Theodore. 2002. Music in Tuva. In The Garland Encyclopedia of World Music, Vol. 6 the Middle East: 979–987. New York: Routledge.

Levin, Theodore and Valentina Süzükei. 2006. *Where Rivers and Mountains Sing: Sound, Music, and Nomadism in Tuva and Beyond.* Bloomington: Indiana University Press.

Lewis, J. Lowell. 1992. *Ring of Liberation: Deceptive Discourse in Brazilian Capoeira.* Chicago: University of Chicago Press.

Lipsitz, George. 1994. *Dangerous Crossroads. Popular Music, Postmodernism and the Poetics of Place.* London: Verso.

Lui, Tsun-yuen. 1968. "A Short Guide to Ch'in." *Selected Reports* (UCLA) 1(2):179–204.

Marcus, Scott L. 2007. *Music in Egypt: Experiencing Music, Expressing Culture.* New York: Oxford University Press.

Middleton, Richard. 1990. *Studying popular music.* Milton Keynes, U.K.: Open University Press.

Mitchell, Tony. 1993. "World Music and the Popular Music Industry: An Australian View," *Ethnomusicology* 37: 309–38.

Monson, Ingrid. 1999. "Riffs, Repetition, and the Theories of Globalization." *Ethnomusicology* 43(1)(winter):31–65.

Moore, Robin. 2010. *Music in the Hispanic Caribbean: Experiencing Music, Expressing Culture.* New York: Oxford University Press.

Muller, Carol and Sathima Bea Benjamin. 2011. *Musical Echoes: South African Women Thinking in Jazz.* Durham, N.C.: Duke University Press.

Muller, Carol. 1999. *Rituals of Fertility and the Sacrifice of Desire: Nazarite Women's Performance in South Africa.* Chicago: University of Chicago Press.

Murphy, John P. 2006. *Music in Brazil: Experiencing Music, Expressing Culture.* New York: Oxford University Press.

Nettl, Bruno. 1954. *North American Indian Musical Styles.* Philadelphia: American Folklore Society.

———. 1975. "The Western Impact on World Music: Africa and the American Indians." In *Contemporary Music and Music Cultures,* edited by Charles Hamm et al., 101–24. Englewood Cliffs, N.J.: Prentice Hall.

———. 1995. *Heartland Excursions: Ethnomusicological Reflections on Schools of Music.* Urbana: University of Illinois Press.

Nijenhuis, Emmie te. 1974. *Indian Music: History and Structure.* Leiden: E. J. Brill.

Nzewi, Meki. 1991. *Musical Practice and Creativity: An African Traditional Perspective.* Bayreuth: IWALEWA-Haus, University of Bayreuth.

Qureshi, Regula. 1987. "*Qawwali*: Making the Music Happen in the Sufi Assembly." *Asian Music* 18(2)(spring/summer):118–57.

"Resolution on the Definition of Folk Music." 1953. *Journal of the International Folk Music Council* 5:23.

Reyes, Adelaida. 2005. *Music in America: Experiencing Music, Expressing Culture.* New York: Oxford University Press.

Rice, Timothy. 2001. "Reflections on Music and Meaning: Metaphor, Signification, and Control in the Bulgarian Case." *British Journal of Ethnomusicology* 10(1):19–38.

———. 2004. *Music In Bulgaria: Experiencing Music, Expressing Culture.* New York: Oxford University Press.

Ruckert, George E. 2004. *Music in North India: Experiencing Music, Expressing Culture*. New York: Oxford University Press.

Russet, J. C., and David Wessel. 1999 "Exploration of Timbre by Analysis Synthesis." In *The Psychology of Music*, edited by Diana Deutsch, pp. 113–69. San Diego: Academic Press.

Said, Edward. 1978. *Orientalism*. Harmondsworth, U.K.: Penguin.

Santosa. 2001. "Constructing Images in Gamelan Performances: Communicative Aspects among Musicians and Audiences in Village Communities." Ph. D. diss. University of California, Berkeley.

Seegar, Charles. 1958. "Prescriptive and Descriptive Music-Writing." *Musical Quarterly* 44(2): 184–195.

Sheehy, Daniel. 2006. *Mariachi Music in America: Experiencing Music, Expressing Culture*. New York: Oxford University Press.

Slobin, Mark. 1993. *Subcultural Sounds: Micromusics of the West*. Hanover, N.H.: Wesleyan University Press and University Press of New England.

Small, Christopher. 1998. *Musicking: The Meanings of Performing and Listening*. Hanover, H.H.: Wesleyan University Press.

Stokes, Martin, ed. 1994. *Ethnicity, Identity and Music: The Musical Construction of Place*. Oxford: Berg.

Stone, Ruth M. 2005. *Music in West Africa: Experiencing Music, Expressing Culture*. New York: Oxford University Press.

Sugarman, Jane. 1997. *Engendering Song: Singing and Subjectivity at Prespa Albanian Weddings*. Chicago: University of Chicago Press.

Taruskin, Richard. 1995. *Text and Act: Essays on Music and Performance*. New York: Oxford University Press.

———. 2001. "Nationalism." In *The New Grove Dictionary of Music and Musicians*, 2d ed., edited by Stanley Sadie, 17:689–706. London: Macmillan.

Taylor, Tim. 1997. *Global Pop*. New York: Routledge.

Théberge, Paul. 1997. *Any Sound You Can Imagine: Making Music/Consuming Technology*. Hanover, N.H.: Wesleyan University Press.

Turino, Thomas. 1993. *Moving Away from Silence: Music of the Peruvian Altiplano and the Experience of Urban Migration*. Chicago: University of Chicago Press.

———. 2000. *Nationalists, Cosmopolitans, and Popular Music in Zimbabwe*. Chicago: University of Chicago Press.

———. 2008. *Music in the Andes: Experiencing Music, Expressing Culture*. New York: Oxford University Press.

Vander, Judith. 1988. *Songprints: The Musical Experience of Five Shoshone Women*. Urbana: University of Illinois Press.

Vishwanathan, T., and Matthew Harp Allen. 2004. *Music in South India: Experiencing Music, Expressing Culture*. New York: Oxford University Press.

Wade, Bonnie C. 2005. *Music in Japan: Experiencing Music, Expressing Culture*. New York: Oxford University Press.

Wade, Peter. 2000. *Music, Race, and Nation:* Música Tropical *in Colombia*. Chicago: University of Chicago Press.

Wessel, David, and Matthew Wright. 2002 "Problems and Prospects for Intimate Musical Control of Computers." *Computer Music Journal* 26(3):11–22.

Williams, Raymond. 1977. *Marxism and Literature*. Oxford, U.K.: Oxford University Press.

Wilson, Olly. 1992. "The Heterogenous Sound Ideal in African-American Music." In *New Perspectives on Music: Essays in Honor of Eileen Southern*, edited by J. Wright, 327–38. Warren, Mich.: Harmonie Park.

Yivo Encyclopedia of Jews in Eastern Europe. <http://yivoencyclopedia .org/article.aspx/ Music/Traditional_and_Instrumental_Music>

Index